ONE OF
THE DAMNED

The life and times of Robert Tressell, author of
The Ragged Trousered Philanthropists

F. C. Ball

Lawrence and Wishart   London

First published by Weidenfeld and Nicolson, 1973

Copyright © 1973 by F.C.Ball

This paperback edition first published by
Lawrence and Wishart, 1979

Reprinted 1980

Lawrence and Wishart
39 Museum Street, London WC1

ISBN 85315 494 5

Printed and bound in Great Britain at
The Camelot Press Ltd, Southampton

Contents

Illustrations

The publishers would like to thank Mrs Kathleen Lynne for kindly loaning pictures for this book.

Acknowledgements

So many people have helped in one way or another with the making of this book that it is impossible to make public acknowledgement to all individually.

I feel, however, that I must make a few special mentions. Thank you, Mrs O'Nions, Hastings Borough Librarian, and members of the library staff, particularly Mr Clive Phillpot, now Librarian at Chelsea School of Art; Mrs Pam Haines, head of the Reference Library, Mr John Powys and Mrs Anne Rowley, and assistants.

And thank you also, Mr and Mrs Kemp, for kindly permitting your privacy to be invaded a number of times by myself and others looking over Robert Tressell's flat at 115 Milward Road, Hastings. And you, Mr Martin Secker, for allowing me to make copies of original correspondence in your possession between Grant Richards, publisher, and Jessie Pope, editor, concerning the first publication of *The Ragged Trousered Philanthropists*.

And thank you, members of Robert's family, without whom this book would not be complete.

And finally thank you, of course, to my typist, stenographer (and wife), Jacquie, for struggling through all the stages of its making with me.

Preface

Robert Tressell was the pen-name of an Anglo–Irish signwriter and housepainter who after various wanderings settled in Hastings, Sussex, in 1901, worked for local builders, and in his spare time wrote a book set in the building trades in a town named Mugsborough, which he called *The Ragged Trousered Philanthropists*, first published in 1914 since when it has become a classic of working class and other forms of life.

The author knew nothing of this; he died in 1911 at the age of forty in the Walton Workhouse, Liverpool.

When a man first lent me *The Ragged Trousered Philanthropists* (it is a book that gets lent around a lot) he told me that Robert Tressell who wrote it had lived and worked in Hastings, where I was born and have lived most of my life, and that he had written the book there. In fact the town he called 'Mugsborough' was meant for Hastings and the people in the book were Hastings people. But even more important for me the book was about the lives of the working classes, the first book about them I had ever seen, and Hastings working class at that, and both sides of my family were Hastings working class. And further, it was set in the building trades, about men at work. We had 'skibs' (painters), 'brickies' (bricklayers), 'chippies' or 'woodpeckers' (carpenters) and 'spreads' (plasterers) in the family and I myself had been apprenticed to plumbing for a time when I was fourteen for five shillings a week and a penny an hour overtime. (They were still paying such wages long after Tressell's day.) And Tressell's people spoke like mine. Words turned back to front, like 'tuneropperty' for opportunity, and many other varieties of our native tongue had puzzled me as a child, or, as my father would say, I couldn't 'under-constumble' them. So it was quite natural that, like many other Tressell readers, I should imagine I must have known some of Tressell's characters, but when they were much older, of course, and perhaps members of my own family might even have worked with him.

Yet till I was lent the book I had never heard of him or *The Ragged Trousered Philanthropists*, although this was nearly twenty-five years after it was published, and neither had my people. It was a kind of underground book: some people knew it well but others had never heard of it even here in Hastings.

I asked in the Borough Library whether there was a biography and discovered no one had ever written one. In fact they knew nothing about Robert Tressell, and I could find no mention of him or of his book in literary histories and encyclopaedias and, I thought, the very same thing had happened with John Bunyan, the Tinker – I suppose it was well over a hundred years before he was accepted by literary critics – and with John Clare the farm-labourer a hundred years, too. And longer still for William Langland's *The Vision of Piers Plowman*, forerunner of all three, and now it would be the same with this house-painter.

This first put into my head the idea that a biography of him was needed and someone ought to write it before it was too late and the living memory gone. I met one or two people who had actually known him and at last, of course, I faced the fact that if I wanted to read this 'life' I would indeed have to write it myself because people who had been his friends were dying while I had been thinking about it.

So in November 1942 I decided to advertise for information in the *Hastings and St Leonards Observer* and a little later in other newspapers, still not seriously believing I would ever write a biography, but I would at least collect the information. Something like nine years went by before at last in October 1951 my book *Tressell of Mugsborough* was published in London by Messrs Lawrence and Wishart. It marked an epoch in the Tressell story – the story of a man whose 'public life' only began after his death and in strange ways has continued ever since. In the first book I was unable to tell much of it as the material was not then available to me and in the twenty-two years since there have been many new developments. This present book entirely replaces that and contains much more and new detail of Tressell's private life, of the writing of *The Ragged Trousered Philanthropists*, with hitherto unpublished correspondence concerning the finding, abridgement and publication of the manuscript in 1914 three years after the author's death; the full story of the rediscovery of the original handwritten manuscript thirty-three years later, the efforts to get it published in 1955; the history of the manuscript itself; of how and why the book was kept alive and became a classic; accounts of dramatizations for stage and television and translations into other languages; the continued and baffling search for Tressell's true identity; stories of members of his family and the extraordinary reappearance of one of them fifty years after being reported killed in an accident; a full account of the strange circumstances of his death; and the long search for and eventual finding of his 'lost' grave fifty-seven years after his burial; and much other material, altogether a story as strange as any in our literary annals.

I have told the story, as I feel it deserves to be told, as nearly as possible in the sequence in which it gradually became known to me, so far as it is known to me, over the last thirty years and have tried to sketch in faithfully the social and historical background of this essentially social writer.

I have for the sake of the record and for Tressell fans told it in as much detail as possible. For the sake of clarity I have used the spelling 'Tressell' all through my own narrative, which is how the author signed himself, although in all the editions of his work till 1955 this was printed as 'Tressall', and I have used 'Tressall' only where that is used in documents and correspondence before that date.

Research was still going on as this book was being written and a few later discoveries have been incorporated into the text out of the chronological order of their discovery but I have given dates.

No biography can truly explain either a man or his work. It can only be a collection of often unrelated anecdotes and opinions about both.

A man has to be known well and his work read often to get anywhere near knowing either. Biographers, critics and commentators often intrude between the man and his work with amateur psychoanalysis. I have confined my work to the known facts about his life and posthumous history and the social and political background to his life and his book, and I hope my book will introduce you to his.

Extract from letter from Len Green, aged eighty-six, friend of Robert Tressell, to F.C.Ball, 5 April 1968.

Well, the first thing I must answer, my Father and Bob Tressell worked together for some time as my Father was the paperhanger on the firm where they both worked.

I come from a family of Paperhangers – my Grandfather and Father and Myself. And my Son is still Paperhanging.

Well, now I will tell you how I first knew how Bob must have written the Book. In 1918 I was in Hospital at Portsmouth waiting for my Discharge from Hospital. I was being invalided from France and one of the Orderlies was talking to me about a book he had got at Home about a Ragged Trousered Man and he would bring it back.

When he came back from his leave he told me little Snatches of the book which meant nothing to me until he said something about the Absconding Secretary of the Light Refreshment Fund then I knew that my old Pal Bob had something to do with it as the job that we were working on a Chap name Dan Pankhurst instead of bringing ½ Gal of Beer back he never turned up till next morning without the Beer, of course it was alright, the rest knew of the temptation and that was alright.

When I got Home 2 days before Xmas on leave I was talking about the book and my Sister in Law went to Hastings Station to Smith Stall and she was able to get a copy of the 1914 Edition which I have got but it is a bit of a wreck now.

That night the Wife started to read it to me until we were dead tired.

I

Who was Robert Tressell?

The editor's preface to *The Ragged Trousered Philanthropists* was signed 'Jessie Pope' and all that it said about the author of the book was that he was a socialistic working-man, a 'house-painter and sign-writer who recorded his criticism of the present scheme of things, until, weary of the struggle, he slipped out of it.'

Miss Pope didn't say how the writer 'slipped out of it' nor when, nor where, nor who he was, nor where he had come from. She left the reader to believe that 'Tressall' as she spelled it, was the author's real name and a lot of readers who have never learned differently still think it is.

If she knew nothing about the author, which seemed very unlikely, why didn't she say so, and if she did know, she should have said enough to do this anonymous author justice. It seemed to me that his name would die with the death of his friends. And the man who first lent me the book told me that Tressell wasn't his real name. It was Robert Noonan.

He was said to be Irish; he spoke with a bit of an Irish accent and said he had come to Hastings from South Africa just after the Boer War. And he had brought with him his little girl Kathleen who had been about nine years old. He never mentioned anything about a Mrs Noonan.

There was always a bit of a mystery about him as if he had secrets in his past that he didn't want to talk about, and what he *did* tell people, or what they *said* he told them, didn't always tally. He never said anything to give a definite idea of who he was, and so very little was known about him even by personal friends.

Some time after I read the book and was already making inquiries, I was sent an old article from the *Daily Worker* for 10 June 1936, written by a J.H.Poynton, who said that Tressell's real name was 'Newland', and they had worked together on jobs in the same trade and in the Socialist Movement of Hastings.

'And he had passed to the Great Beyond', said Poynton, in Biblical language, 'three years before his book saw the light.'

This, of course, was mystifying because now I had Robert Noonan and Robert Newland.

This article was the first mention of any name other than 'Tressell' that I had seen in print and the printed word is generally regarded as official, but here were two men claiming to have been workmates and friends giving different names for him.

How could I prove a man's name and identify him with it? Short of a relative I had to link him with a place or event, and if that were impossible, find more people who knew him and learn what name *they* knew him by, and look for *that* name in the directory.

Tressell died a few years before 1914 according to Poynton's article, so I worked back from there and sure enough it cleared up nothing for there was Robert Newland as large as life and living at 100 Milward Road – and Tressell had lived in Milward Road! So which name was the right one? There was never a mention of Robert Noonan as far back as 1907 but as 'Tressell' was said to have come to Hastings just after the Boer War I kept going back and in 1906 a Robert Noonan appeared as living at Flat 5, Grosvenor Mansions, 115 Milward Road, and he was there back in 1903 which was the earliest reference to a Noonan in Milward Road.

Then a Mr Ward, Master Signwriter, wrote to me. He had worked with 'Bob Noonan' who wrote *The Ragged Trousered Philanthropists*, and a little later I also received a copy of what I believe is the earliest reference to Robert's identity in print.

This was an article from the *Painter's Journal* for December 1922 by Mr J. Walsh, the Chairman of the Executive Committee of the National Society of Painters.

'The author's real name', he says, 'was Robert Noonan. Very little is known of his early life but he was an Irishman rather small in stature.'

These laconic details were all that were given about Tressell's identity but I was ready now to conclude that 'Newland' was an idiosyncrasy of Mr Poynton's. His article gave no information about Robert's origins and although I met him many times he could add nothing further.

Mr Ward said he didn't know much about who Noonan was, nor where he came from, and as far as *he* knew nobody else did. Bob, as he called him, didn't talk of his personal affairs but he did once say that he was born in Cleveland Street off the Tottenham Court Road, about 1870, and on one occasion after a trip to London told Ward that he had visited his birthplace up there.

This Cleveland Street account was given with the assurance that Tressell himself had said so and Ward wasn't the kind of man given to romancing. Cleveland Street lies partly in the Borough of St Pancras and partly in that of St Marylebone and I tried for a birth certificate, but as I couldn't supply his parents' names I couldn't get one.

I advertised with no luck in the local papers there, and then it occurred to me that if Tressell was Irish he might have been a Roman Catholic so I wrote to Roman Catholic churches in the area, and eventually from the Church of St James, Spanish Place, I obtained a copy of a certificate of baptism of one Robert Noonan, born 5 December 1868, baptised 12 January 1869, son of Timothy Noonan and Helen (*née* Antle), but it gave no address for the parents – no particulars whatever to give a clue to the birthplace or even Timothy's occupation, which I discovered later was in fact that of a tailor.

But it was something and I worked out quite a picture of the London Irish of the 1860s as Tressell's forebears, and after the fashion of some economical thinkers, I thought I could deduce much of his character from it.

I made inquiries about schooling with no result, I tried to trace Timothy in the registers, I even wrote to all the Noonans listed in the *London Telephone Directory* – and without result.

Of the few of his surviving friends I had by now managed to trace, none had heard of Cleveland Street as the birthplace, or knew anything whatever about his origins, but there remained Ward's marvellous guess, if not memory, supported by a certificate.

Poynton had said in the article that Robert died in the Royal Free Hospital, Liverpool, although he only gave the date as three years before the book was published; but the Royal Liverpool United Hospital was able to furnish a certificate which stated that Robert Noonan was admitted there on 26 November 1910, and died on 3 February 1911, aged forty.

This meant a discrepancy of two years in ages given in the two certificates. By this time a few other people, too, had confirmed that it was said that Tressell had died in Liverpool in 1911 and he himself must have given his age, and this cast further doubt on the baptismal certificate.

Then one day a man asked me whether I had been in touch with

Robert's niece. I had never heard of her, or any other living relation. Tressell, he said, had had a sister who kept a special school for handicapped children over at St Leonards and her daughter was still alive. He didn't know her name but the school had been somewhere in Upper Maze Hill.

The directories of Tressell's day didn't show any school under her name in Upper Maze Hill, but the directory for 1940 did, and through this I discovered this niece, by then an elderly lady.

I was very surprised to talk to her on the telephone – she spoke like a lady, with a cultured voice, and I was expecting a house-painter's niece, though I was ready to admit that she could have learned to speak like that at elocution class. But when I met her I was even more surprised because she was a lady if I could tell one. At least she was middle-class.

I had the impression that she wasn't particularly excited to be discovered (she had kept silent about my advertisements) nor to learn that a biography of her uncle was in preparation. She told me that her uncle, with whom it was obvious she hadn't been very close, was very reticent and would not wish his biography written, to which I replied very diffidently that Tressell by writing his book had put himself before the public and that a public figure must expect to arouse interest and publicity.

The same air of mystery and secretiveness was here as had been described to me about Tressell, but here there was one more family skeleton, and in the cupboard of the author of *The Ragged Trousered Philanthropists* himself. And perhaps I was going to open that door! It took about five minutes to disillusion me – all that her statement said essentially was that Tressell was not a working-man.

She asked me to publish nothing she had told me, said that she trusted me, that she had given me facts and where she wasn't sure, her opinions. I agreed to protect her only by refraining from mentioning her and her mother's name. There was no point in withholding her statement anyhow, for no one could connect it with her except herself!

As the lady is now deceased and to my knowledge no living person can connect Robert with any other surviving relations, and I don't know of any, I am released even from this undertaking. But it wasn't the end of her story.

I was to listen to another version of it – equally inconclusive – from an extraordinary source twenty-three years later and many years after her death, and however valueless as evidence her unsupported statement seemed at that time it became valuable taken with this second account.

About his origins his niece told me:

I know very little about Robert's parentage and background as this subject was hardly ever referred to by my mother, his sister.

Robert was not a working-man in origin; his father was a well-educated Irishman of Dublin, I rather think an officer in the British Army but am not sure. He was said to be a good scholar, to be able to read in the original Greek Testament and to have studied law.

He was a very good father to his three girls and three or four boys. I think Robert was the youngest child and, I should say, was born in Dublin. His early childhood was very happy and he was a very sensitive and impressionable child. He was very fond of his father.

His sisters were educated at a convent in Dublin but where Robert was educated I don't know as there were great changes in his boyhood consequent upon the death of his father, somewhere about his sixth year. Robert grieved very deeply, despite his tender age, and never forgot his father. His mother married again, sooner than was then thought proper, and apparently the family was split up, and certainly this marriage had a profound effect upon Robert, who never, I believe, agreed with it nor took to his stepfather and the stepfather never took kindly to the children. Also, Robert's education seems to have been seriously interrupted, for he complained in later life of his stinted schooling, that is compared with that received by his brothers and sisters when his own father was alive.

I know of nothing of any residence in London and of no connections with the Roman Catholic Church in the district of Cleveland Street. I don't think the Noonans in that area are connected, certainly not, I should say, a tailor named Noonan mentioned by one of your informants. The Noonans of Dublin were of a gentleman's family.

They were, it is true, Roman Catholic and Robert was brought up in this faith. The whole subject of the family history was taboo in the later life of the sons and daughters.

Robert was extremely self-willed and in my opinion left home in youth unable to bear living at home. I do not know his father's Christian name, nor his residence in Dublin, but I think Robert probably came to England, but whether he left home without leave or whether with parents' assistance as he was under age, I don't know.

Some of his sisters and probably his brothers had already left Ireland for England and I don't know whether Robert found a home with any of them, but he never saw his mother again and by tacit consent her name was never mentioned among members of the family afterwards.

This apparently was as much as the niece knew of her uncle's family, her own mother's family, and in fact she had never even heard her grandmother's Christian name.

It seemed that the brothers and sisters had managed to complete their education and to enter professions, but that Robert did not. None knew where he went nor how he lived. He was launched into the world a callow half-educated youth suddenly finding between himself and the future little but his own brains and energy. He certainly could have had no profession – he was less than twenty years of age and probably much younger and it is unlikely that he had been trained as a tradesman or craftsman at home.

His niece stated categorically that he was never apprenticed but that his skill as an artist was probably developed by some systematic lessons at some earlier period.

What he undoubtedly did have were the severe handicaps which his upbringing would impose upon him in these changed circumstances. He was now a working-man without having been nurtured as one.

I had to admit that the niece's story was conclusive evidence of her relationship with Robert despite the lack of verifiable information, names, places, dates, etc. Her mother was known as Tressell's sister to many of his acquaintances although none that I knew had met her, and the story is supported by chance remarks of Robert's.

He complained to others of his poor schooling; he once joked that his ill-health was due to the age of his parents, and he told friends that he had not been apprenticed to trade – a most unlikely omission if he had been born into a working-class family of any standing. Yet none of his friends, my informants, suggested that there was anything about him to lead them to think he was anything other than a skilled artisan of working-class origin.

It took something like four years to get such information as I did from the niece when I could persuade her to see me, or reply to correspondence, and a year after the statement quoted there came another twist in the story.

In December 1945 as a result of an appeal I made there, the South African newspaper *Forward* published an interview with Mr Stewart Ogilvy of Johannesburg, who claimed that he had worked with Robert there from 1897 till the outbreak of the Boer War, and undoubtedly had done so. In the course of his statement and correspondence I had with him following it, Mr Ogilvy said, 'Because of our intimacy I knew something of Noonan's private life. To the best of my recollection his full name was Robert P. Noonan and he gave me to understand that he came here from *Liverpool, that his father had been an Inspector in the Royal Irish Constabulary.*'

This was indeed becoming a bewildering story. I now had three distinct accounts of his origins from three people who had undoubtedly known him, one his own niece and two purporting to have got their stories from Robert himself.

Although I had already found a Robert Noonan in London, I now had to begin looking for another in Dublin and yet another in Liverpool without any other particulars than plain Robert Noonan and a birth date somewhere about 1870 if, as the death certificate said, he was forty in 1911.

I wrote on chance to the Registrar-General, Dublin, and was told that I must supply parents' names, mother's maiden name and exact place of birth as there were many Noonans in the registers. This, of course, I was unable to do and I tried at Somerset House but found no one who could be my Robert Noonan.

And then in 1947, three years after our first meeting, the niece told me that the father's name was Samuel and even then, as I was to discover ten years later, she left out what was even more vital.

So now I began looking for Samuel Noonan in British Army Lists at the Public Records Office, which even searched Navy Lists for good measure, and I also, of course, tried to find him in the Royal Irish Constabulary in case the niece's 'Army officer' was also Ogilvy's 'Inspector in the Royal Irish Constabulary'. And I searched on and off for years but entirely without result.

As the evidence stood, I neither knew who Robert's family were, nor where he was born, nor more tantalizing still, whether in fact his name was 'Robert Noonan' at all. For his niece now made one very cryptic remark in a letter. 'I do not', she wrote, 'at all rule out the possibility that Robert did not take his father's name.'

I had by this time been looking for Robert 'Noonan' for nearly four years with her help and this sudden pronouncement could only mean that in an uncontrolled moment the family skeleton had actually managed to peep out of the cupboard door.

And it was just as rapidly locked up again for I could get neither the surname that Robert might not have taken or anything else in explanation, so I was left looking for a Robert Tressell who, at least, didn't appear to be a Robert Noonan as we had believed.

2

Who *was* Robert Tressell

'It was always taken for granted throughout his life,' said his niece, 'that Robert would go off somewhere and then reappear at long intervals giving no explanations. None of his family knew where he was or how he earned his living in earlier years. He was a true rolling stone.

'However, we know that he emigrated to South Africa some time in the early 1890s and that for a while he lived and worked in Johannesburg.'

This was the first mention of any specific part of South Africa and enabled me to discover Mr Ogilvy, but Ogilvy didn't meet him before 1897 and by that time he had already lost his wife and had a daughter, Kathleen, about five years of age. Had he been in Johannesburg all that time or if not, where?

Robert's daughter believed he had gone to South Africa direct from Ireland and not from England as his niece thought, and that he worked his passage, but she didn't know why he chose South Africa.

South Africa was still in the throes of growing and great recent discoveries of new wealth on the Rand must have made it appear more exciting than other Colonies or the United States in which vast numbers of new immigrants found themselves in conditions of extreme poverty and/or committed to the slavery of primitive factory life, a prospect which I do not imagine appealed to Robert Noonan.

On the meagre information I had I tried to discover some facts about the marriage and the birth of the daughter in Johannesburg but without success and it wasn't for another twenty years that I learned he had been first in Cape Town and that his daughter Kathleen was born there on 17 September 1892, in Mowbray – then a suburb.

At that time he was believed to be twenty-two and probably had married in South Africa, although this was not known for certain and no record of the marriage had been found either there or in England.

His relations believed he emigrated as a single man and this would mean at least 1890/91, but as there is no knowledge of him from the time he left home till the birth of Kathleen he may well have gone there before 1890. I am inclined to think so because he remarked later in Hastings that he thought his standard of skill might not be high enough for England, and this seems to indicate that he received most of his training in the decorating business abroad; because of the art lessons mentioned by his niece, and the systematic home studying which we know he was still doing when he was in Hastings. It seems to me very unlikely that he worked in the trade in Ireland if he had just left the home of a 'Dublin gentleman'; and, his words suggest that his first experience of English conditions was on his return from South Africa.

I had already known Kathleen's birth date from an old autograph-book given to me twenty-five years ago by a schoolgirl friend of hers; but her birthplace didn't come to light until 1967 from a sworn declaration made to the Superior Court, Montreal, Canada, in lieu of a birth certificate on the occasion of her marriage fifty-three years earlier. This declaration deposed that these particulars of her birth were taken from a birthday-book given her by her father on her sixth birthday and were in her father's own handwriting.

It is curious that in this declaration Kathleen gave her mother's Christian name as 'Madeline' which she believed it to have been. For Robert extended the family reticence, even to his relations with his daughter. Kathleen wasn't told either her mother's Christian name or surname, and her father never told her his own mother's name either. He seems to have wanted to bury the identity of these two women in his life.

With this new information I wrote to the local authorities in Cape Town and Johannesburg and the central authorities in Pretoria, for information about the marriage and Kathleen's birth, but nothing was found in such records as were searched. Registration of births was not compulsory in Cape Colony before 1895, but there was perhaps a chance of finding a record of Kathleen's baptism – if she had been baptised. According to the niece Robert had been brought up as a Roman Catholic and Kathleen believed her mother to be a French woman and a Roman Catholic and that she herself was baptised 'Kathleen Noonan' in that faith; but a search of church registers in St Mary's Cathedral and the Roman Catholic churches of Rondebosch and Woodstock produced no record of her birth or baptism, nor any evidence of the marriage, nor of the death of Mrs Noonan.

In the Cape Town Directory for 1889 there appears a Mrs M. Noonan living at 22 Constitution Street, gone by 1891, who perhaps might be our Madeline, but who, I thought, could hardly be Mrs Robert Noonan at that date. But she is the only Noonan mentioned for the period.

It then occurred to me that Robert's father was Protestant, I believe the niece told me this but I had no other record of it. Perhaps Kathleen had in fact been baptised a Protestant. As late in this story as July 1969 I obtained a list of all the Protestant churches in Cape Town and wrote to each for a search of parish records and in December, from St Peter's, Mowbray, a church not on my list, I received a certificate of the baptism. It recorded:

> Kathleen Noonan, born 17.9.92, baptised 7.4.95, father Robert Phillipe Noonan, mother Elizabeth Noonan; Address Rosebank; sponsors, Blanche Willmit, Joseph Slack, Elizabeth Noonan; Administrant, A.Daintree, Rector; Quality, Trade or Profession of father, Decorator.

There was no record of the marriage although all the churches replied.

So her mother's name was Elizabeth. Unfortunately records of baptism do not give the maiden names of mothers. Strangely Robert's second name, 'Phillipe' as written on the certificate, sounds more French than his wife's 'Elizabeth'. Also at the time of baptism Kathleen was two-and-a-half years of age, which seems to indicate that Robert was not a regular church-goer. He may not even have attended the baptism, and if particulars for the certificate were given by his wife, the spelling of 'Phillipe' would support Kathleen's belief that her mother was French.

The certificate seemed to disprove the theory that the mother was Catholic: it is barely likely that a Catholic mother would have consented to have her child baptised a Protestant, let alone act as sponsor!

Her Christian name was all I could discover of this woman, apparently the only one to play any significant part in his life besides his mother. And then in May 1971, I finally uncovered a record of the marriage which gave the particulars:

> Robert Phillipe Noonan, Bachelor aged 23 of 78 Strand Street,

11

Cape Town, occupation Decorator. Elizabeth Hartel, Spinster, aged 18, of Cape Town. Married, after publication of Banns, on October 15th 1891 at the Church of The Holy Trinity, Cape Town, witnesses N.G. and W.H.Eckovoff.

The copy states that the signature of the officiating priest is illegible on the original and in the item 'Consent given by:' it states 'Parents' in each case, although why Robert at twenty-three years of age should be required to make such a declaration or should state 'Parents' is mystifying. His parents, or at least his father, were supposed to be deceased.

His wife's name, Hartel, seems more likely to be Afrikaans than French, and Holy Trinity is a Protestant church, none of which supports Kathleen's assumption that her mother was a French Catholic named Madeline. And what had happened to this girl of eighteen years? She was with Robert at most five years for she didn't go with him to Johannesburg in 1896.

The niece said that he never referred to his wife and that she probably died in South Africa soon after her child's birth, but Kathleen believed that her mother died in Cape Town in 1895, the year of the baptism, of typhoid fever.

Ogilvy, however, in Johannesburg, said that: 'Noonan's domestic life had not been happy. He was separated from his wife though on what grounds I cannot recall.'

Little else is known about the marriage or the five years or so that Robert lived in Cape Town. The absence of his name in directories seems to indicate that he was not a householder in Cape Town or that alternatively he was nowhere long enough in residence to be recorded. He describes himself on both certificates as 'Decorator' which doesn't indicate whether he was employed or self-employed; and Kathleen speaks also of 'mining' or 'ranching' interests because he told her that he believed his chest condition to be due to drinking whisky and then getting chilled when riding across the veld on cold nights – as if he were making habitual journeys on horseback. This again may refer to a period before his stay in Cape Town.

Finally, there is a delightful studio portrait of him with his daughter which Kathleen says was taken when she was about three years old. Robert, in straw boater, bow-tie and a flourishing fair moustache and looking very young is riding a studio bicycle with Kathleen in frilly bonnet standing behind him with her hands on his shoulders. This photograph bears the trade-mark Blomfield Studios, Cape Town, and did not come into my possession till 1967.

Within a few months of losing his wife he decided upon another move. Perhaps he wished to break with the sad associations of Cape Town, and to get right away to where there seemed to be something going on. And Johannesburg in the 1890s must have looked like just such a place.

Although ten years earlier only a cluster of shacks it was already one of the richest districts in the world, third in production of gold and developing rapidly. But Johannesburg was a tense and divided city with all the worst features of capitalist development and was about to become the scene of the final eruption of the long-standing conflict between British and Boer. This eruption deepened not only the hatred for British Imperialism which Robert already seems to have felt as an Irishman, but his disgust with capitalism – he had left home, according to his daughter, because 'he would not live on an income of absentee rentals'. And it was to end the new life he was making for himself and bring him to Hastings and the naked class structure of England, and so, had he but known it, to 'the Ragged Trousered Philanthropists'.

In the two Boer Republics, all foreigners were registered in the Fields Cornets' (Town Magistrates') Registers, and in 1968 after many unsuccessful searches for our Robert Noonan, the following entry was found, of all places, in the archives of the Commissioner for Mines, Johannesburg.

Name:	Noonan.
Christian names:	Robert.
Date of Birth:	17.4.1871.
Date of arrival in Z.A.R.:*	15.8.1896.
Date of arrival in Johannesburg:	15.8.1896.
Last place of Residence:	Ireland.
Date of Registration:	9.1.1897.

This document raised straight away questions I had hoped were answered. I was satisfied that it was my Robert Noonan, but his second

*Africaans—Zud (South) African Republic.

name Phillipe was left out and the entry gives his birth date as 17 April 1871, and not 1870, and further, he had given his age as twenty-three at his marriage which would make the year of his birth 1868. And his last *residence* before entering the South African Republic, and Johannesburg itself, he gave as Ireland and not Cape Town, yet he had been in Cape Colony for five or six years and the South African Republic was a foreign country. The whole business seemed to be thrown wide open again.

The move to Johannesburg itself seems, in the light of recent events there, difficult to account for, especially for a man with a four-year-old child. And as he would discover, 1896 was the most unpropitious time to choose to go there.

3
Emigration and marriage

Alongside these two official references to Robert in South Africa I managed to find only one person, Mr Ogilvy, who remembered him there.

In correspondence with me following the article in *Forward*, Mr Ogilvy corrected one or two misstatements and added a few more reminiscences and in 1946 I managed to get an English WAAF, Miss Roberts, who was in Johannesburg, to interview him and this is Ogilvy's story.

During the years 1897 till the outbreak of the Boer War, I worked with Robert Noonan who was foreman at Herbert Evans. He was a very good signwriter indeed, one of the best I have ever known, and he had the makings of a brilliant artist. Noonan was an extremely pleasant fellow and the best of company and we became very friendly. We spent many evenings together and almost all our Sundays. Johannesburg, which was still very much of a mining camp, offered little, outside of hard drinking, by way of amusements, and I found Noonan an interesting and entertaining companion.

There can be no doubt that he had a brilliant and versatile mind. Noonan had some queer foibles arising from his interest in his fellow men. For example, he had an eye for queer characters, and he would follow them about endlessly listening to their conversation and taking voluminous notes of how they looked and what they said. When, many years afterwards, a copy of his book came into my hands, I had no difficulty whatever in identifying some of the characters portrayed as being derived from the oddities Noonan had subjected to such close examination and study during the years he lived on the Rand.

Because of our intimacy I knew something of Noonan's private and domestic life, which was not happy. He gave me to understand he came here from Liverpool, that his father had been an Inspector in the Royal Irish Constabulary.

15

Concerning his family affairs he was extremely reticent. I gathered from his conversation that he was separated from his wife. He had a little girl who was a boarding scholar at the old End Street Convent.

Noonan was very attached to his child and he used to visit her every Sunday, mostly taking her out for a day's outing. I often accompanied them on their excursions.

I don't know anything of his coming to South Africa. While I knew him he had rooms in Pritchard Street, between Smal and Van Wiellegh Streets. I surmise his wage would be about £7–£7. 10s. od. per week. His standard of life was good – a very solid sort of man.

To the best of my knowledge, he did not belong to any club, and as for his political opinions, he kept them to himself. Trade unions were very much in their infancy and I don't know that Noonan worried about them. He lived in a little world of his own and was very fond of writing, especially articles dealing with everyday life. He wrote for various publications and his writings gave ample evidence of the literary power that flowered so prolifically in his masterpiece on working-class life.

I recall even now how deeply I was impressed by his sketches of life on the Rand.

When and where his articles were published I don't know, excepting one entitled 'All Meals a Shilling', which appeared in a little paper dealing with local topics, the title of which I have forgotten. This was distributed gratis, the advertisements paying for publication. Noonan intended to write a book of his impressions of the people of Johannesburg. I think it was shelved owing to the troubled times.

This was just before the Boer War and although he was British, Noonan was very much opposed to the war and it is said that when he returned to England he carried on a vigorous propaganda against it. But this hostility went beyond protests. I know for a fact that he was active in the formation of the 'Irish Brigade' which fought on the Boer side during the war. The leader of this movement was an Irishman named Mitchell who had a small dyer's and cleaner's shop between Pelvers and Smal Streets. This shop was, at the time I speak of, the headquarters of the 'Irish Brigade', and here Mitchell and a lot of other wild Irishmen used regularly to meet and concert their plans.

Noonan disappeared into the blue very shortly before the Boer War broke out and we never met again, although in later years someone mentioned in the course of conversation that he had seen Noonan in Cape Town during or shortly after the war.

To this Mr Ogilvy added:

To the best of my recollection his full name was Robert P. Noonan and his daughter's name was Nora or Noreen.* Noonan was short and well built. We used to call him 'little Noonan'. He walked with a sharp energetic step and a slight roll or sway. His speech was good and accent very slightly Irish. He did not mix much with his fellow employees but on the whole he was a good little chap. He spent much of his time in the compilation of his book about Johannesburg, which was shelved owing to the war. He was last heard of in Cape Town with his little girl.

Four years after Ogilvy's account, I received the only other personal reference to Robert in South Africa. The General Secretary of The Amalgamated Society of Woodworkers of South Africa sent me the names of two ladies, Lock and Hendricksen, at one time of Salisbury, Southern Rhodesia, who were said to have known him in South Africa, but an attempt to find them through the *Southern Rhodesia Herald* brought no result, and I could get no further information about them, where and when and in what connection their lives had crossed Robert's. They remained in the shadows, two disembodied names dredged up from an old man's memory after half a century or more.

A few other details are given by Kathleen.

In 1897, the date mentioned by Mr Ogilvy, she was in her fifth year and was in fact boarded at the Convent of the Holy Family and not the End Street Convent where, she says, she was accompanied by her own nurse and where the day girls used to be brought to school in carriages, and where she remained during the whole of their stay in Johannesburg.

The Convent of the Holy Family was, of course, Roman Catholic, but, says Kathleen, this may have been in Robert's opinion the only 'suitable place', that is, suitable for her education, or, she said, it may have been that her mother expressed a dying wish that she should be brought up in a Catholic school although, as she says, her father 'had

*Mr Ogilvy probably confused this with the 'Nora' in the book.

no use for them'. But as her mother had her baptised as a Protestant, this 'last wish' seems very unlikely.

The convent also had a farm out in the country where convalescent children were sent. 'It was a school of high repute,' said Kathleen, and added, 'I don't suppose I would have been permitted to have my own nurse in a nondescript school.'

These remarks help to throw light of a kind upon the status and the social ideas of the Noonans, although the nurse could have been a necessity until Robert got the child into an institution. Her father used to visit on Sundays and it seems probable that Ogilvy accompanied them upon country picnics, probably to the farm – Kathleen remembers walking through long grass, and on other occasions she says, Robert's visits were a joy to the other children as well because he used 'to give them races and prizes'. She also says that her father had a 'black servant' who was named 'Sixpence' and of whom he was 'quite fond', but Ogilvy mentions nothing about this, although according to Kathleen, Sixpence was with Robert during the whole period of his stay in Johannesburg.

I don't know whether Sixpence lived with his master in Pritchard Street or whether he lived out nor whether Robert 'christened' him with his nickname.

Kathleen quotes her father as saying that the only thing Sixpence ever stole was the emerald-green sash he possessed as member of the Transvaal '98 Centenary Association, and Robert used to imagine Sixpence strutting around in front of his wives wearing nothing but his loin-cloth and the sash of the United Irishmen.

Kathleen tells another curious story. Robert was going home in the early hours of the morning on one occasion after a party and saw a man lying in the road apparently hurt or drunk and went over to see if he could help or move him to the side where he would be less likely to get run over. But it was a gang set-up and as he reached the man he was set upon, robbed and battered. Kathleen says:

> I don't know how he got to hospital, but he was found to have a broken nose and was operated upon. While under the anaesthetic, although unable to move he heard the doctors saying 'The books describe this as an easy operation but we're not finding it so.' When it was all over Robert said, 'You didn't find it as simple as you expected, eh?', and a doctor replied, 'Perfectly simple', and Robert

surprised them by repeating their conversation. It seems our family doesn't take well to anaesthetics. My Aunt Mary Jane was treated with morphine as a pain-killer for neuritis and the doctor told her she had taken enough to kill anyone else.

Kathleen didn't know where her father lived or how he earned a living but thought it possible that he learned his trade in South Africa and it is interesting that she had doubts as to whether he in fact ever followed his trade in Johannesburg; and Herbert Evans and Co. where, according to Ogilvy, he was foreman, can find no reference to his employment with them. The Johannesburg Public Library has a copy of *The Paint House* – a history of Herbert Evans and Co. Ltd, in which there is no mention of R.Noonan and the firm's address is given as at Kruis Street, but Ogilvy is talking about the workshop. It would appear that Robert worked for Evans's for something between two and three years and therefore, perhaps, not long enough to be recorded in a history of the firm, and Mr Ogilvy himself looked up and questioned five old men who had been employed by Evans's but as Ogilvy put it, results were nil. And Ogilvy himself finished up as managing director! But he undoubtedly knew Robert and knew him as a signwriter and decorator and many points in this account are conclusive – Robert's trade, his daughter, his walk and appearance are instances – and tally with other accounts.

It is possible that Robert worked as a jobber on contract for Evans's and that as Ogilvy was working at that time in the wallpaper department, they met in the course of business; but on the other hand he is quite positive that Robert was foreman there. And since this statement was made to me in correction of the report in *Forward* that Ogilvy himself had been foreman, it indicates that he well remembered.

But if Ogilvy is right about his income and Kathleen is right about the nurse and the servant, he was in good circumstances, although the cost of living was extremely high.

According to Kathleen he also owned some land on a Stand (or site) No. 16, Forest Hills, 'somewhere in South Africa', but I have been unable to confirm this although the fact that his entry into Johannesburg was registered by the Commissioner for Mines perhaps bears her out. Forest Hills is a suburb of Johannesburg and he may have owned a site there at a time when fortunes were being made in land. Creswicke's references to land prices in his description of Johannesburg in his *South Africa and the Transvaal War* illustrate the phenomenal increases in land values with the opening up of the gold-fields. When first the natives were driven off their traditional lands these might change hands among the Boers for as little as ½*d.* per acre, but over the period of British infiltration prices rose from as low as 1*d.* per acre to as high as £1 and by Robert's time to £40,000 paid for one site in Pritchard Street.

Nothing has been found in records of any Johannesburg writings under Robert's own name but he may have used a pen-name, though it is likely that he made little money, if any, from writing in the Johannesburg of the 1890s.

The loss of Ogilvy's newspaper-cuttings and his photographs of the author are indeed a loss to all Tressell readers. That title 'All Meals A Shilling' sounds as if he was already sharpening his pen, but with good humour.

I must say that I find it difficult to imagine that the evenings spent with Ogilvy were of a purely social nature and that Robert kept his political views to himself. It seems hardly likely that they didn't discuss the affairs of the day, for the situation in Johannesburg could hardly be ignored; or that they didn't find themselves at loggerheads over the question of the Boer disputes with the Uitlanders – the foreign adventurers who had flocked to Johannesburg after the discovery of gold on the Rand in 1886. Technically Robert himself was one, though perhaps as an Irishman didn't consider himself so. Undoubtedly Ogilvy considered himself so because he left hurriedly when the war came.

Ogilvy mentions Robert's participation in 'the Irish Brigade' as a known fact but not his proven association with fellow Irishmen in the Transvaal '98 Centenary Association. This was, of course, named in honour of the risings of 1798 in Ireland when with French and Dutch aid and Napoleon's good will, the Irish fought another round in their centuries-old war against English oppression and the Protestant religion, and after sporadic and mutual and indiscriminate murder, an army 'of 14,000 assorted Irish were literally caught napping in camp at Vinegar Hill near Enniscorthy, Wexford, in May, and crushed'.

In 1898 the Transvaal '98 Centenary Association no doubt still looked forward to a consummation of the work of the patriots, and there were some in that very society in Johannesburg who were to die fighting England on South African battlefields, and one of the men on the committee of six was to die facing a British firing-squad in Dublin after the Easter Rising of 1916.

Among the other five committee-men was the name of R.P. Noonan, and his own membership card gives us the first authentic example of his signature.

One cannot but admire the paradoxical twist of history that set Robert's own ancestry, if either Kathleen or Ogilvy is right, on the side of the British Crown, but of such is the politics of Ireland.

4

Sad South Africa and the Boer War

Robert must have watched the growing tension between Boers and English with alarm and with his Irish anti-British sentiments it wasn't far to becoming pro-Boer. Indeed, it appeared to many liberal-minded people in England that Britain, as she had done all through the nineteenth century, was waging another colonial war against a small nation. As early as August, two months before war broke out, some of the non-British Uitlanders had offered their services to the Transvaal Government,* so high was anti-British-Empire feeling among foreigners.

The cover story used by the British in the quarrel with the Boers concerned the limitations on civil rights and restrictions on the franchise imposed on the Uitlanders. But in reality both British and Boers were determined upon gaining control of South Africa for themselves. Apart from the historical rivalry between the two peoples, the very logic of the economic conflict, in this virtually 'undeveloped' sub-continent, between two ways of life, industrial and pastoral, made war inevitable.

There is some confusion about Robert's reasons for and the order of his leaving the Republic. It is not at all certain that the war was the chief reason for his going or in fact a reason at all, although all accounts but Kathleen's suggest that it was and Kathleen herself is not conclusive.

Ogilvy's assertion that Robert was 'active in the formation of the "Irish Brigade" which fought on the Boer side', would seem to be corroborated by the niece, who said she understood that he was in some trouble in South Africa caused by pro-Boer activity; and by a remark by Kathleen that had he not already by then sent for his sister and gone to meet her in Cape Town 'he may have remained in South Africa and taken part in the war'. Although I have been unable to

*Samson Low, *Times History of the War in South Africa*, London, Vol. 2, p. 86.

confirm it, the Transvaal '98 Centenary Association must have been a leading mover and a rallying-point, if not the central organizer of the Irish Brigade.

I have been unable to confirm Ogilvy's statement that 'the leader of this movement [to form an Irish Brigade in Johannesburg] was an Irishman named Mitchell who had a small dyer's and cleaner's shop between Pelvers and Smal Streets.' The Directories do not show the existence of Mitchell or the shop for the years 1892 to 1899 and none of the officials or committee-men of the Transvaal '98 Centenary Association is named Mitchell, although of course, this is no conclusive evidence that Ogilvy is wrong, and Michael Davitt, Irish MP and prominent Irish Nationalist, founder of the Land League, in his book *The Boer Fight For Freedom*, gives an interesting account of the formation of the Irish Brigade(s) which seems to suggest that Ogilvy was somewhere near the mark about Robert's association with their formation.

'The Irish Brigade', says Davitt, 'was organized in Johannesburg chiefly by the exertions of Mr John McBride, a native of Mayo, who was at the time employed as an assayer in one of the Rand mines. He was warmly supported by other Irishmen on the Rand.'

Davitt's 'John McBride' can surely be none other than the 'J. McBride' who was Robert's fellow committee-man in the Transvaal '98 Centenary Association.

P.S.O'Hegarty, the Irish historian, in his book *History of Ireland Under The Union*, says that John McBride was commander of one of the Irish Brigades. And the British had long memories; in 1916, they caught him in Ireland during the Easter Rising and took the opportunity of executing him off-hand *for his part in the Boer War** all those years earlier. But the brave Major's immortality in Irish and Boer history is assured by his inclusion in Yeats's poem 'Easter 1916'.

Robert could thus well have owed his life to the fact that his sister Adelaide, whom he had gone to meet in Cape Town, had been first to England for a holiday.

Adelaide, who was living in Chile, had been recently widowed and was supporting herself and her son Arthur by teaching English in a convent school there, and Robert had invited her to South Africa, says Kathleen, so that Adelaide could keep house for Robert and be a mother to his daughter, and he could take the place of Arthur's father.

*C. Desmond Greaves, *Life and Times of James Connolly*, London, 1961.

But so far as she knew, it wasn't intended that they should set up home in Johannesburg.

At his expense Adelaide and Arthur, who was five years younger than Kathleen, left Valparaiso for South Africa. But they stayed on in England to see their relations, where they managed to prolong their visit beyond Robert's expectations and to spend the money which was to pay their fares on to South Africa. This obliged him to send more.

Kathleen concludes from this considerable expenditure that he must have had other sources of income than his job 'or how could he have sent Adelaide so much money merely from signwriting'.

But unless he had *some* property or at least prospects of work in Cape Town it is difficult to understand why he should leave Johannesburg where he was apparently doing well. Neither does Kathleen's memory of his intention accord with the accounts of his niece, Ogilvy and other friends.

According to Kathleen, Adelaide and her son finally arrived in 1898 or possibly early 1899, and Robert left Johannesburg to meet them in Cape Town, where they were all to settle, leaving Kathleen at the convent to be brought down later. But I can think this probable only if he had no alternative, for instance if he had to leave hurriedly on the eve of war and was faced with a dangerous journey. The Convent of the Holy Family was run by a French Order, the Holy Sisters of Bordeaux, and therefore presumably neutral, and Kathleen would be safe there if her father left in emergency.

There seems no other valid reason to leave her behind although she explains that he first had to find a home for the four of them.

The accounts of others appear to contradict Kathleen's. Ogilvy, the niece, and also Mr Ward, all unknown to each other, affirm that he left on the eve of the Boer War – Ogilvy says, 'disappeared into the blue', suddenly. The niece says that Robert himself stated that he travelled in an open train and it was such a bad journey that he ascribed his subsequent chest trouble to that. Ward goes further still and says that Robert told him he travelled on the last train out of Johannesburg and that the journey was 'terrible', and these stories could only have come from Robert direct or second-hand from Adelaide.

Of the trains carrying the Uitlanders – the Natal newspaper *Newcastle Chronicle* gives a figure of thirty to forty thousand leaving Johannesburg – Michael Davitt says, '. . . trains for Natal and Delagoa

Bay were being crowded every day with refugees. They rushed off in needless panic before the war broke out. No immediate risk menaced their persons or liberties – they rushed into cattle trucks in their hurry to be off. They fought for places.'

The direct line to the Cape, which had only been connected with Johannesburg in 1895 ran, of course, through the Boer Orange Free State.

While Michael's picture of the refugees may be correct, he doesn't give their motives; that they were already in the position of aliens, that they were apprehensive of what would happen to trade and industry and their livelihoods, and that they feared that the British, should they win, could construe their remaining in the Republic as trafficking with the enemy, especially in the case of dissident Irishmen. And what would happen if the Boers won – in a war ostensibly fought on account of these perishing Uitlanders?

There were many, mostly non-British, who *did* stay on and some who took the oath of allegiance to the Transvaal Government, but Robert Noonan's name is not among these in South African Government records.

Another remark of Kathleen's that she was seven or nearly seven, she's not sure which, when she left the convent, seems to indicate that Robert left the city very near to the outbreak of war. Kathleen's seventh birthday was in September 1899 and war broke out on 11 October, three weeks later, and this would seem to place the date of his departure later than the 1898 or early 1899 that she links with Adelaide's arrival.

British troops were already on the Transvaal border in September. It seems to me that all accounts probably add up to this: that Adelaide's long delay – the journey from South America to England, the protracted stay there and the journey out to South Africa – had brought her arrival very near to the outbreak of war, and that Robert had to leave in a hurry to stop her from going on to Johannesburg. Kathleen herself says that had it not been for Adelaide's arrival he may well have stayed and taken part in the war and this contradicts her idea that they had already decided to settle in Cape Town.

There is another important point. In August, as war appeared certain, Herbert Evans had closed down his business, leaving a German as caretaker of the premises; and Robert may then have had to make

25

rapid alternative plans about Adelaide if it had been intended that she should come to Johannesburg.

The first 'Irish Brigades', largely composed of Irish–Americans, were already formed by the outbreak of war, and on the eve were stationed at Sandspruit, twelve miles from Laing's Nek, and if Robert was at all concerned in their formation he must have been in Johannesburg in the weeks immediately preceding this. Incidentally, it may have been from these Irish-Americans on the Rand that he picked up the American expressions such as 'say', and 'hoodlum', which he frequently used among workmates but which do not, however, appear in his book.

I can find no evidence that he fought with the Brigade. But with a young motherless child in his care it is very unlikely that Robert considered fighting. He may have been excused on that account.

As for his being in trouble with the British authorities as his niece believed, the South African Police have been unable to find any records of this. And if he was in trouble when he left Johannesburg for Cape Town he was going in the wrong direction – towards the British – so one can only presume that no hint of his activities reached their ears.

Kathleen says that 'for years' she possessed some kind of deed for the site on Stand No. 16 and it looks as if Robert couldn't dispose of this property. Perhaps it was confiscated by the Boers, but if so, there is no evidence that Robert tried to reassert his claim when he was in England after the war; and if he did and was successful, his financial situation in Hastings showed that he couldn't have got much for it, and surely he would have had to surrender the documents. I have been unable to discover what happened to 'Stand No. 16'.

The niece says that Kathleen travelled in the care of 'the Consul's wife' from Johannesburg to Cape Town, and I assumed at that time that this meant the British Consul's wife, but as Kathleen says the lady was a Madame Vaillant, she could well have been the French Consul's wife, and this too gives substance to the belief that Robert had left hurriedly as a result of the war. The French Consul's wife could have been bringing out a party of British and other alien children.*

They travelled by boat from Durban, Natal, and Kathleen re-

*Since the above was written I have ascertained that the French authorities have no record of a Madame Vaillant connected with the Consulate at that time.

members that a tug took passengers out to the ship and they were then hoisted aboard 'in a large basket'.

Instead of meeting Kathleen at Cape Town himself from the Durban boat, Robert, who 'had some business to attend to' as Kathleen put it, sent Adelaide who was, of course, a complete stranger to her. 'We got off on the wrong foot from the start', says Kathleen.

> I had been travelling with a Frenchwoman [Madame Vaillant] probably very smart, fashionable and chic. My Aunt turned up in a white tailored suit which, no doubt, looked like a 'maid's' uniform to me. Every now and then afterwards she reminded me that I had taken her for a 'maid'. I was used to people with a more fussy kind of clothes. I would only remember that I'd expected my daddy to come for me and absolutely refused to go with a woman I'd never seen before. My whole trip from Johannesburg had probably been one long anticipation of seeing my father again.

The little boy, Arthur, had been left with the maid, said Kathleen, so it appears that Robert could still afford a servant. Sixpence had been left behind in Johannesburg and had lost a kind-hearted master. Robert had taken a house in Rondebosch, Cape Town, where all four lived until they came to England.

The district of Rondebosch was on the site of one of the original Boer settlements after the 1652 landings and took its name from them. Almost nothing is known of their stay there, but according to Kathleen her father decided to move to England so that she could be 'properly educated';

> There probably were good schools both in Cape Town and Johannesburg, but colonials living abroad nearly always sent on or brought their children home to be educated – many still do. I do not think there was any question of his not being able to afford to send me to a good school in South Africa. The convent was far from being cheap. He probably did not know the great difference he would find in English conditions and by that time it was too late to return to South Africa.

There are other versions of why he left.

Edward Cruttenden, a friend, says that he came here because things were 'upside down' as a result of the war and Walsh says, 'During the war business became so dislocated that he came to this country', and this is probably nearer the mark. There were three other people to consider besides Kathleen and possibly, also, Adelaide may have wanted to live in England where her sisters were. To me it all sounds a far cry from the poverty-stricken decorator who wrote *The Ragged Trousered Philanthropists*.

In September 1901, they travelled by Union Castle on the s.s. *Galician*, having stayed for a short while at the Hotel La France, where Kathleen was bitten by someone's pet monkey in disobeying her father's orders.

There are a couple of stories told of Robert on the ship. As a practical joke he wetted a fur stole, probably one of Adelaide's or the victim's own, and put it into someone's bunk where it looked like a big black snake and terrified the occupant, for, says Kathleen, Robert was sorry afterwards for doing it.

And, as 'George Washington', Robert edited *The Evening Ananias*, a hand-written 'bulletin' produced on flimsy octavo sheets and containing items of news and comment in keeping with that title.

Kathleen had her ninth birthday on the ship.

I wonder about his feelings as he left South Africa. It had given him and taken away his wife; it had given him a daughter. And he had seen the Boer cause defeated by numbers ten times their own – an army estimated at double the entire population of the two Boer States – at a cost of over 120,000 British soldiers dead, missing and invalided out, or twice the number of the entire Boer forces.

As for the British soldier, his own people had sent him out with inferior weapons and not trained in the tactics of this kind of warfare. (Another case, as the German Chief of Staff said of the British soldier in the First World War, of 'lions being led by donkeys'.) And for some, the shame of the experience was to last a lifetime. Fifty years later, I was interviewing a friend of Robert's in Hastings, an old man, blind and over eighty years of age when, talking of the Boer War, he suddenly broke down and cried bitterly. He had been a soldier and in one of the innumerable skirmishes which were so much a feature of the fighting, had mortally wounded a Boer, and when he came up to him, the dying boy, he was only about sixteen, said to him 'Why did you shoot me brother?'

The Boers lost less than four thousand killed but 17,627 of their women and children died in Kitchener's concentration camps from

July 1901 to February 1902, and it took a public outcry organized by a civilized English woman – Miss Emily Hobhouse – to force on the Government the reform of the camps; for which Kitchener called her 'that damned woman', but the Boers buried Miss Hobhouse at the foot of the Women and Children's Memorial in Bloemfontein, late capital of the Orange Free State.

But what had been happening out there on the veld had already decided Robert's future for him.

5

Mugsborough, England

On a particularly wild and wet stormy day a few years later Robert was explaining to Bill Gower why he found himself standing in the rain holding his hat on in a gale at a holiday and residential resort on the English Riviera.

Apparently upon his return from South Africa he and his party stayed a little while in London, no doubt wondering where to settle and how to earn a living in strange England, where probably he had never been and from which in any event he had been absent for at least ten years and more likely twelve or thirteen. Besides Adelaide there were two other sisters, Ellie, living in Liverpool, and Mary Jane, in Hastings.

And it was Mary Jane, said Robert, who had written asking him to come to '. . . dear, sunny Hastings', as her letter called it, and here he was, he said, waiting.

So Adelaide, Arthur and, of course, Kathleen, travelled down in one of the old green and brass coaches of the South Eastern and Chatham, or 'Slow, Easy and Comfortable', Railway, as it was called in the old days.

They stayed at 38 Western Road a while and Robert must have decided that Hastings would be a good place both for himself and his daughter to live in, and perhaps better for his bad chest than the cold north. For already there was another shadow cast over his life – he told Gower that in South Africa a doctor had told him he had tuberculosis.

At Western Road, there was a partial reunion of the family – the three sisters, Adelaide, Mary Jane and Ellie, who came down from Liverpool, and Robert of the three or four brothers. As far as I know this was the only time these four got together, and it seems that Robert never saw any of his brothers again, and Kathleen makes no mention of them.

So at thirty-one, Robert Noonan, later to become once and for all Robert Tressell, was already into the last phase, the last decade, of his life in the setting which was going to have a more profound effect on him than all the grisly farce of the Boer War and the macabre revels of Irish 'history' – the doltish brutality of English class society in the town which he was to immortalize as 'Mugsborough'. God knows what he would have made of the industrial slums we called 'factory towns', but in Edwardian Hastings he had a perfect example of the smug humbug of Imperial gentility with everyone understanding the proper place to which apparently it had pleased God to call them.

But the town was recommended in medical journals especially to sufferers from bronchitis and 'incipient pulmonary weakness' as they put it, and this was probably mentioned to Robert and may have decided him to stay on the South Coast among the yachts, the bandstands, the steamers, the rowing-boats and the Pierrots and Columbines. So they stayed awhile with Aunt Mary Jane. 'How long,' says Kathleen, 'I don't know, but my aunt probably thought we had money and when she found we hadn't our welcome wore out.'

The four, Robert, Kathleen, Adelaide and Arthur, found a house at 1 Plynlimmon Road on the West Hill, Hastings, a house with a fine prospect of the castle and the gas-works. Robert had, of course, to find something to do for a living and I believe he moved over from St Leonards because he had found a job with a builder in Hastings.

Someone once asked him why he didn't start his own business in signwriting and interior decorating but was told that being entirely unknown here and unused to English conditions, Robert considered that he stood no chance. I believe this would have been so at that time although his special skills might have turned the balance had he received the full prices as self-employed.

I believe also that the simple reason why he did not was lack of capital: with competition what it was he might have had to live for a long time on his own money. But I'm also convinced that there were deeper reasons which unfitted him for business.

And even as a highly skilled workman he couldn't have come at a worse time for a job. It is true that Hastings had become a 'superior' resort, although not so superior as Eastbourne, but with no basic industries, with a higher than average of retired and elderly inhabitants (it still has) and an economy best described as taking in one another's washing. St Leonards, originally laid out by James Burton, a nineteenth-century speculator, had many streets built for the new gentry, many of which in my time became the one- or two-roomed homes for hundreds of lonely remittance women – the spinster relations of the aforesaid gentry, so much thicker than blood is water.* But the only industrial buildings were the gas-works retort-houses, built almost in the centre of the town by the cheeky founders, and which belched smoke and the sickly smell of gas over the populace.

The old catch, which would be added to any list of wonders of the world, expressed the feelings of the more patriotic working-class inhabitants, examples, 'Well, we've got so and so and a photo of the pier', or 'What would you like and a photo of the pier', or, 'Yes they presented him with an illuminated address – and a photo of the pier.' For all I know, of course, they have the same sense of civic pride in Wigan.

The town being entirely without factories and industry, the working classes lived off the Corporation (and men literally fought for jobs there), the public utilities, the railways (and horse-buses), shops and hotels (the two worst-paid occupations), and domestic service, or the 'kiss-me-Aunt trades' as they were referred to by an irascible elderly working gentleman of my youth who used to carry the hod.† And last of all there was the building.

And Robert was dependent upon this, the worst of the lot. The trade was at its lowest ebb for twenty years in Hastings following the developments in Victoria's reign when most of the town had been built – the population at sixty-five thousand was nearly four times as great as fifty years earlier. But sixty-five thousand was the limit, in fact the numbers actually declined by five thousand during the eight years Robert lived here.

And there was the aftermath of the Boer War. Consequently new building during the whole period was very limited, in fact there wasn't an undertaking in the town that subsisted only on building, and none that could undertake a large project. Many made no pretence of ever building a house in their lives but those who *had* dignified themselves with the name of 'builder' were little more than jobbers. And in such a set-up it could not be expected that craftsmen of exceptional and varied skills would find much scope. I don't know how long Robert had to wait before finding work, some time late in 1901 or early in 1902. His first employers told me that they had no knowledge of him and I couldn't search their records, but it was for Bruce and

*See F.C.Ball, *A Grotto for Miss Maynier*.
†My mother's father. See F.C.Ball, *A Breath of Fresh Air*.

Co., Electrical and Sanitary Engineers and Builders of 2 York Buildings, Hastings, just off the Prince Albert Memorial (clock-tower) that he started, and we first see him through the eyes of William Gower, an apprentice.

Gower remembers arriving at the shop one day and seeing a new 'hand' doing something in the shop window. Gower, when opportunity arose, passed a remark by way of conversation as apprentices do, and received such an 'unusual kind of reply coming from a workingman' he says, that he became curious about the new hand. And although he can't remember the reply, he never forgot his first meeting with Robert Noonan. But their real acquaintance began at 10 Stockleigh Road, St Leonards, home then of Professor W.C.T.Beasley, RA where, when Gower arrived on the job, Robert was graining the Professor's front doors. Gower himself was a Premium apprentice, his mother paying ten pounds for that privilege, and the character Bert White, the painter's boy in *The Ragged Trousered Philanthropists*, is partly drawn from him although Gower was an apprentice electrician. Robert apparently was on top rate for Hastings, sevenpence halfpenny an hour, and it is said that after the firm acquired his services it was able to undertake jobs of interior decoration for which, till then, London firms or London craftsmen had been contracted. His reputation as artist soon got around and his varied skills placed him virtually in a class of his own among the local house-decorating fraternity and seems to have surprised him. He had expected very high standards in England, apparently, and was surprised that he could surpass the average.

And it must be remembered that a house-painter in those days really was a skilled man and many more processes were used in ordinary house-decorating than now. He had to mix and match colour, grain, gild, varnish, etc. Paint out of pots had only just been introduced. Yet both Gower and Ward speak of Robert's diffidence about his work and this lasted all his life. This diffidence is expressed in the book through Frank Owen, especially in Chapter Eleven – 'Hands and Brains'. This diffidence also suggests that Robert had in fact had no previous experience in England. But, says Gower, he never presumed by virtue of his extra talent; and indeed, 'never gave any inkling that he was other than an ordinary member of the working class'.

In fact no one ever raised the question with me that they suspected he might not have come originally from the working class. I think his mates in Hastings wouldn't associate his slight Irish 'twang' with the cut-glass accents they expected of gentlemen. 'And in appearance too', said one, 'he always looked like a skilled artisan and never a decayed gentleman.'

His very skill, of course, would add to their convictions that he was from a working class background, but they did recognize a difference.

'He was wearing a house-painter's apron and a stetson hat', said Gower. He never wore the common cloth cap, perhaps because said Albert Sellens, who knew him later on, 'it would have fitted too tightly round the active interior'.

Gower wasn't alone in recognizing that here was someone different, someone, he said, who had his own ideas, ideas rather different from the run of the mill workman, who so often spoke in newspaper headlines much like his betters, someone who was educated and had been around and liked conversation. But Gower himself was not quite the run of the mill, either. Says he,

> I was myself something of a critic of existing conditions, and I did not hesitate to express my youthful opinions to the men on the job there. I used to like to start arguing with Noonan to hear his answers and we became great friends. I always endeavoured to get myself sent on jobs with him and so did the other lads. He always treated us kindly and was an interesting man to work with. He said he had just returned from South Africa where 'Things were very unsettled following the Boer War.'

Talking of Bert White, the apprentice, in the book, Robert says, 'He soon became a favourite with Owen, for whom he conceived a great respect and affection. . . . Bert in his artful, boyish way, would scheme to be sent to assist Owen, and the latter whenever possible used to ask that the boy might be allowed to work with him.' And he seems to have got on with most of the men and made some friends among them and it was on this first firm that he made the ambiguous remark 'sorry to do anyone out of a job'. True he seemed a bit of a mystery and didn't say much about himself, but his workmates soon discovered he was a skilled man and could express himself on a number of other subjects besides his trade.

Robert, of course, was a man who wore his heart on his sleeve, where it ought to be, and by all accounts, and as Gower noticed upon their first meeting in the shop, he had a completely open and natural manner with people, but kindly and considerate of considerate people. And openness of character is the last thing required in our society, especially in business and official relations, and poor Tressell, I believe, made a discovery in England that he hadn't made before. Not because he was naïve (although he was one of 'God's fools' as they used to call such open people)* but he had been a self-employed man in South Africa, was highly skilled, was well read and of considerable education and, I believe, had had no direct experience of English class society and working conditions and could not know that, as in the Armed Services, for a man even to look intelligent is considered an affront.

I was told that this first employer never addressed an employee directly but always through the chief foreman, Robert's 'Misery', and actually sacked a man for presuming to approach him in the street about a matter concerning a job the men were engaged upon. It was something to do with prestige. This kind of thing is still widespread although some of the new youngsters are erasing the word 'Sir' from their vocabularies.

Half a century after Tressell I was myself stopped for saying 'Good morning' to the manager of the local Gas Board without adding the 'Sir'. And I suppose the chairman at the top is 'My Lord' or even 'Your Majesty', but you can get a medal or a gold watch for it if you hang on for forty years. Poor Tressell, he got a pain in the neck and was punished with early death.

One can imagine the effect upon a skilled man from a frontier town in South Africa meeting with these phenomena in England. Whatever status he enjoyed in South Africa, he was about to begin making the discovery that in Britain, working men in that day were only used as doormats, and he would be regarded by his betters with much the same lofty sentiments of contempt and distaste as the black Africans had been in South Africa, but without the same consideration he appears to have given his aptly-named 'servant' Sixpence.

He was about to discover too that an important field of psychological and sociological study may be afforded by the 'business' man. With a tinge of unconscious snobbery he gives a pen-portrait of his first boss.

'He was a man', he says, 'who took himself very seriously. There was an air of pomposity and arrogant importance about him which – considering who and what he was – would have been entertaining to any observer gifted with a sense of humour.' 'Considering who and

*My saintly grandmother told me.

what he was', says Robert, as if that is the qualification, but perhaps an angry man may be understood – and incidentally, despite his 'gift of humour', his portraits of his employers are too angry and contemptuous to be 'humorous'.

6

The dignity of labour,
as the man said

He was also about to make the discovery that in England builders'
general foremen of the more obnoxious kind were sometimes obliged
to stuff their bowler-hats with newspaper, especially on big jobs, or a
displaced brick might accidentally put them in hospital among the
nurses. It was at Bruce's that he got half of the character, habits and
predilections of his chief foreman – Nimrod, Misery, Hunter – of
whom he wrote that 'If one were to make a full-face drawing of his
cadaverous visage it would be found that the outline resembled the
lid of a coffin.'

I am told by many that this simile described the ground base, as it
were, of the face to the life, the face itself an embellishment by nature,
as it were, and as described by Tressell, of the coffin idea suggested by
the base.

And I say that he got half of the character and habits of Misery at
Bruce's because he is known to have got the other half at Adams and
Jarrett's later on.

This Misery seems to have made a set at Robert almost from the
start, that is, as soon as he discovered Robert's skill and what manner
of man he was.

It would soon be passed on to Misery, of course, that this Noonan
was some kind of radical; and any appraisal, let alone criticism of life
to people like Misery, who was also a Chapel-man, was worse than
blasphemy, like questioning the very laws of God. And also I have
never met nor indeed heard of a foreman who cared for the idea of
one of his hands being more skilled than he was himself.

Because of his additional skill, Robert was given regular employment during slack periods when some might be stood off and then
Misery would give him all the dirty unpleasant jobs he could invent,
even when not strictly necessary. There is no indication that Robert

expected special treatment, but Misery very pointedly discriminated. One old hand remembers seeing Robert whitewashing filthy cellars while another painter worked exclusively on decorating the upstairs rooms, and another remembers him painting garden railings while Misery took the opportunity to make a pointed but after all perfectly true remark about the dependency of the man of independent mind.

Little is known that can be directly traced to his employment with Bruce and Co., but many of the incidents in *The Ragged Trousered Philanthropists* are, I am told, based upon his experiences there, although some didn't feature in the book in the setting in which they occurred.

One incident, particularly, reveals the kind of violent storm produced in the feelings and the complete change in psychological climate for the little man of whose life on the Rand Ogilvy gives a carefree and even placid picture. Robert was working with a gang on the Post Office, King's Road, St Leonards, and had arrived a little after six o'clock at the 'shop' where the men had to report first and was reprimanded by Misery for being late. Apparently there was a little dust-up between them. Robert went along to the job seething with rage despite the fact that he was in the wrong, but very few men are of a philosophic turn of mind at six o'clock in the morning and in the course of walking a couple of miles before getting on to the job. They say it wasn't the fact of the ticking off which upset Robert, but the manner of it and, of course, the bad blood between them, and, I believe, this new sense of shock I speak of.

At the Post Office there were two forty-foot ladders, one at each end of the building for the men were working on the roof, and later in the morning Robert from his perch aloft was warned by a voice 'Look out, 'ere It comes', and looked down into the street to see Misery approaching. Robert was still fuming over the earlier encounter and to his mate's sudden and almost unbelieving surprise he grabbed a piece of lead piping and with a vehement curse said: 'If that bastard comes up this ladder and starts again I'll knock his brains out with this!'

His mate said he was in such a passion and there was such a look in his eyes that he was shocked to see him and feared there would be murder done. And he wasn't worried for Misery's sake. But as luck would have it, Misery went up the other ladder and stayed away. Robert's immediate passion subsided as quickly as it had arisen and suddenly realizing the awful danger he had been in he exclaimed in great relief, 'Thank God for that.'

'Why?' asked his still shocked mate, 'would you have hit him?'

'Yes I would have done,' said Robert, 'but thank God he went up that side.'

Such people as Robert, of course, challenge the very structure of class society simply by insisting on being treated as human beings. He was too deeply interested in his work, as all craftsmen are, to be a mere 'troublemaker', but the employer must know his place and by God keep it.

In his book Robert describes a visit from Misery which is obviously a reflection of the situation that day at the King's Road Post Office and Owen's experience is so obviously his own.

Owen is working in a room by himself and presently

he began to feel conscious of some other presence in the room; he looked round. The door was open about six inches and in the opening appeared a long, pale face with a huge chin, surmounted by a bowler hat and ornamented with a large red nose, a drooping moustache and two small, glittering eyes set very close together. For some seconds this apparition regarded Owen intently, then it was silently withdrawn, and he was again alone.

He is so surprised and startled that he nearly drops the blowlamp and he feels the blood surge into his cheeks. 'He trembled with suppressed fury, and longed to be able to go out there on the landing and hurl the lamp into Hunter's face ... he would like to take him by the throat with one hand and smash his face in with the other.' But what of his family? 'If it were not for them! ... he would seize him by the collar with his left hand, dig his knuckles into his throat, force him up against the wall and then, with his right fist, smash! smash! smash!' into Hunter's face. And so our author takes Owen through the throes of a very frenzy of rage until it is over and he 'leaned against the wall, white-faced, panting and exhausted.' If only it weren't for his wife and child.

With this kind of malarcky going on it was only a matter of time before the job blew up, and according to Ward so it did in less than a year and Ward added ingenuously that it appeared Robert 'had left under a cloud', but wasn't certain whether he was sacked.

I don't know whether this derogatory comment, the only one from a fellow workman I ever heard of, explains how Robert changed jobs. 'Him,' he said, 'if he didn't like a job he just walked out!'

This came to me second-hand from this man's son, but there is some truth in it for he left 'under a cloud' at least one other job, where he had worked for four years.

I wonder whether later when writing the book he gives a kind of backward-looking preview, as it were, of his leaving, in Chapter Seven with Crass, sub-foreman, speaking:

> 'Between me an' you an' the gatepost, as the sayin' is, I don't think Mr bloody Owen will be 'ere much longer. Nimrod 'ates the sight of 'im. . . . 'E's 'eard all about the way Owen goes on about politics and religion, an' one thing an' another, an' about the firm scampin' the work. You know that sort of talk don't do, does it?'

And of course it don't do, it don't do at all, especially that bit about 'scampin' the work'.

And here Robert explains how he got his jobs in Hastings.

'' 'Unter would have got rid of 'im long ago', says Crass 'but . . . it was Rushton [the boss] 'imself as give 'im a start. It seems Owen took a lot of samples of 'is work an' showed 'em to the Bloke.'

And Crass's jealousy of these special skills is an echo from real life and explains much of the hostility which Robert experienced from foremen and some of the men – a more potent factor than his socialistic views and merely aggravated by them.

I don't know whether he had a new job before leaving but Ward says that he was out of work for a while and tried London, though it had been thought that an autobiographical passage about London in the book refers to his return from South Africa. In 1922 in the *Painter's Journal*, organ of the National Society of Painters, Mr J.Walsh, General Secretary, wrote a short article on Robert and says when he came to England after South Africa

> he remained for some time in London, where, his physique being against him, he had a bitter struggle for an existence. We get a glimpse of this period in the book where in giving us a picture of Frank Owen, he says, 'He found London, if anything, worse than his native town. Wherever he went he was confronted with the legend: "No hands wanted." He walked the streets day after day; pawned or sold all his clothes save those he stood in, and stayed in London

for six months, sometimes starving and only occasionally obtaining a few days' or weeks' work.'

Raymond Postgate, in his fine book *The Builders' History*, on page 340 gives an account of how Robert came to Hastings after South Africa. He says that he joined one of the London branches of the Painters' union apparently before even getting a job, and that the 'impossibility of getting work sent him on the tramp to Hastings'.

It seems very likely to me that this account follows Walsh and derives from accounts obviously current in the trade which Postgate would have come across in compiling his *History*.

Walsh's account, he tells us, 'comes from a friend very closely associated with him [Tressell] in Hastings', received 'some three or four years ago' which was probably information sought in connection with the 1918 cheap edition, which really brought *The Ragged Trousered Philanthropists* to the notice of the unions.

I mention this because Walsh's notice is the earliest reference to Tressell that has come to my knowledge from union sources. I myself think that the passage refers to the period after leaving Bruce's. When first here from South Africa Robert had some resources even if very few. Kathleen had been sent to boarding-school in Kent, St Ethelburga's at Deal, and this must have been more expensive than maintaining her at home. Perhaps, as she said, they *had* come to England for her education.

What is certain is that their circumstances in England were soon very different from what they had been in South Africa, particularly in relation to Robert's prospects of becoming a Master Man. He makes another reference to London in Chapter Six – 'It is not My Crime', where Frankie Owen and his mother are discussing unemployment: 'Well, I suppose we'd have to go without, that's all, the same as we did when Dad was in London.'

His own account of the situation in London is corroborated by the experience of a couple of friends. These two were stood off and decided to make the trip to 'London-on-Thames', to get work, as it was, and is, generally believed in these parts that there's plenty of everything up there.

They packed up food for a week, took enough money to hire doss-house beds and bought single tickets.

In London, however, they found the streets, paved with building-workers (as everyone was well housed) and at the end of their week they were broke and stranded and reduced to sleeping in doorways, staying on in desperate hope which they at last realized was a joke and so started for home – on foot. But Hastings is sixty-three miles from London and it was in fact several days later before they arrived, sore in foot and mind after living rough on the road and sleeping out.

I've no doubt that Robert himself had real experience of London, and this, together with Bruce's cured him of any illusions about work in England and the status of the workman, whether craftsman, artist or labourer.

And it wasn't his temperament alone which made him detest the set-up and the lack of a real human relationship between employers and men. All the old men (and their wives) I interviewed had evil memories of the three main firms he worked for: the mildest of them spoke in terms of disapproval of the bosses and many of the foremen and the wrongness of it and some damned them out of hand in bitter language, and all spoke of the low wages and harsh conditions imposed upon them.

That his reactions weren't peculiar to himself is also, of course, proved by the rise of the Trade Unions and Labour Movement.

I have dealt first with his work, with the impact of this first job because of the obviously profound effect his new working life in England had upon him, making him put work and conditions of its performance at the centre of his book. It is from the shock of his experiences with Bruce and Co. that I date the real origin of the passionate sense of outrage which was to inspire and light up *The Ragged Trousered Philanthropists*; and, perhaps, the beginning of the deep sense of loss which he was to feel over the rest of his short life.

Robert Noonan Tressell and his young daughter Kathleen, photographed against a painted landscape, in Cape Town, 1896.

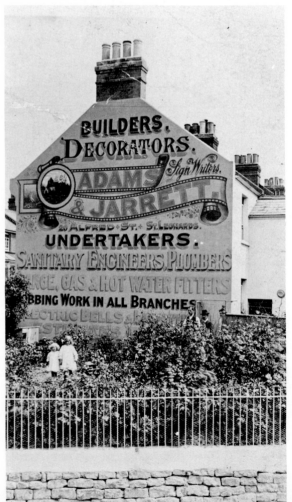

Wellington Place in Hastings – the Mugsborough of Robert's book. The scene is still recognizable in present day Hastings.

Robert, in a trilby hat, stands below an advertisement he designed and painted in about 1907. Tressell worked for Adams and Jarrett for some years.

7

Robert at home

In the same year as he left Bruce's he moved to the top flat of five in Grosvenor Mansions, 115 Milward Road, in the same area. Milward Road runs along the west side of the West Hill from the Castle and from the top flat of number 115 one has something of the same prospect as at Plynlimmon Road but with a better view of the gasworks. Both of Robert's main residences here consisted of top flats, a little cheaper than those lower down probably, but hardly what I would have thought a man would choose who suffered from what his friends and relations called 'asthma'. The four remained together, Adelaide apparently acting as housekeeper, and here they were to remain for four years or so.

The flat, an architectural curiosity of three attics, allowed for a small room for Robert, a separate bedroom for Kathleen and a room for mother and son, plus a communal sitting-room, but no bathroom of course in those days. It was quite a journey up and down four floors from the front door and a long flight of high-rising steps from Stonefield Road, off Queen's Road, which Robert would walk up from the builder's shop of his new employer.

The floors, said Gower, were without carpets and Robert himself had painted designs on the floorboards to take their place, supplemented I believe, by mats, but Kathleen says they had linoleum and both accounts are probably right for different periods and flats.

Some of the walls, too, had been painted quite elaborately and artistically. One with a curved ceiling, says Kathleen, was 'painted in the style of Louis XIV period with cherubs and scrolls and things', and in fact as late as 1969,* when I last saw the interior, traces of these decorated ceilings remained – after about sixty-seven years!

In Kathleen's room the wallpaper had a motif of poppies which, she says, '[I] drew faces over as much of the wall as I could reach because I saw faces everywhere'.

*See Robert's brief reference in Chapter Six – 'It is not My Crime'.

Gower and others describe his various homes as very poorly furnished; in Robert's own room 'were mostly books on the floor, books on the chairs and some of the "furniture" was made of boxes'. Kathleen says that this is something of an exaggeration. I think that Gower would be impressed by the unusual number of books, but nevertheless, being himself from a working-class home, he would not have remembered that the furnishings were poor unless noticeably so by his own family's standards, and these were humble enough. Gower also said that he had often seen Robert writing at a 'table' made from a large box and with a pile of books for a seat, but Kathleen does not confirm this, although Gower mentioned seeing her sitting at the only table, by the window, doing school homework, with Robert in the middle of the room surrounded by books. Kathleen, however, mentions a sideboard and a round table on which was a green-shaded lamp.

The only other possession Gower mentioned was an 'Irish harp on which Robert would strum while he sang old songs, mostly Irish, to amuse himself', but Kathleen said that it was 'an Italian harp decorated with rams' heads round the top of the fluted front column, and it only had five strings. I was supposed to learn the harp at one time, but one day my aunt was in a temper and slashed the five strings and that was the end of the harp.'

But Robert wasn't above doing a bit of singing even if it wasn't to the harp. He had quite a deep singing voice, said Kathleen, and she mentions 'The Diver' – 'To the depths of the ocean cold', words which at this distance sound worthy of Sankey and Moody themselves. 'He also had a wonderful sense of humour' she said.

He rarely called us by name – always by some funny or insulting one, 'Funny Face' or some outlandish name he'd invented. When out walking with us he would make up names from signs and notices to amuse us, like 'Isn't Sally a lucky girl?' 'Who's Sally?' 'Why look over there, there's a house for sale(y)', and he used to come home and for little Arthur's benefit hang his hat on an imaginary nail on the wall and walk away and of course it would fall to the floor. We used to think it very funny. I can remember Arthur and I doing drawings and sticking them on the wall by the sideboard and underneath we had written, 'Drawn by hand', and Dad coming in and saying about them, good thing we had put 'by hand' or people may have thought we had done them with our feet.

The lavatory window of their flat opened high above the steps from Stonefield Road and Kathleen was able to teach the little boy how to pour water on the heads of people climbing slowly up, until one lady had to buy a new hat and called at the flat to congratulate the parents whereupon Kathleen locked herself in the lavatory fearing a spanking but Robert was at work and Adelaide had to pay up.

And sometimes, the flat being very high, almost perched on top of a building, the birds used to get into Kathleen's room and once, she says, she came home and found it full of visitors and part-time residents sheltering from the rain, and the adults had to get them out, by removing a window-pane as the birds got caught between the sashes.

'One piece of "box" furniture we had,' said Kathleen,

was our coal-box. It was half the size of a large packing-case and covered with 'Lincrusta' paper as though it was an Oriental piece. It had a lift-up lid at the top and a drop-leaf in front about a third of the height. In it we kept our Pandroculus which we fed with 'Smithydanders', and they belong to a land in which Arthur and I lived a long time ago with many other creatures and people – Leprechauns and changelings included.*

And then she adds: 'Entering into our make-believe must have been a relief from the tragedy of everyday life.'

After a short period in a private school and for some reason unknown, considering that she was baptised a Protestant, Kathleen was sent to a Roman Catholic school, the Convent of the Sacred Heart in Old London Road. The Roman Catholic scholars used to walk up the steps opposite the flat and over the green West Hill, Hastings, and down the other side to the Old Town and, says Kathleen, they would meet the Protestant scholars coming down to St Andrew's School which was situated right under the Noonans' back windows. And they would call out, says Kathleen:

Roman Catholic ring the bell,
When you die you'll go to hell.

And the Catholics would reply:

Proddywhack, Proddywhack, Quack, Quack, Quack,
Go to the devil and never come back.

*Philpot plays this wild beast, the Pandroculus, for the benefit of the children at the Christmas party in Chapter Twenty-nine – 'The Pandorama'.

'Then', said Kathleen,

there was Christmas time when Santa Claus used to come and see us and I remember he was always 'annoyed' because although my father knew he was coming he always used to go out. I believed faithfully in Santa Claus. We always had a Christmas lantern in the hall at Milward Road and at that time an oil-lamp with a green china shade, being green on the outside and white underneath and we children would be round the fire with this lampshade and the Christmas Tree on the side somewhere when Father Christmas came.

Our lantern was one of those that opened like a concertina and it had six panes above and below with little scenes of Christmas, and lit by candle. There was one time when Santa Claus had a glass of magic wine and he gave it to us each to drink and none of us could drink it. It was a magic glass of wine all right for when *he* took it he emptied it right away.

It was probably a wine-glass with a hollow stem, corked. We of course couldn't drink it – Santa removed the cork surreptitiously and no doubt caught the liquid in a handkerchief.

For Christmas presents Dad often used to give me prints of famous pictures. I remember I had a whole lot of Gainsborough's. And then, of course, I had a print of the engraving showing Dr Johnson coming to the rescue of Oliver Goldsmith from his land-lady who wouldn't let him leave his room until he paid the rent. Dr Johnson sent a guinea for immediate relief until he could call but when he called later that day Oliver had already changed the guinea to buy a bottle of wine with instead of paying the rent. Someone visiting us saw this print and admired it and Dad was going to give it to them but I said, 'Daddy, that's mine!'

Kathleen already had a love for reading and her father seems to have had a high opinion of her ability and expressed to more than one of his friends that he hoped she would become a 'lecturer' or teacher. What he didn't foresee was what she in fact became.

With the boy, Arthur, he was on terms almost of father and son and many of the incidents about children in the book are based upon these two children and in some cases use their actual words, such, for instance, as where Frankie, Owen's young son, is lying in bed talking about his new kitten and he hugs his father very tightly.

'Oh, Dad, I love you so much, I could squeeze you to death.'

'I'm afraid you will if you squeeze me so tightly as that.'

'That *would* be a funny way of showing you how much I loved you wouldn't it, Dad? Squeezing you to death!'

The boy would watch for Robert to come up the road from work or up the long steps running down past the flat to Stonefield Road and when Robert arrived would run out and throw his arms round his uncle's neck regaling him with tales of the day's events.

Gower says that Robert used to go into the children's rooms and stand awhile looking down at them. He often spoke bitterly and sadly of the fate of drudgery and want which so many children had to endure and of the future blunting of their fine perceptions, of the loss of the happiness and gaiety natural to childhood.

The relationship between himself and the children is delightfully brought out in the book in different ways through the various child characters. But between brother and sister it appears the atmosphere was neither as free and easy nor as cordial. They weren't apparently on very brotherly and sisterly terms. Kathleen remarks that Adelaide always called her brother 'Robert', and never 'Bob', as his friends did,* and she disapproved of his ideas.

Gower said that on one occasion Robert was 'sternly rebuked' by his sister when he made a bitter attack upon religion in the presence of the children, to which, says Gower, he merely replied that 'children should always be told the truth'.

And he remarks in the book upon the almost unanimous opinion that whether it were true or not 'religion' was a nice thing to teach children. He despised this dishonest attitude.

He was always full of fun and gaiety with children, believing that they must be made happy while they were young, for the future would bring suffering enough without their having it inflicted upon them in childhood.

One day, walking with Gower, and passing ragged children he burst out 'God is a devil who lets little children suffer.' His fears for Kathleen's own future and those fears that went back deep into his own childhood gave a poignant cutting-edge to his compassion. Such sights hurt him – compassion can hurt strong men. And for this reason

*None of his sisters called him 'Bob'. It was always 'Robert'.

Robert, who was fond of Arthur, became much more of a father to him than Adelaide ever became mother to Kathleen.

I got descriptions of Robert's physical appearance at this period from various friends and workmates. He was about five feet three inches tall and, in his early years here, well knit and compact in build, about nine stone in weight. His hair was of a sandy colour and he sported something of an 'Old Bill' moustache, but with 'military' points, as I believe our ancestors called this type of decoration.

His complexion was 'fresh' but both Gower and Ward spoke of the 'pink spots' which appeared in his cheeks in moments of excitement.

Ward described his expression as lively and animated and the eyes as 'piercing'; 'the eyes of a genius', he said, and Ward spoke soberly, but of course, in English folklore and the newspaper world anyone with an animated expression must be mad – or a genius. This 'piercing eyes' look is very marked in a photograph taken by William Gower one Sunday morning sometime in 1907 in the district known as 'Old Roar'; though different photographs may show different aspects of a face, and in fact may often appear not to be of the same person. I make the point because where the friendly Ward in real life saw 'the eyes of a genius', a hostile correspondent, a pupil of Lombroso,* cited the photograph as evidence of unpleasant attributes of character in Tressell.

Kathleen talks of other visitors to the flat. Her father, she says, 'used to bring people home to tea and was just as likely to bring somebody like the crossing-sweeper and a bishop at the same time'. And he was always giving things away. His friends were as mixed as a Christmas pudding, especially later, but in the early days there were the youth, Gower, and a priest, Father O'Callaghan, both regular visitors, and Kathleen, who was sometimes present when the priest came, said he and Robert would probably be sitting up half the night talking.

Other visitors, probably for Adelaide and the children, were two ladies, the Misses Haggard, who are not mentioned in the local Directories and whom I can't identify although Sir Rider Haggard, who was living in St Leonards, had three daughters. There were also a Miss Zillah, Marie le Verrier, miniature-painter, and a Miss Lowe, who, Kathleen says, 'was a writer and illustrator of children's stories

---

* Cesare Lombroso (1836–1909), Italian criminologist who tried to tell us that 'criminal types' could be picked out by anatomical, for instance, facial characteristics, to which one may only reply, God help a vast part of the human race.

who introduced herself when she could not manage to get into conversation with Arthur. (Don't talk to or go with any stranger!) She came to call on Aunt Addie to get permission for Arthur to model for her.'

This 'Miss Lowe' was, perhaps, Constance M. Lowe, writer of books of children's verse, the only Miss Lowe I can discover in the catalogues, and she does not appear to have illustrated her own works, books with such titles as *Amusing Pictures, Little Folks Fun, The Round & Round A.B.C., What A Surprise* and so on, all illustrated by others.

In 1906, when they left Milward Road, Arthur would be about nine years old, so if he was the subject of the illustrations, they were probably done a few years before, but he couldn't have been very young because Kathleen says that Miss Lowe saw him in the street alone. Kathleen at one time possessed one of the books, but it was lost with most of her possessions in Canada.

'Arthur had long curls and was a very pretty and attractive little boy', she says.

> I remember we used to go out together and he always believed in fairies and goblins and when he wouldn't do what I wanted him to do I used to knock on the railing posts to get the goblins listening and tell them all about him and then he would do what I wanted to do. And another thing we did. You know they have hung up in places the leaflets for sailing-boats, the *Albertine* going out for a sail or whatever it is, well I would pull them down and make him go and tell the people sitting on the front and they would give him a ha'penny or we would go and sell them to people for a penny.

Gower tells of a little incident which well shows off Robert's whimsical humour and his free and easy attitude with the children. When visitors were chatting one Sunday morning, Arthur, who was playing with his uncle while the talking was going on, got a little too boisterous and Robert said to him, 'Now, Arthur, you just go to the door, will you, and close it on the outside.'

Gower was a frequent visitor and there was a touch of hero-worship in his feeling for Robert – for this fellow workman full of stories both from real life and from books, with his profound concern for the quality and nature of social relations and his conviction that a man's deepest duty was to struggle for a just and humane society. He was as ardent and enthusiastic as a youngster and talked of everything under the sun.

In their talks there was surprisingly little nattering about horse-racing and women, says Gower. It was politics, economics, history, socialism, flying, books, and so on over a whole range, and in their animated discussions Gower was enthralled – and educated. Even meals were a secondary consideration, he says. Robert would brew a quantity of coffee and they would drink that and carry on talking. Gower remembered Robert once in a moment of peckishness going to the cupboard to look for something to eat, taking out a bowl of cold porridge, having one look at it and putting it back.

He was an intelligent youth, this electrician's apprentice, and eager to learn from Robert what he could never learn from his school-masters, and Robert became both his mentor and friend.

He told me that he always felt, as he put it, that 'some submerged genius lay in Robert'.

What this might be exactly and how, if ever, it would be expressed, other than in Robert's gifts as mentor and conversationalist, Gower couldn't guess at that time. Working-men hardly think of numbering among their friends someone capable of outstanding achievement and in any case Robert's friends thought of him first as a craftsman and what they called a 'gifted artist'.

There's nothing to support Ogilvy's remark that Robert carried on vigorous propaganda against the Boer War after his return to England, a remark which seems to imply 'public' propaganda; and in any case, I don't see how Ogilvy would have heard of it. It's possible that letters were exchanged; but more likely that years later, after the book appeared, references may have been made in England to Robert's anti-Boer War sentiments. And there is Kathleen's memory of being taunted at school as pro-Boer.

The war ended a few months after he came to Hastings but the horrors of the final guerrilla phase, with the British measures against the Boer civilian population, may well have led him to voice his consistent anti-war attitude among friends and acquaintances. In this he wasn't alone, of course, nor was he merely voicing Irish anti-British sentiments. Not from a single person I interviewed nor in any reminiscing about Robert did I ever hear of any hostility to English people because they were English.

Not only is his book entirely free from mere nationalism, but he shows the tragedy of the British soldiers and their dependants and families in references to the old soldier carrying sandwich-boards in Chapter Thirty-two – 'The Veteran' and in Chapter Five – 'The Clock-case', where he describes the death of the young reservist in the war and the circumstances in which his wife, children and aged parents were left.

8

Work, boys, work, and be contented

There are rumours of short terms of work with other firms but sometime in 1902, or early 1903, he started working for Burton and Co., Builders and Contractors, Funeral Directors, Decorators, of 88 Stonefield Road, Hastings, which is still in existence.

Says one of the directors in a letter, 'the writer of this letter has often heard of Bob Noonan as being employed by this firm. We have records that confirm this and that he also wrote coffin-plates. His book is said to be a composite write-up of another firm Bruce and Co. and ourselves. We hope that conditions as revealed by Noonan were not wholly true as far as we ourselves are concerned.'

There was in fact one more firm to make up the trinity which was to inspire *The Ragged Trousered Philanthropists*. In response to the director's hopes about his own firm – well, true or not in Robert's day, the conditions portrayed don't apply today in most respects. But it was another member of this firm who described Robert as a mere illiterate workman who wrote a bad-tempered book. He hadn't, however, known Robert, and it hardly sounds as if he had read the book, and as he wasn't born when Robert worked there his comment is at least evidence that Robert's reputation was still a living memory.

Apparently in Robert's own time it was the old boss of Burton's who described Robert as a 'difficult' man, and few bosses put up with a 'difficult' man unless that man is more than worth his money.

This boss was a typical *Ragged Trousered Philanthropists* character himself – another 'pillar' of the local church (that is, local to where the firm was known) as you had to be in those days, of course, if you wanted to stay in most businesses. He had a peculiar habit, probably due to nightmares brought on by his employees, of getting down to the workshops at 6 a.m. when the men began work, issuing his orders and then going back to bed to finish his nightmare.

He wouldn't allow an 'annual beano', which was an almost universal event in many trades.

'You'll have enough holidays in the winter,' he told the men.

He also enforced a no-smoking rule and I have no doubt many of the references in *The Ragged Trousered Philanthropists* to Misery creeping around trying to catch the men smoking are based upon experiences here.

At one job up on the West Hill, Hastings, the men were more than usually uncomfortable (as people seem to be when deliberately watched at work) because, knowing their old man, they swore he used to sit in his office watching them through a telescope, probably bought for the purpose, they said, for no one ever saw him on the sea-front with the coastguards and so far as their knowledge went he wasn't an astronomer.

This firm kindly let me have a complete set of ledgers for the period of Robert's stay and these show that he spent a good deal of his time on general work, but in places he is mentioned as on a separate job.

As regards the writing of coffin-plates mentioned by the Director, this was one of Robert's jobs on all the firms he worked for, being the signwriter as well. There were many pathetic entries in the ledgers for the writing of coffin-plates for children's funerals, evidence of the higher rate of child mortality then. This random entry, in its own laconic ledger-like manner, is the stuff of *The Ragged Trousered Philanthropists*:

Mr B . . . . 2 W . . . H . . . Cottages.
1904

January 18	To making strong covered Child's Coffin with inside fitting, etc., complete for the late J . . . H . . . B . . . Fees paid for ordinary grave, one interment.	Noonan 1 hour 1 Taking Home 1 To Funeral.
January 22	Single Horse Carriage to Cemetery and Driver's Fee. Undertaker's expenses arranging and conducting Funeral as agreed.	£2 0 0

Settled 22nd January 1904

This, I suppose, would be Robert writing the coffin-plate, and the 'Single Horse Carriage' the type in which the parents ride with the coffin for an infant or young child on a shelf in front of them, and the '1 To Funeral' would no doubt be one of the 'hands' who, as Robert illustrates in his funeral scene, become for the occasion professional mourners and assistants.

I possess a faded, mutilated newspaper-cutting, given me by a friend of Robert's, taken from the *Weekly Dispatch* for 13 August 1905 headed:

DEMENTED FATHER

Kills His Children Because He Could Not See Them Starve.

STRESS OF POVERTY

This story somewhat altered was to find its way into *The Ragged Trousered Philanthropists* in Chapter Four – 'The Placard', in the episode where Owen on his way home from work sees a placard headed:

TERRIBLE DOMESTIC TRAGEDY

and goes into the newsagent's to buy the paper.

The firm's ledger for 1905 carried an entry for Christmas Day:

'Dec. 25th. R. Noonan, writing coffin-plate, one hour'.

Robert explains that funerals were very 'popular' with bosses and, of course, most of the men, because they were paid extra for funeral work. For '1 Taking Home', for the purpose of placing the body in the coffin, or one 'lift in' as this was called, they were usually paid one shilling unless it happened to be a 'high-class'* funeral when they sometimes got one shilling and sixpence. They were never paid by the hour. Likewise Robert's remuneration for the coffin-plates differed according to the 'class of work'.

In Chapter Thirteen – 'Penal Servitude and Death', he illustrates just how beneficial all round a good crop of deaths was, and that children's funerals especially were a kind of bonus. Philpot is speaking of Misery, the chief foreman, to the sub-foreman, Crass:

' 'Ow's 'is temper this mornin', Bob?'

---

*There are, of course, high-class, middle-class and lower-class corpses, as there are people.

'As mild as milk,' replied Crass. 'You'd think butter wouldn't melt in 'is mouth.'

'Seemed quite pleased with 'isself, didn't 'e?' said Harlow.

'Yes,' remarked Newman. ' 'E said good mornin' to me!'

'So 'e did to me!' said Easton. ' 'E come inter the drorin'-room an' 'e ses, "Oh you're in 'ere are yer, Easton", 'e ses – just like that, quite affable like. So I ses, "Yes, sir." "Well," 'e ses, "get it slobbered over as quick as you can", 'e ses, " 'cos we ain't got much for this job: don't spend a lot of time puttying up. Just smear it over an' let it go!"'

' 'E certinly seemed very pleased about something,' said Harlow. 'I thought prap's there was a undertaking job in; one o' them generally puts 'im in a good humour.'

'I believe that nothing would please 'im so much as to see a epidemic break out,' remarked Philpot. 'Small-pox, Hinfluenza, Cholery morbus, or anything like that.'

'Yes: don't you remember 'ow good-tempered 'e was last summer when there was such a lot of Scarlet Fever about?' observed Harlow.

'Yes,' said Crass with a chuckle. 'I recollect we 'ad six children's funerals to do in one week. Ole Misery was as pleased as Punch because of course as a rule there ain't many boxin'-up jobs in the summer. It's in winter as hundertakers reaps their 'arvest.'

This extra money, especially in the case of a high-class corpse, when extra men would change their painter's togs for a collection of frock-coats, could make all the difference in their weekly budgets, and, of course, in the firms' solvency.

Kathleen mentions her father talking about the episode, which is described in the book, of the rival undertakers Rushton and Snatchum when Philpot is killed, and the bamboozling of Philpot's landlady over who should get the funeral job which ends in Misery, Crass and Sawkins (Philpot's own fellow employees) going to the dead man's room with a coffin, where he is already lying in Snatchum's coffin, and removing the body from Snatchum's to their own and carting it away on a hand-truck.

It is a quarter to eleven at night and Crass and Sawkins just have time to get a drink before the pub closes, and they leave the truck and the coffin standing by the kerb. While drinking they discuss the problem of how to write out their time-sheets because, as Crass says, if they put one 'lift in' as usual they will only get a shilling and finally Crass comes up with the answer 'one lift out and one lift in' and 'taking corpse to carpenter's shop'.

Kathleen says, 'I remember about them taking the corpse, lifting it out from one coffin and into the other and Dad saying "one lift out and one lift in". I don't remember whether Dad was one of the men who had to do that or whether he was referring to one of the other men who had to put it on his time-sheet.'

I'm not sure on which firm this incident took place but Robert vouched for its truth.

Someone once asked Robert what he earned and he named a sum and the questioner remarked that it was very good to which Robert replied, 'Oh, that's not what I *get* – you asked me what I *earned*.'

Robert makes many mentions of the men tramping the streets to and from jobs, dressed in an assortment of old clothes, pushing hand-trucks or carrying tools, but he hasn't the occasion to mention how long were the journeys they often had to make.

Employers in those days took it for granted that our forerunners were long-distance walkers and nocturnal in their habits. Any job within about a ten-mile radius had to be reached on foot – and six o'clock was the time on the job. Men sometimes had to start from home at three and four o'clock in the morning and pad it, rain, snow, thunder or lightning, often arriving saturated, to work in empty houses or on building sites without fires for warmth or cooking. Luckily, builders don't feel the wet and cold as other people do. The secret is that they varnish the naked skin before dressing. In summer you might be on a job for thirteen or fourteen hours, when you were then at liberty to walk home, and if your wife was still up and hadn't locked you out, she would serve a meal for you. Work was broken for short periods of sleep during the night, no method having been discovered of working men for the twenty-four hours and keeping them alive. Just the kind of life for a man with a weak chest. Men who worked with Robert tell me of such journeys to villages like Ninfield, Mountfield, Crowhurst and Netherfield, all many miles outside Mugsborough.

And if the job was too far, even as employers calculated mileage, then the men would pack a week's food in the time-honoured wicker-basket and live on the job, sleeping at night on the floors amid the dust and the paint-pots, the plaster and the shavings. One can picture the old building-workers tramping through the dark overhung Sussex lanes, dressed in their drainpipe trousers, caps and bowlers, and a rare collection of second-hand clothes, the rain dripping off their walrus moustaches. One can sympathize with their imprecations on work and the weather and the size of the country, and the slowness of time.

Many men who couldn't get work in Hastings managed it in better-off Bexhill, where the rate, by one of those strange quirks, was a penny an hour higher, and walked there by six o'clock in the morning and left for home at half past five in the evening – unless there was overtime! And Bexhill was only four and a half miles. My maternal grandfather for a long time walked to and from Crowhurst, about five miles from his home.

And with the men, of course, would be the 'apprentices', perhaps lads as young as fourteen years dragged out of bed at four or five o'clock in the morning, with a margarine breakfast, threadbare clothes, and, if they were 'lucky', hobnail boots, which chafed the feet and toes, often causing bleeding, but kept the feet dry. If they were 'unlucky', they might be wearing a thin pair of worn boots or even slippers or an old pair of mother's shoes if nothing else was available, and there was many a battle between mothers and sons over the wearing of women's shoes, they somehow lowered one's dignity.

For dinner, perhaps several slices of bread and an onion, in some cases the men each putting a small contribution from their own baskets to make up a meal for the boy. There were cuffs and curses for these lads from their rough and ready seniors, but always quick aid and sympathy in any real difficulty, as Robert shows. On the whole, semi-starvation, exposure, and the blunting of the mind by such a life were the greatest enemies of the very poor.

The worst condition of such 'apprentices' applied only to the poorest where proper 'indentures' weren't part of the contract; but such conditions were by no means uncommon and the apprentice's real welfare depended upon the economic standard of his home. If father had a fair job his son might eat reasonably and be clothed for the English climate and not the Bahamas. His condition certainly didn't depend upon his earnings nor his boss's kindness.

Robert's 'apprentice' Bert was at least paid 2d. an hour overtime. Twenty years later than Bert, after the First World War, I was paid 5s. a week and 1d. an hour overtime – 4½d. for a Saturday afternoon.

A 'green' apprentice might have other 'temporary' problems. He might (but only once) be sent with great urgency to get a rubber hammer for a piece of delicate work in soft material, or a left-handed screw-driver for a left-handed carpenter. On this firm one of the youngsters was sent across the road to a builders' merchant for some spotted paint for rocking-horses (as I daresay thousands of apprentices have over some centuries) and was asked by the (experienced) shopman whether the painters wanted white-spotted paint for black horses or black-spotted paint for white horses.

Robert was to stay with this new firm for about four years and to get to know the town. It is with the atmosphere of Hastings that the book seems most closely associated, in all the scenes of the locale and of Owen's domestic life, especially those involving his child. Arthur, Robert's nephew, was about the same age as Owen's Frankie and undoubtedly a model for him. And although most of the book was written in the St Leonards area and many of the work anecdotes relate to his last employment there, the whole atmosphere is of Hastings and the town centre and environs, and a great deal of incident dates from the years before he moved to St Leonards. Ogilvy, Gower and Poynton all agree that he kept notes.

A few other anecdotes which didn't go into his book are told of his period with Burton's.

At a large house in Hollington Park, the firm had a job for a boot-manufacturer, Upson, a prominent figure in the town, a fiery Tory gentleman disliked by all workmen who had the misfortune to work at the house – they said he had an eye like a 'stinking eel'. He used to amuse himself by standing watching them at work, passing highly critical remarks, though there is no record that he ever had his head shoved into a bucket of whitewash.

On one occasion Robert started singing 'Work for the Night is Coming', and the men began singing with him, an incident later recorded in the book, but given to Philpot.

This man used often to be seen being driven along the sea-front in his coach and four to the glory of Mugsborough. The workmen who told me this story asked whether I would be glad to hear that the men, during their long stay (and his absence) burned three tons of his coal and one of coke, to save him the bother, and, of course, to keep themselves warm.

It was at Val Mascal that Robert is said to have decorated the

Moorish room and some have told me that this was the famous 'Cave', the setting for the book. The job lasted a long time, from September 1903 till June 1904, and most of the firm's staff were employed on it and Robert thus had a well-varied assortment of crafts and men under one roof.

Here it was that when Philpot and the others were picking losers as they do in the book, they used to hide the paper and themselves in a large cupboard to avoid sudden interruption.

And here Robert played one of his practical jokes on the foreman carpenter. This man was in the habit of sneering at the degree of skill required by a house-painter but in a slack period he suggested to the boss that he should fill in a little time at painting. Robert fixed up an effigy resembling the foreman (and his effigies *could* resemble people) dressed up and painted, hung a characteristic 'watch' across its waistcoat and erected it in the drive leading to the house. On it he put a placard saying, 'Please, sir, I want to be a painter.' It was duly seen by the carpenters' foreman with, it seems, chastening effect.

All accounts agree that there was only one Robert Noonan and not 'two faces under one hat', as he quotes about Crass in the book. He wore this face to men, bosses and customers alike. Green described him as a very friendly little man, who used to repeat a rhyme which explained everything:

> Oh! the sadness of his sadness when he's sad,
> And the gladness of his gladness when he's glad.
> But the sadness of his sadness and the gladness of his
>   gladness
> Are nothing to his madness when he's mad!

And apparently they weren't.

Both his character and his views enlivened the plain issue between the traditional Tory and Liberal partisans among the men. In his time the radicals were turning to socialism, himself among them, which his openness of character could not and would not hide, and although he never intruded his views, he also never hid them and this added spice to his relationships both with the men and with employers who, of course, were told.

He wasn't unique in this habit of frankness but he was virtually a colonial to whom a free and easy manner was natural at the level of ordinary men. But his workmates knew their England better than he did and only the undefeated, uncorrupted among them managed to keep their manhood intact. These recognized this incorruptibility in Robert and accepted the vulnerable colonial as an honest man. He doesn't perhaps make enough of them in his book – but it was a case of watch your step and they knew what happened to any workman who imagined he was living in a free country.

He was free to starve.

9

Artist and artisan

On Sundays he dressed smartly, almost dapperly, usually in a grey 'fashionable' suit, 'soft' hat or a stetson, set at a tilt, and he liked carrying a walking-stick.

He walked with a jaunty step – a slight roll – and friends pulled his leg with nicknames. Len Green writing years later said, 'As I write this letter* I can see Bob and hear his cheery laugh, he always seemed to be a very Happy Man. My Dad and him got on very well together. Our family always called him "Dolphus", he had a very Harty Laugh but would put his hand on his Chest and I ask him once what was the matter and he said I am "One Lung" in Chinese and I knew he was a Tubercloses Victim.'

This 'tuberculosis', was called 'bronchial asthma' by Kathleen and apparently by others but Gower didn't think Robert was quite so sure.

He had a habit of illustrating his argument with drawings and diagrams – at work, in the dirt on the floor with a tool or on glass with chalk from his pocket kept for the purpose, or in the dust of the street and even on the sand of the sea-shore with the walking-stick. So if you met him out for a walk on Sunday or ran into him anywhere, you might find yourself looking at the pavement while this little man drew diagrams in the dust for you illustrating the proportions of drones to worker-bees, or bishops to itinerant mendicants, and very likely to the great curiosity of passers-by, for the English as a rule aren't given to making themselves conspicuous.

On one occasion, as he was rounding the Memorial with the lad who was assisting him on a job at St Andrew's Church, he absent-mindedly paused to illustrate some point with a drawing on one of the windows of the York Hotel. A policeman spotted him and ordered him to 'pretty soon rub that out or I'll run you round the corner', 'round the corner' being the near-by police station.

*Of reminiscences to me for this book. I've left Len's own style.

It was, as one of his characters says, 'due to his reading all them books'.

In the same letter Mr Green says, 'Bob was very fond of reading and used to buy cheap books at the bookstall and I use to pay him a 1d. for the use of one a week as I was fond of reading. One of them was called "The Waters Of Lourdes" where people went to bath in the waters for Health Cures.'

Gower gave me a list of authors he remembered Robert quoting in conversation. Among these were Dickens, Swift, Fielding, Shakespeare, Shelley, Byron, Whittier, Oliver Wendell Holmes, William Morris and John Ruskin, who was a favourite. Robert also lent him Sir Edwin Arnold's *Light of Asia*, and Haeckel's *Evolution of Man*. Robert would often quote the English poets, though he makes no use of the great ones in his book except for Tennyson's *In Memoriam*.

According to Gower, the literary figure for whom he had the greatest admiration was Dean Swift, another redoubtable Anglo-Irishman.

On many a fine Saturday afternoon, said Gower, Robert would take a walk over the West Hill, sometimes with Gower, sometimes alone, down into the Old Town to browse among the second-hand book-shops and this is principally how he built up his little library.

He loved these outings and besides his black trilby hat (for he was never seen hatless) he usually sported a buttonhole, being partial to flowers, and liked to stand looking in the florists' shops, said Gower, because he wished that he could afford more flowers for the house. Or he would walk down to the sea-front and along to where the fishing-smacks were drawn up beyond the harbour wall. The harbour had only this one wall for though a ton of money went into building a harbour, it proved too expensive and the sea was declared the winner.

In Robert's day the Hastings Old Town, little of which is now left, was still largely its old self, and the most interesting part of the town, although it was here that Robert would have seen some of the worst poverty and hardship.

Although he liked a drink, his drinking was mostly confined to meetings with friends and other social occasions. Until he joined the Social Democratic Federation his recreations were mostly walking or talking with friends who came to the flat, reading, and working on ideas and designs for interior decoration which was his hobby as well as his profession.

The following romantic account was collected while the memory was still fresh among his friends. In the 1922 article in the *Painter's Journal*, Walsh says·

He was a brilliant scenic painter and signwriter and also a grainer, and was in great demand in decoration of local churches, where his work received much admiration. He loved his Art for Art's sake. He shared with William Morris and Walter Crane a desire to give to the world the best that was in him, so that the beauty of his work should be an inspiration to all in striving for that which is most beautiful.

Like Morris and Crane, he found himself in revolt against the degrading conditions of labour imposed on the workers by Capitalism.

He had a hard struggle with failing health and poverty. His gifts brought him no extra remuneration. Art was not wanted. Much of his time was spent in the less skilled work of washing off, distempering, etc. Nothing distressed him more than the scamping of his work. He, like the rest of us, was not permitted to do his best. Everything was sacrificed to the god of profit.

Apparently it was the men at Burton's who first gave him the nickname 'Raphael' in reference to his artistic skills. One of his foremen, too, remarked that he was really an artist, not a house-painter. He was always working at designs for imaginary mural decorations and spent much time studying technical books on the arts and interior decoration, and those long browsings in second-hand bookshops were often made in course of searching for these.

More than one man, and also his niece, told me that Robert was a better artist than indicated by any examples of his work then surviving, and though I hadn't the chance to see any other than wall advertisements and such-like, these too were pretty impressive examples of the signwriter's craft. And, of course, there is the surviving photograph of St Andrew's Church, and many signwriters would have been glad to have done a piece of work like that once in a lifetime. But he seemed essentially a muralist – there was little danger in any case of his affording the materials for much canvas painting. But he was interested in the human figure because when Gower called one day Robert was drawing and asked him to sit for a study. Gower said that he seemed to be diffident, even apprehensive, of someone entering and finding him trying to draw the portrait of a man. Poynton, however, says that he was quick and bold in his sketching. By all accounts, including his own in the book, his mural designs were worked out carefully and painstakingly at home and then stencilled on to the walls. Even his signwriting was elaborate. A huge one, now painted over, on a wall at Perth Road included a little landscape of Hollington Church-in-the-Wood inset, and also an inset of a landscape with birds.

Such examples as are known of his murals are very much Victorian-Edwardian. They were of course all commissions via his employers, but I don't think in any case that he had any real originality, or even interest in the art of painting as a means of revolutionary experiment and discovery.

It has always been a curious omission to me that no one ever mentioned him making any reference to art and artists, and in fact he makes none in the book. Not a word has come to us of any interest in the great painters or in the art itself, except for his interest in William Morris and Walter Crane – and that, it seems to me, was chiefly because of their views on the social duty of the artist to make the environment more beautiful for his fellow men.

He was essentially conservative in his work, I believe, because for all his delight in his skill painting was not his true means of expression.

The most elaborate piece of work of which we have an existing record – a photograph – was carried out in St Andrew's Church, Queen's Road (next to the gas-works) and was a gift from his employer Mr H. Burton, to the church. The gift took the form of a redecoration of the chancel and is a comprehensive and in many ways remarkable example of the work of Tressell the signwriter-artist. In elaborate floral settings and scrolls it seems to exhibit every variety of script as if in glorification of his craft.

He worked out his own designs in his own time in the evenings and cut stencils for them in cardboard, an extremely exacting task over such a large area, embodying many thousands of separate stencils of a variety which it would take a book to describe and illustrate in detail. The stencils were traced on the walls with a pounce of muslin and whiting. They were then painted. In the episode of the Moorish room in the book, he describes something of his method. He says that long after bedtime, and all night if necessary, he worked searching through old numbers of the *Decorator's Journal* for examples, and going through books from the Free Library. Kathleen says that he possessed a folio of William Morris designs and he may well have used Morris motifs or similar models for St Andrew's, but he was still responsible for his own over-all designs, as is clear from the book when he talks of Owen giving much thought to designs and roughing out general plans.

The general design is a mosaic effect, the segments consisting of floral and foliate motifs with some formal designs based upon these; and along the whole base of the work a row of large panels, beautifully written in many scripts, of the Lord's Prayer and the Apostles' Creed, with excerpts from the Bible; and the whole crowned with great scrolls with the words 'Holy, Holy, Holy', wreathed in a leafy setting. The whole gave a marvellous effect of an illuminated manuscript on a large scale, say twenty feet high and forty feet round the chancel. It was typical of the style of the Late Victorian period inherited from the Pre-Raphaelites and from William Morris particularly.

The designs of Morris and his associates, with their ornate foliate tracery, appear even in the designs for membership cards of socialist organizations of the period, such as that of the Social Democratic Party illustrated. It doesn't follow that Tressell was self-conscious about the influence nor that it was direct, but Morris was already an influential industrial designer and theorist when Robert was a boy, and Robert's training, whatever it was, must have incorporated the older artist's ideas. And I believe that Robert became particularly interested in Morris's work for the Socialist Movement and in his theories on the arts, craftsmanship and industrial design.

We get a little historical glimpse of him at work at his craft – exactly the kind of scene he depicted in his book – through a lad who assisted him, an old man when I spoke to him, who remembered Robert and the occasion well. Robert was working at night in the church to get the job completed by Easter. And the days and the quiet church too were enlivened with arguments between Robert and a verger of the church who made efforts to 'convert' him. This, said Robert's assistant, who described him as 'a bit of a firebrand', led to rows. I'll bet it did. It was an imposition on the part of the verger and it put Robert at a great disadvantage, as indeed it would put any man questioned about his religious and political views at his place of work.

I prefer to think of the scene when the verger was safely tucked up and the artist could work on in peace into the night. It must have made many passers-by, and policemen, too, wonder at seeing the church lighted into the early hours, and the artist by himself working in the eerie stillness, and tired at last locking the church and walking up the steps opposite St Andrew's to his flat at the top of them at three and four o'clock in the morning, as his daughter says.

And as he says of Owen and as Gower and others say of Robert himself, the question of what he 'made' out of it was 'unimportant', was truly unimportant. The work was the thing, a notion which may strike many practical people as entirely romantic. He describes in a passage about the Moorish room how in his imagination he saw the reredos, the walls from floor to ceiling, the whole chancel, the plain stone Victorian church itself, 'transformed and glorified'.

For the magnificent work at St Andrew's, later whitewashed over,* the artist got eightpence an hour (an extra penny) plus an agreed number of hours for overtime (a negotiated percentage of actual time) and was apparently trusted to put in a correct time-sheet for night-work.

Upon the completion of the work, evidently for the Easter Festival, the Vicar of St Andrew's presented Robert with a present of five pounds and a testimonial:

> Mr Robert Noonan
> from Rev. Henry W. Jeaves.
> (Vicar)
> As a souvenir of his most artistic renovation of the Chancel of St Andrew's Church, Hastings. Easter 1905.

His wages did not in fact cover the real time worked. Often he didn't show all the time he worked in the nights, and the honorarium represented in fact only something like a fortnight's extra pay, or three weeks' ordinary pay at the number of hours put in. Nor did it take into account the harm that the great physical effort must have done to his health.

---

*For the subsequent history of the mural see Chapter Forty.

10

Linguist and model-builder

A quite extraordinary accomplishment mentioned by Kathleen, but strangely enough by none of his friends, was his linguistic ability, but this could merely mean that he had no occasion to mention the fact to these working-men. There is evidence that he knew something of French, not perhaps in the fact that he signed a letter to Kathleen 'Je vous aime toujours' for she had learned some French herself, but that he used the phrase without comment. This is Kathleen's own account:

> Robert could speak several languages and tried to keep Kathleen's French (her mother's tongue) alive by mealtime conversations. He himself could speak French, German, Dutch, Spanish, Italian, Gaelic, about seven. The Dutch was real Dutch not Afrikaans. He spoke French fluently.
>
> He probably learned them at home – remember his father was supposed to be a scholar. Latin would make French and Spanish easy. German, of course, is different but he probably picked up Dutch in Africa. I don't remember that we had many Greek books but we had French and German ones.

English made up the seven but if he knew Latin and Greek the number is greater.

I am not surprised that a man who by the time he was about twenty had mastered a half-dozen skilled arts and crafts and was soon writing pieces for publication should find the life of a house-painter in Hastings galling; I am only more than ever mystified as to his motives for remaining in the trade and the overbearing circumstances which prevented a man who *was* well read and could speak several languages from getting some kind of teaching or professional appointment even in those days of limited opportunity. But both Kathleen and his niece say he deliberately chose to become a worker.

I am also not surprised that despite his natural friendliness, some of the sardonic spirit of his book and some of the violent reactions of

Owen are attributed to Robert himself. He may well have exercised his linguistic abilities with Father O'Callaghan, for since we can be certain that the priest wasn't there as Father Confessor, a mutual interest in languages may well have been the basis of their friendship. Robert must have met Father O'Callaghan as a result of Kathleen's attendance at the convent school, and we can assume that the priest was a man of liberal views. Robert would never have made a friend of a religious bigot.

It may equally have been that these expatriates had a mutual senti-mental attachment to Ireland. There is nothing to suggest that there was any deeper ideological or personal meaning to their relationship.

Sometime in 1905 Father O'Callaghan was transferred to New York, to the Church of Our Lady of Mount Carmel, 448 East 116th Street, N.Y.10029, USA.

But Robert's wide-ranging discussions, his reading, languages, writings and his murals were still not the complete range of his truly active mind. He had another favourite interest – the subject of aircraft and flying then in its exciting pioneer stage.

'Robert, Arthur and myself were all mad on flying,' says Kathleen. Gower says Robert read 'Everything the library had to offer on the subject of aircraft.' And Walsh says, 'Tressell was convinced of the utility of heavier than air machines long before they were invented and spent much of his spare time making aeroplane models.'

Some of his friends have mentioned model aeroplanes he was building between 1902 and 1908 but Gower, who was most likely to know, says that he couldn't remember any, although Robert may have experimented with designs.

The public interest in flying was at its highest during the ten years Tressell was in Hastings, the first decade of the century, when the basic 'problems' of flying were about to be solved, and every kind of experiment was being made by many of famous name as well as by unknowns and many prizes for different feats were offered by news-papers, individuals and institutions.

In the Boer War, Britain had units of military observation balloons in use. Airships and aviation were the talk of Europe, the French-Brazilian Santos-Dumont won a prize in 1901 for ballooning round the Eiffel Tower, and by November 1902, the French had made long flights in the first practical powered airship. In 1903, Santos-Dumont, who used to run round Paris in what was virtually a balloon-taxi and land in his own garden, visited England and it was undoubtedly about then that Robert began to think of using his own inventive powers. There could be prize-money or commercial possibilities in airships and England was beginning to take some interest.

Just how interested Robert himself was is shown by the fact that he wrote an article 'The Evolution of the Airship' and illustrated it with his own drawings. This was probably written in 1901-2 as it takes the history up to 1900. Whether it was ever published or was even written for a publication I don't know. It is the first of his writings that survives and the only other besides *The Ragged Trousered Philanthropists*.

Whatever his own interest, if any, in heavier-than-air craft, it was a model airship which he finally built. Gower speaks more than once of helping, it seems, in 1905-6.

Says Gower: 'I used to go along to 115 Milward Road to help with the soldering.' He remembers Robert sending him on errands; 'Bill, just slip along to so and so's and get a packet of Melachrinos, [cigarettes].' When Gower returned Robert had made a jug of coffee and they sat and smoked and talked over the job in hand, as was their habit.

Two items in the local *Hastings and St Leonards Advertiser* are interesting in this connection. The first on 3 April 1905 said:

Channel air race ends near Hastings. Three Balloons came down at Robertsbridge, Westfield and Hollington [the latter a district of Hastings] on their way to cross the Channel. At Hollington the 'Vera' at 6 p.m. in Jessie Oliver's field. The balloon was packed up and sent to London by train from Warrior Square Station, St Leonards.

And again on 4 October 1906, headlines said: 'Balloons from Paris Pass Over Hastings'.

The balloon 'Britannia' narrowly misses Plynlimmon House,* West Hill, Hastings. Sand ballast was thrown out over the Old Town and also a telegram to be forwarded on. The telegram fell in the garden of a house and was retrieved by the dog.

Robert's own airship – a scale model, six feet long – was evidently

*Plynlimmon House is only a few yards away from Robert's house at 1 Plynlimmon Road.

of his own design. I've seen none like it and histories show every conceivable size and shape. It was power-driven, but unfortunately no specifications remain and I forgot to ask Gower all about it while I had the chance. It seems to have been driven by three pairs of three-bladed propellers; it had a large rudder at the rear and in shape it resembled from the front the prow of a ship and from the side it was suggestive, to quote my friend Clive Phillpot, of a 'Walt Disney whale'.

The prow was decorated with a design representing the rising sun and other formal designs were painted on the stern and the rudder, all geometric in character. Along one-third of the ship was painted the name inset, topped by a rising sun. Robert called it 'Martian'.

It was 'manned' by small wooden Dutch doll figures for which Adelaide had made uniforms. The ship was painted over all in aluminium with decorations in red, green and gold and flew a green flag proudly bearing the harp of old Erin.

The decoration reminds one of the popular art most associated with fairground decoration and also in some degree of modern Pop art.

His airship like most of his other hopes had a sad history and a tragic end, says Gower. He tried to interest various well-known people in it but without success. He wrote to newspapers with the same results and it stood in his room almost forgotten for a long time until, the story goes, a *Daily Mail* Model Aircraft Competition of 1907. This gave him fresh hope and he dug out his specifications and drawings and submitted them, and some of his friends say that he heard nothing and some that his plans were rejected. Some say that he wrote to the War Office and that they wanted a scale working model before they could consider it.

Kathleen says that a 'friend' suggested he should offer it to Germany, but in spite of being a wicked Irishman (she says) he wouldn't.

'Sometime afterwards,' said Gower, 'he told me that he took a hammer and smashed it all to pieces.'

11

Bread and circuses, 1906

The year 1905 ended with a General Election campaign, with polling day on 15 January 1906. The last General Election had been just before Robert arrived in Hastings.

By 1906, the majority of the male population had had the vote for just about twenty years – even the elements of democracy were that recent. This election was to bring Robert into direct contact with the political movements and personalities in the town and with the local socialists.

The election was fought against the background of a declining standard of living for the working classes, but not for the rich. Purchasing power in 1905-6 was well below that of 1900, but profits were soaring. Taxation was mostly indirect and on articles of common consumption so that, as now, the heaviest fell on the ordinary people.*

Taking into account all trades and jobs and all factors – type of work, state of trade, weather, sickness and accident, spells of unemployment, etc. – the average wages for men varied considerably. A fairly large section could expect to take home twenty shillings or less per week over the year, a middle section about twenty-five shillings and a smaller number of skilled men about thirty shillings for basic hours of anything between fifty-six and seventy or more per week, and there were only jobs for a limited percentage of skilled men. A good example this year was that of tram-conductors at eighteen shillings. Women were in an even worse position and child labour was widespread among the poorer.

I collected many examples in Hastings of the kind of exploitation which horrified Robert.

Joe Hodd did a two-hour paper round before 'school', and then worked all day Saturday and five evenings a week in a grocer's shop for half a crown and would often go home crying because of the pain in his feet. His wife at ten years of age had to go out and scrub steps

*G. D. H. Cole and Raymond Postgate, *The Common People*, London, 1966 edition.

before school and take the money on to teacher to look after. Mother worked in a laundry from 8 a.m. to 8 p.m. and her baby was looked after with others by a neighbour, and Mrs Hodd used to have to wheel the baby round to the laundry at dinner-time and after school for its mother to breast feed it, and then wheel it back to the neighbour's.

Even for these efforts the family were sometimes obliged to break-fast on a slice of bread and a cup of hot water 'flavoured' with salt and pepper. And these were 'respectable' working-class families.

Mrs Quaife's father, a carter, on fifteen shillings a week, cottage rent three shillings and sixpence, often managed to get a share in carcasses of drowned sheep pulled out of the marshes.

Ragged, barefooted, rickety children walked the streets in this bleak winter weather and groups of down-at-heel and dejected-looking unemployed haunted the street corners. People in the Ore district were used to the sight of a file of old women hobbling through the streets to collect their weekly bread ration at the Workhouse. Average expectation of life was forty-four years.

There were three hundred and ninety workhouse inmates and a hundred and forty-seven vagrants registered in the town during election week and in addition many hundreds receiving some kind of assistance from the charity organizations, not to mention those at the soup-kitchens. Robert had seen nothing like it among white people in South Africa, and this was Imperial Britain.*

For contrast, King Edward VII and his pals in one season at Sandring-ham shot 25,397 birds, hares and rabbits aside from the grouse season. And the King was no exception. Yet over vast estates belonging to the rich an English working-man dared not catch a rabbit if his family was starving.

The *Primitive Methodist Magazine* commented of the period: 'The country was never so wealthy and never so poor as now.'

The rich candidates who were to represent these people were Harvey Du Cros, Conservative, and Freeman Freeman-Thomas, Liberal, the sitting Member since 1900, both connected with finance and big business. William Harvey Du Cros was born in Dublin of old

---

*And indeed twenty years later than this he could have seen had he been here, a family of young children living and eating with their mother the crumbs of Parish Relief in a small room where on one side was what they called their 'boat' on which they laid their plates, this 'boat' being their father's coffin and he in it, and over which their mother, keeping the secret from them, sprinkled disinfectant until it was taken away nearly a week later. This told me by a man who had been one of the children.

Huguenot stock and with his son, Arthur, founded the pneumatic-tyre industry from an invention of John Boyd Dunlop, a Scot of Belfast, and Freeman Freeman-Thomas was son-in-law of Lord Brassey and later to become Lord Willingdon and Viceroy of India (1931–36). He too was connected with the motor trade and with insurance, a Tweedledum and Tweedledee, if ever there were, for local electors to rave about.

The campaign was the usual Mack Sennett affair described so well by Fielding, Dickens and yet to be described by Robert himself. He had only to record it. Although there was no socialist standing, the candidates, the speakers and the newspapers, belted away at the evils of being 'taken in' by these subversives, showing that socialist ideas were growing.

The *Hastings and St Leonards Observer* (Robert's '*Obscurer*') printed some profound observations by the then head of the Rothschild family giving the benefit of his money-lender's intelligence to the barefooted and rickety children of England. He offered the journalists what he thought was a shattering argument with an imaginary socialist: 'I own, as you say, £30 million. I estimate that if my money was divided as you say, it would work out at a franc a head. Here is a franc each – good afternoon.'

The paper quotes another genius in the same cause: 'A working-man may possibly be a socialist on Thursday, but he can't be one on Saturday when he gets his wages.'

Robert's ironic examples of anti-socialists are not in the least exaggerated – they are taken from life.

The principal difference in policy between Conservative and Liberal dated from 1903 when the 'Radical' Joseph Chamberlain, after joining the Conservative Party, introduced his Tariff Reform and Imperial Preference policy – Protection as against the traditional Liberal Free Trade – and finally got it adopted as Conservative policy in the 1906 Election. The fiscal questions arising from this are the subject of violent argument among Robert's ragged trousered philanthropists in the book where they are pronounced as 'Fissical' and 'Fistical'.

Robert's 'Big loaf' and 'Little loaf' were actual political terms used throughout the country.

Du Cros had turned the ground over thoroughly in preparing for his candidature over the past year – fifty pounds to be shared among the slate clubs; supporters working round the pubs with the free beer;

school teas at the schools and teas for the 'old people'; and good advice
about Empire and 'Imperial Destiny' (the new catch-phrase) and
promises of jobs in his London factory for the workless. There was
much talk of 'lies' and 'dirty tricks' and 'unfair tactics', exactly as
Robert recounts.

A Liberal councillor complained of hooligans at meetings and said
that the Tories were 'importing scoundrels' from London. See Robert
on scoundrels from the Seven Dials district hired at ten bob a day to
scare hecklers. In Tressell they were hired by the Liberals but it was the
same difference, as they say. One of the more heroic duties of the
aristocratic candidates was the kissing of working-class babies-in-arms
presented by chosen mothers carefully picked at random from the
crowd.

This kissing showed that the candidate was a true democrat and
when his befeathered and bejewelled 'lady-wife' (as popular journalists
would refer to her) brushed the infant cheek with her scented lips,
admiration 'knew no bounds'. And even the attendant spivs and
deserted maiden ladies might go so far as to chuck a few of the washed
under the chin.

It was often difficult to choose for charm between Liberal and
Tory and this is where a presentable younger son as candidate was so
useful, or in the case of an old stone-face, a good-looking young wife.
But she had to be a lady, mind you, although at least half of the voters
could be relied upon to vote as they had been brought up to believe,
even for a set of baboons – so long as they were labelled 'gentlemen'.

The Liberals at a meeting at the bottom of High Street fixed a white
sheet against the wall and showed film slides with the words of anti-
Tory slogans and songs such as 'No More Joe' (Joe Chamberlain) and
'Stamp, Stamp, Stamp on Protection', which the Liberal crowd sang,
while Mr Hermitage, the papers reported, led from the platform with
his cornet.

A Liberal headline said: 'Simply Work and Sleep. A Timely Remini-
scence of the curse of Protection. Appalling Picture.'

Mrs Freeman Freeman-Thomas and party, said the ecstatic papers,
were drawn through the streets in their coach by magnificent white
horses and 'Master' Gerard Freeman-Thomas stood on father's platform for people to admire. But a local sartorialist complained: 'Why
will the Liberal Candidate persist in wearing a brown suit!' No-one
answered this embarrassing question.

A Social Democratic Federation meeting on the beach in front of the Queen's Hotel, Hastings, in June 1907, showing Robert and Kathleen Tressell in the audience.

Robert photographed on one of his cycling rambles in 1908, by William Gower.

Kathleen Noonan, in August 1913. Kathleen was a serious young woman, as dedicated to social change as her father.

Some of the philanthropists. A group of workers from the Hastings building trade. Second from the left, front row, is the author's grandfather, George Easton, a radical socialist.

The Board of Guardians had a collective fit and agreed on the need for 'State Employment'. Letters signed 'Workingman' and such-like titles appeared, one from the very poorest quarter of the town in those days, Sandown, congratulating Mr Du Cros upon the Tory Aliens Bill. It and other literate letters from men who could barely write their own names caused a lot of merriment and some sadness among the socialist and radical working-men. The Liberal campaign ended with a monster procession. Five thousand people, men, women and children, with banners and torches, streamers, hats and rosettes and pans of coloured fire, marched through Hastings headed by Freeman Freeman-Thomas himself and a brass band of fifty-four instruments and with five thousand voices, singing to the tune 'Tramp, Tramp, Tramp, the Boys are Marching':

> Vote! Vote! Vote! for Freeman-Thomas!
> We'll hang old Du Cros upon a tree!
> Freeman-Thomas is our man,
> And we'll have him if we can,
> Then we'll always have the biggest loaf for tea.

And Kathleen takes us inside the Noonans' house:

> I remember it was at Milward Road we stuck our heads out of the top flat window shouting:
> > 'Don't vote for either of the bounders,
> > Throw old Thomas in the sea.
> > Du Cros he is no good
> > He wants to tax your food
> > Socialism is the thing for you and me.'
> And I remember my Aunt coming and dragging us back in saying, 'Just because your father wants to live that kind of a life there's no reason why we shouldn't live like civilized beings.'

No wonder the book pointedly describes the 'respectable classes' in the flat and in the street – he must have been very conscious of their eyes daily on his back.

In the book he had merely to fill in different names for his election scene. He describes the fever and anxiety among Tory and Liberal partisans, and the fighting, brawling, black eyes and boozing, the cockles and whelks and pease-pudding suppers and the party colours in coloured fire.

In the book, Robert describes the long wait for the election result by the crowd, as it is swept by one rumour then another. The *Hastings and St Leonards Weekly Mail and Times* reports Freeman-Thomas saying at one meeting that: 'Only last week there was a certain suspicion among Liberals that the Tories were catching up.' Then on election eve it was rumoured for the poor Tories that the Liberals had won and one prominent Tory left the scene believing this to be so and the papers reported that the Old Town Liberals had already begun to celebrate victory. Polling day was 15 January and the Central Cricket Ground adjoining the Town Hall in Queen's Road, was opened to the public for the result.

During the very moments of the announcement a rumour went round the crowds (there used to be crowds then) that the Liberal was in by six hundred votes, but it was finally revealed to the breathless that Du Cros had won the seat for the Tories.

In *The Ragged Trousered Philanthropists*, Robert reverses the result and elects a Liberal (with almost the same numbers of voters) and makes another little aside of which I found evidence in the local Press.

'Sir Graball', the beaten Tory, shakes hands and refers to 'Adam Sweater', victorious Liberal, as 'my friend' in a passage symbolic of the essential understanding between gentlemen in front of the mob.

'The Buried Hatchet. Political Enemies Fraternize', said the newspaper. 'At the Jenny Lind Public House in High Street, 40 Liberals and Tories from the Old Town, including the Deputy Mayor, met for dinner. The King and Queen were drunk [toasted] with musical honours and the greater part of the evening was spent in harmony.'

By 'harmony' the reporter meant songs and sing-song.

Although the Conservative turned out the Liberal in Hastings the country turned out the Conservative Government and elected a Liberal. This result was regarded by Free Traders as the saving of the country and by the Non-conformists, a powerful group, as support for non-denominational religious instruction in State schools, and by the increased working-class vote as the hope for promised social reforms. But there was something else, a sense of greater forces at work. The defeated Tory Prime Minister, A.J.Balfour wrote to Lord Salisbury:

If I read the signs aright what has occurred has nothing whatever to do with any of the things we have been squabbling over the last few years ... what is going on here is the faint echo of the same movement which has produced massacres* in St Petersburg, riots in Vienna and Socialist processions in Berlin.

Incidentally Hastings and its neighbour, Rye, had the distinction of registering the only Conservative gains in the country.

This election was to bring Robert into direct contact with the political movements and personalities in the town and with the local socialists.

*Of workers by the Tsarist Government.

12

The rise of the Labour
Movement

Although there were individual socialists in the town they began to organize only after the 1906 Election and then at first as part of an attempt by local radicals (left-wing Liberals) to organize a new ginger group in the Liberal Party, spurred by its defeat and by growing disillusionment. The Labour Party had been officially formed nationally in February after years of working through the complicated questions involved in developing the basis of a mass working-class party, yet Hastings went back twenty-five years for its models and repeated the whole process locally, and I think this throws light on *The Ragged Trousered Philanthropists*.

A brief account of the rise of the modern Labour Movement nationally will put the local background in perspective. Although the development of the working-class movement was continuous throughout the nineteenth century, the 1880s marked a new stage.

Several factors had led to this: the growing influence of socialist ideas, the long gradual recognition by many in the unions of the need for direct 'labour' representation in Parliament, the winning of the vote (partially granted in 1867 and extended to about five million workers in 1884), and the growing disillusionment with the Liberals.

In 1881 the Democratic Federation was founded, this in 1884 became the Social Democratic Federation (SDF). Its inspiration, says Cole,* 'was Marx's, relayed through his most eminent English pupil H.M.Hyndman' (he was, however, disowned by Marx and Engels), and its membership cards stated as aims 'The Socialization of the means of Production, Distribution and Exchange.' William Morris and Walter Crane, both of whom had some influence on Robert, and Marx's daughter Eleanor, were members, but Morris and many others left in 1887 to form the Socialist League.

*G. D. H. Cole and Raymond Postgate, *The Common People*, London, 1966 edition.

Also in 1884, the Fabian Society was formed, with Shaw and Beatrice and Sidney Webb among its leaders, to achieve democratic socialism by constitutional, peaceful and gradual means – hence 'the inevitability of gradualness'.

In 1888 Keir Hardie formed the Scottish Labour Party (the first 'Labour' Party) and in 1893 the Independent Labour Party (ILP) emerged to struggle (like the middle-class Fabian Society) not for socialism but for 'social changes pointing in a Socialist direction'.*

There were also many other groups of various persuasions. Yet not only did no single socialist party exist, but the basic organizations of the working class, the trade unions, while their personnel overlapped into the political parties, had not as a body fought out the political battle. In fact they resisted the idea of political commitment although they had a Parliamentary Committee. But at last 'after years of ineffective debate and with much new blood and an increasing number of socialist resolutions',† the Trades Union Congress (TUC) in 1899 passed a resolution drafted in the ILP office, but stemming from the Railway Servants' Union, calling for a special conference of all working-class organizations.

The conference, though it wasn't supported by the Co-operative Movement, the Miners' Federation and some other big unions, met in February 1900 at the Memorial Hall, London, and was an almost unique event; for trade union leaders sat together with ILP, SDF, Fabian and other delegates and a 'Labour Representation Committee' was formed which was at once colloquially called the 'Labour Party'. The new Labour Representation Committee (LRC) set about recruiting trade union branches to its support (there was no individual membership of the Labour Party till 1918 but only 'affiliations'). The SDF however, denounced it as 'in no way consciously socialist and as a result likely to be an obstacle and not an aid to Socialism'.‡ And the SDF walked out.

On 12 February 1906, just after the General Election, the new 'Labour' (LRC) MPs, twenty-nine in number, elected Keir Hardie as Chairman, and Ramsay MacDonald as Secretary of the group and on 15 February the Annual Conference of the Labour Representation Committee adopted the official name 'The Labour Party'.

*Cole and Postgate, *op. cit.*
†*Ibid.*
‡*Ibid.* – Cole's words.

Already in 1906, the Labour Party had 998,000 affiliated members at a two shilling subscription fee and was the only party in the country with any real basis or potential for fighting for the interests of the working classes. But it was the visionary socialists – many of whom remained suspicious of Labour's essentially reformist policy – who had brought the new fervour to the political scene which was attracting more and more people from the working classes, as well as leading intellectuals and even honest fugitives from the upper classes to the hope of a completely new society.

It was this vision which involved and absorbed Robert Tressell, and it was to him at once an ideal and a rational solution, which he was amazed that humanity didn't recognize.

The vision wasn't new. Men had dreamed it for ages, probably since the break up of primitive societies and the beginning of social division and exploitation. And it has come right through our own history in one form or another. John Ball, priest of Kent, and one of the leaders of the great Peasants' Revolt as long ago as 1381, had preached: 'My good friends, matters cannot go well in England until all things be held in common; when there shall be neither vassals nor lords; when the lords shall be no more masters than ourselves. Are we not all descended from the same parents, Adam and Eve?'*

And for many socialists such ideas plainly had their inspirational authority in the Prophets of the Old Testament and the original early Christian conception of the equality of all men before God which had long been abandoned.

Robert was extremely conscious of, and concerned about, the social and moral predicament humanity had got itself into. Phenomena accepted as 'normal' by this society were to him horrifying revelations of its abnormality – class divisions, immense social inequalities, exploitation of men and nations and the world's resources with the degrading purpose of amassing personal wealth, and the plight of the vast majority of the working classes who throughout history had always lived in almost total economic, political and social subjection. He saw all men as in some way spiritually corrupted by this, those who acquiesced in it as much as those who exploited it.

Robert's socialist views weren't suddenly acquired: they were part of his nature, arising from his humanity and his intelligence – as both his daughter and his niece told me.

*See R. H. Hilton and H. Fagan, *The English Rising of 1381*, London, 1950.

His niece says:

I saw little of him but I knew his extreme socialist opinions. He had always been extremely vehement and very very bitter. We believed this to be partly temperamental (self-willed, headstrong, idealistic, high-principled, etc.) and partly the disappointment and disillusionment of his early life, though, of course, his intellectual power and strong sympathies would naturally incline him to socialism.

This niece was herself a devout Christian with little liking for either Robert or Kathleen, which makes her statement the more valuable.

He had been a convinced socialist for a long time, although except for one or two friends he had lived in some isolation in Hastings, both from the Trade Union Movement and from radicals and socialists. Only when the socialists finally began to organize independently did he find the organization and comradeship to meet his need, and it seems to me no accident that this should have been the impulse needed to call out his particular kind of talent and give it direction.

13

Robert joins in

George Meek, of Eastbourne, one of the early socialists of that period in the south-east and author of *George Meek, Bath Chairman*, published in 1910, says that he had a friend who had 'kept the socialist flag flying for many years in Hastings'.

This was Edward Cruttenden who was to become a close friend of Robert's. 'For some years,' says Meek,

> being the greater part of the time the only socialists in our respective towns [Hastings and Eastbourne] we maintained a regular correspondence and Cruttenden used to bike over. Then he formed a branch of the SDF in Hastings which fell through after a time, but it put him in touch with E.J.Pay, a very active socialist worker who has been invaluable to the Movement in the South East ever since.

Cruttenden's daughter Rose says of her father: 'He was a great one for writing to the press on various matters and was the founder of the earliest workers' movement in Hastings.'

Mr Cruttenden, whom I met thirty years ago, claimed that as a result of correspondence initiated by him in the early 1890s, the Hastings and St Leonards Trades and Labour Council was formed in 1894, but Rose is referring to an attempt to form an earlier branch of the Social Democratic Federation sometime in the nineties and of which her father became secretary.

Says Rose, 'I remember my sisters and I, when children, holding the red flag at meetings.'

Cruttenden, a shopman at Brooker & Jepson's Fancy Goods Shop, still in existence as Jepson's, and his wife Phoebe, ardent radical-socialists, advertised in *The Clarion* and possibly in *Justice*, both of which they read, for any local readers to make themselves known to them.

There's a saying that you must live in Sussex ten years before you discover the names of the people next door and the result of the

Cruttendens' advertisement illustrates it. The first reply came from the E.J.Pay mentioned, living two doors away and this is how the Cruttendens were 'put in touch with him' – in Meek's words. They had a good laugh over it and soon arranged little meetings in the Cruttendens' house. Pay was also a shopman – in a baker's in Robertson Street. Soon a Mr Taylor joined them with one or two others to form a branch of the Social Democratic Federation.

The branch doesn't seem to have functioned for long and some while later it was decided to form a branch of the newly created National Democratic League, a much more broadly based organization with Labour sympathies supported by elements drawn from both the socialist and Liberal camps. The Editor of *Reynolds News*, W.M. Thompson, was President, Lloyd George was Vice-President and Tom Mann was Secretary! But the main bodies of organized socialists, the ILP and the SDF, stood aloof because of the League's Liberal connections and its refusal to accept a socialist programme.

Cruttenden's daughter Rose says, 'I remember as a very small child a large yellow poster with black lettering outside our house at 12 Russell Street, headed NDL which said "Vote for King and Lamb". This must have been in the late nineties.'

Lamb was a member of the Trades Council who played a part in trade union organization here and in early working-class politics.

King was Toby King, a very colourful and most famous local character of the time, a good example of the old type radical and freethinker – fighter for the vote; a free press; universal education freed from the Churches; the freeing of children from mines, factories and prisons; in fact for most of what we know as humane and democratic.

Cruttenden's entry in Rose's autograph-book, written when she was in her 'teens, shows the kind of idealism which animated many of these men.

> For the world is for ever improving,
> All the past is not worth one today,
> And whatever deserves our true loving
> Is stronger than death or decay.

Toby, a giant of twenty-two stones in weight and prodigiously strong, with his white ten-gallon hat bedecked with rosettes and his face wreathed in flowers, was famous in all radical campaigns both in

Hastings and London where it is recorded that even the mounted police gave him friendly winks of recognition.

Toby held classes in his house near Hollington Church-in-the-Wood, where he taught working-men to read and write so that they might study politics and history and learn their way about in this blind world.

His house became notorious in Mugsborough among the 'unco guid' as a kind of Devil's kitchen where freethinkers gathered.

To liven up the superstitious he had his own coffin made to his specification and stood upright in the corner of his room where he could speculate upon the vanity of human wishes. He had himself photographed standing in his coffin.

To cure his children of any deference towards the so-called 'better classes' which they had drilled into them at church and school as one of the laws of God, Toby would not allow his boys to salute nor his girls to curtsy as was the expected custom and his daughter said that her children in turn were threatened with a hiding if *they* did so, to keep up the family tradition.

As a consequence of visits to Ireland, Toby wrote a pamphlet *Ireland's Woes and Ireland's Foes*, which had a great circulation among radicals.

During the agitation for the reform of the House of Lords, he had an inspiration which matched the occasion. He rigged out a wagon and in it he put half a dozen or so donkeys wearing coronets. He then got some working-men to harness themselves in the shafts and the townsfolk were treated to the spectacle of this symbolic tableau drawn through the streets labelled 'House of Lords'.

He died in 1899, just before Robert Tressell reached Mugsborough, but Toby's pupils* were there and the links with Toby's work carried straight through to the new socialism and so to *The Ragged Trousered Philanthropists*.

The first NDL branch died out as most of its members were really socialists but after the 1906 Election, a new organization, The Hastings and St Leonards Democratic Association was formed to be an 'educational medium' for the workers. F.H. Willard became secretary and it was intended to put up candidates for local elections. In a fortnight it had a hundred members and the Trades Council agreed to form

*My mother's father was one of them.

with it a Municipal Labour Representation Committee and donated five pounds towards funds.

But this unity of the democrats didn't last long. It was found impossible to fill in every Sunday with League speakers and Willard apparently arranged for socialists to speak on vacant dates. This scared away many members and at the quarterly meeting Councillor March moved that they should become a branch of the Social Democratic Federation, but the matter was dropped.

And then one evening in September 1906 a few men met in a room at the Cricketers' public house in South Terrace overlooking the cricket ground to discuss the formation of a branch of the Social Democratic Federation, which seems of all the Labour and socialist groups to have been the most uncompromisingly anti-capitalist. To this meeting came Robert Noonan and the one-time apprentice William Gower, now in his early twenties, and among others Edward Cruttenden and a gentleman named Alf Cobb, a kind of local Till Eulenspiegel.*

Cruttenden says that only two meetings were held at the Cricketers', and these seem to have been convened by a small group for preliminary discussion, for the *Hastings and St Leonards Observer* of 13 October carried an item stating that on the previous day, Friday, a public meeting to form a branch of the SDF had been held at the Beehive Tea-rooms at 32 Pelham Street (just off from the Prince Albert Memorial) with F.Owen† in the chair, and that 'there was a good attendance'. J.M.Kerr was elected Secretary and J.Hutchings, Treasurer. Subscriptions were twopence per week.

Within two days, the branch held its first public meeting at the Fishmarket with George Meek as speaker.

Meek had formed a *Clarion* Fellowship in Eastbourne which sold Robert Blatchford's *Clarion* and his book *Merrie England* in cheap reprint and he also formed a group of *Clarion* Scouts, one of those heroic and dedicated bands of cyclists who toured the towns and countryside of Britain holding socialist meetings and distributing literature and of whom Robert gives a memorable little picture.

One of the National *Clarion* Vans, with Tom Kennedy as chief

*Flemish not Straussian version.
†Robert may have got the name of his hero from this F. Owen.

speaker, spent a week in Hastings in November, holding meetings every evening at the Fishmarket or at the yacht stade at Harold Place where the tripper yacht *Albertine* was beached.

The old name of 'Beehive' for the tea-rooms seems to hark back to the 1860s when the only national Labour journal the *Beehive* was founded in 1862.

The Beehive Coffee-House first appears in local directories in 1867–8 owned by J. Haisell a bootmaker, and E. J. Hobsbawm* mentions boot and shoemakers 'as always artisan intellectuals'.

Within a fortnight of this example of socialists actually organizing themselves in Hastings, the *Hastings and St Leonards Weekly Mail and Times* and the *Hastings and St Leonards Observer* started violent anti-socialist propaganda – and Robert found a new, and as it were official, source for his notebooks on the subject.

The organizing of the 'Marxist' SDF branch worried others too. Some union branches said they wouldn't support socialist candidates of the LRC, and the Trades Council left both the LRC and the NDL because they were 'socialist'. But in contrast to their national predecessors, the local SDF remained in both. Others formed another sect, the Christian Social Union.

The SDF had internal problems too and Robert was present at an early meeting which had to make a decision described by Mr Sellens.

> When the SDF was first formed there was trouble over Alf Cobb. The Puritan element thought he should not be in the SDF because he was living apart from his wife and was living with another lady, whom he later married. I remember Cobb leaving the meeting at Phelps Coffee House and waiting while the question was discussed. The result was that the majority considered that his living with this lady should not bar him from serving the cause. Most of those who disagreed with the verdict left the SDF and together formed the Hastings branch of the Independent Labour Party with Frank Willard as secretary.

So there were now socialist and Labour groups all over the town and all disunited. Many years were to pass before there was a Labour Party. In the meantime the SDF was the most active, concentrating

*E. J. Hobsbawm and George Rude, *Captain Swing*, London, 1969, p. 63.

on exposing local and national politics to public gaze and on taking socialism into the streets.

I believe this local situation played a part in determining how Robert was to portray the role of socialism and socialists in the book.

14

Democracy Ltd

The year 1906 was also a year of change for the Noonans. Sometime during the year Robert left Burton's and I don't know why. The boss with the spy-glass may have spied once too often and this time at the wrong man.

A present member of the firm describes an altercation between the boss and Robert. 'Noonan was a hot-tempered man and on one occasion when working he got himself into an argument with Mr Burton (the head of the firm) who finished up by calling Noonan a blackguard and Noonan finished up by locking Mr Burton in the room.'

I got another account of this incident from a workmate, who said that Robert was working at a house in Trinity Street, behind the church, and the boss, as was his habit, thought the job was taking too long. He went along to see and started on about it and Robert, who resented the impertinence, got into an argument with Burton, both men becoming more and more angry until the boss called Robert something, probably 'blackguard' as described, and Robert threatened to 'knock his bloody head off' and may have actually struck him.

At any rate he finished up by storming out and turning the key in the lock on the outside leaving Burton locked in the room.

Clearly this incident wasn't on any account of Noonan's personal honesty and integrity but simply on account of his detestable views and his habit of expressing them, whether they were matters of personal belief or to do with his opinion of the job in hand. It is very likely that this particular incident was the immediate reason for himself and this firm parting company.

It is said that he worked for short periods with other firms but the next definite news of him is with Adams and Jarrett's, a firm with showrooms in Norman Road, St Leonards, and workshops in Alfred Street, right behind Christ Church, of which Kathleen tells the story of how the Wind and the Devil were walking past the very windy corner of the church and the Devil said: 'Wait a minute, I want to go in here', and the Wind had been waiting ever since.

At Adams and Jarrett's Robert was to meet the other half of his character 'Misery'.

Sometime, too, this year the four left 115 Milward Road, and moved over to St Leonards, where they stayed at Warrior Square and St John's Road but I don't know the exact addresses.

He now threw himself into the work of the new SDF branch.

George Hicks, one-time General Secretary of The Amalgamated Union of Building Trade Workers, in his preface to the 1927 edition of *The Ragged Trousered Philanthropists*, says:

> Those early agitators and propagandists of SDF and ILP working amongst their fellows carrying on in the shadow of victimisation and dismissal from their employment endeavouring to make those with whom they came in contact see the necessity of organisation and economic and political enlightenment, must have been heroes indeed possessed of lion-hearted courage and faith that conquers.

This is no exaggeration.* They were mostly unknown and humble men spread throughout Britain who had been conditioned by society, their masters, Church and State, over centuries to fear authority, to believe they were cast in the role of inferiors. As an 'educated' lady once admonished Alf Cobb – 'But Mr Cobb, what are the working-classes for, if not to work?'

They were conditioned to believe that master and man was the natural order of things and the will of God and that there was no wickedness comparable to that of forgetting their station in life and trying to change society. They had been taught to believe that poverty was the result of their own inadequacy. The harshness and cruelty of industrialism to men, women and children, the obscenities of wealth and power, were explained away in specious tracts, homilies and sermons from earliest childhood. For countless thousands of working people who had seen through this mockery the idea of their own political party was like a new and healthy religion in place of the degradation and hypocrisy of the old, and it lifted them up with untold hopes.

Mrs E.M. Hogg of Tunbridge Wells summed up for me in a letter

*Even though George lays it on a bit.

exactly what it was that sustained the early Socialist Movement: 'In the days I have written of, which were the Pioneer days of the Movement, there was always a feeling of Becoming Something which these stalwarts were trying to attain.'

'Becoming Something'! Did it not now seem possible in Britain and not only in Britain? After all were there not as early as 1893 three million socialist votes in Germany and fifty MPs sitting in the Reichstag? And the people themselves were proving that they could be the real heroes of their own struggle – for it took great courage to dare even to take out a union ticket or distribute a socialist handbill.

George Gallop, a foundation-member of the NDL and then of the SDF, told me that many members used to go one at a time to secret meetings held at the old Central Hall in Middle Street, near the Memorial, a small hall and later one of our early cinemas.

'If I met Tom going down Middle Street,' said George,

I used to go down Havelock Road. If we both arrived at the same time, one used to go in and the other walk on a bit, then turn round and come back in. If there was a speaker arriving from London for a Meeting, we used to meet him from the train to act as bodyguard in case of any trouble. Branch meetings were kept secret after a time as there would have been trouble as the town was all Tories and Liberals.

The word 'socialism' had first appeared in 1835 in connection with Robert Owen's ideas, and had been increasing the incidence of apoplexy among the 'unco guid' ever since. Even an old membership book of the Tressell period I have in my possession gives no indication as to what organization it refers to, nor the secretary's name nor even a date. It is merely headed 'Members' Names and Addresses', but is known to have been of the SDF.

According to Police Constable Burr, who later became secretary of his branch of the old Municipal Employees' Association, the police used to intimidate people by taking the names of those attending SDF meetings and posting lists of names in the police station. This name-collecting had been a police method against trade union movements for a very long time all over the country.

In addition to police lists, employers' associations then and since kept 'blacklists' of such people, who could then be refused employment all round and forced to find other kinds of work outside their trade, usually to their great disadvantage.

E.J. Pay whom I have already mentioned, of Hastings, was one such who was finally obliged to leave the town and go to Tunbridge Wells where he again joined the SDF and became a well-known 'agitator', this time sustained by his own little pedlar's business.

Alf Cobb was also forced out of his employment and had to take a street barrow to get a living.

The fate of such blacklisted men was a warning for their comrades of the real value of 'free speech' in England – a warning they often ignored.

With its 'revolutionary' insistence upon 'socialism', the organization was also under attack from the new-style 'Parliamentary' Labour Movement which had to deal with all shades of outlook and policy, the trade unions, religious elements and a non-socialist public opinion in order to attract a mass vote.

Against this kind of background as the going got tough and after a number of withdrawals and changes of secretary, the SDF branch developed a hard core of militant socialists in 1907, among them Robert Tressell.

Meek who is a useful guide to opinion in the rank and file at local level says that as early as 1907 the *Clarion* crusade was beginning to grow 'respectable' (although the local stalwarts in the SDF weren't). Meeks says of the *Clarion* Fellowship: 'Nowadays we have to conform to the manners and are expected to have the intelligence of Sunday School Scholars. I wonder how many *Clarion* Fellowships would consider a man like Pay tame and respectable enough to be admitted to their membership.'

Meek had earlier tried to get SDF, ILP, Fabian and other socialist groups in Sussex to work together in a *Clarion* Fellowship, and the main papers, *Clarion*, *Justice* and *Labour Leader* gave support to the Federation but after a time the support of *Labour Leader* was withdrawn. Meek wrote to Francis Johnson, National Secretary of the ILP asking why and was told that the National Committee was forming ILP Federations throughout the country and did not believe in hybrid Federations.

Meek also says J.R. MacDonald wrote saying that he would advise the ILP not to co-operate with the SDF whenever asked.

Thrown out of work on Monday 13 May 1907 Meek decided on

a walking tour to seek work and on the way to visit branches of the SDF and says that he waited till the following Thursday before starting off on foot as the SDF branch of Hastings held its weekly meeting on that night. He says that he was kindly received by the Cruttendens and by the branch. The Cruttendens put him up and the branch gave him three shillings and he then went on to Ashford.

I can't discover whether Robert was at this branch meeting but he knew of and met Meek who occasionally spoke at Hastings and around whom a little story grew in connection with his own book and *The Ragged Trousered Philanthropists*. Incidentally Rose Cruttenden gives the popular explanation as to why the name of 'Social Democratic Federation' was changed to 'Social Democratic Party'.

'It was,' she says, 'I believe, because our opponents used to refer to us as Silly Damn Fools.'

The SDP brought Robert a few more friends among them Edward Cruttenden and his wife Phoebe, Rose's parents, very gentle and compassionate people who nevertheless possessed that determination not to allow the obscene social abuses to go unchallenged which marks the best of the British people and the old pioneers.

Robert became a frequent visitor for some time at their house at 16 Wellington Square; and in their daughters, Kathleen, too, found friends.

Rose says, 'Meetings were sometimes held at our house at 16 Wellington Square and after meetings we frequently used to sing songs from the *Socialist Song Book*, my elder sister playing the piano. In fact our house was known as "Liberty Hall".'

In 1906, after much resistance, Hastings had introduced school breakfasts of skimmed milk and bread and margarine for poor school-children thereby proving that not only a national scandal but an emergency existed. The Tories had said that school breakfasts would mean the destruction of the home but a Fabian Socialist Tract pointed out that 'the Eton and Harrow boy is kept at school not only for meals but for the whole of the term yet no one fears for the homelife of the plutocracy'.

The local school boards fought every provision which might weaken local Church of England hold on them. The Reverend Durnford in Hastings moved a resolution sent to the MPs for both the Hastings and the Rye Constituencies urging them to oppose the Provision of Meals Bill for Elementary Schools on the grounds that all relief should be in the hands of the local School Board and not the Board of Education. In practice, this meant that sectarian prejudice would continue to dictate the school life of the working classes, the nature of their education and the health and hygiene of their schools.

Rose says that during school holidays when no breakfasts were forthcoming for the children she, her mother, the other girls including Kathleen, and other socialists, collected enough to continue to serve the breakfasts at Ore and Hollington until the schools opened for the new term.

Meanwhile the Reverend R.F.Hessey, Canon of Winchester, was circulating his pamphlet *Socialism*, in which he said 'They are clamouring for the Old Age Pensions of five shillings all round with no distinction whatsoever, and for the feeding of all children at school.' And he purports to quote 'A mother' as telling a 'Clergyman's wife' that she was thankful her children were grown up before the feeding of children came about. 'My husband cared for his children and nothing but that made him spare a penny from the drink', said this poor lady.

From such parsons' hypocritical, or plain callous, falsifications of principle Robert was gathering material for his long hard look at such 'Christians' in *The Ragged Trousered Philanthropists*.

15

Raw material for a book

Before the building of the high promenade the beach came up to the roadway and the yachts *Skylark* and *Albertine*, the rowing-boats, and, further along, the fishermen's luggers and trawlers would be drawn right up on to the shingle. On Sunday evenings this stretch of the beach was a regular sideshow and crowds of people would go along to see the fun.

Various religious bodies would be there, as Gower said, nearly in one another's pockets in order to shout each other down.

Mr Hubbard, the evangelist, would be bravely contending against the Salvation Army Band who, said Gower, tried to drown him out, and stood right alongside his rostrum blowing the guts out of their instruments; but the evangelist would carry on belting out his warnings of Hell and damnation. Often his meetings would be broken up because people didn't care to be told outright that they were damned anyhow and on the way to Hell; but when driven off the beach, Mr Hubbard would continue accosting passers-by.

The famous scene in the book in which, at a beach meeting on a summer Sunday evening, two students offer a phial of poison to the evangelist and challenge him to drink it taunting him with his belief in miracles while themselves claiming belief in the efficacy of the scientific antidote, is based upon a scene with Mr Hubbard, and it was Robert himself who issued the challenge. This account is from Sellens and is confirmed by Kathleen. (Sellens in 1952 still signed his correspondence with me and as far as I know with other people, 'Yours for the Revolution'.) He says:

I remember Bob once telling me how he enjoyed himself at Mr Hubbard, the beach preacher's, meeting. You knew, of course, Mr Hubbard, the preacher, who attacked nearly all religious bodies. He was bitter against Atheists and Agnostics. He declared one evening that he believed every word in the Bible to be true. Bob challenged Mr Hubbard stating that he could prove that Mr Hubbard did not believe the Bible. Mr Hubbard accepted Bob's challenge. Both were present at the appointed time. Hubbard was asked to read a certain part of the Bible,* this he did. In it, it stated that those who trusted God could drink poison and it would do them no injury. They were, of course, words to this effect. Bob then challenged him with a bottle labelled 'poison'. He said, 'Now, Mr Hubbard, I have a bottle of poison enough to kill several people. If you drink this and it does you no harm we shall know that the Bible is true and that you are indeed a prophet sent by God.'

Mr Hubbard hesitated, protested, and the crowd of religious opponents, Catholics, Anglo-Catholics, who were always bitter against him, cried out – drink it, Hubbard, drink up, drink up! hoping apparently to get rid of a pest to them. Hubbard refused to drink. Bob then stated that though Mr Hubbard could not trust the Bible, he himself could trust science which Hubbard condemned, whereupon Bob drank the contents of the bottle followed immediately by a drink from another which Bob said was an antidote invented by science. The fact was both bottles contained only water or other harmless fluid.

But that night Robert went home and said to Kathleen, 'I shouldn't have done that to the poor old chap!'

Kathleen later commented: 'Just think how wonderful it would have been for the preacher if he *had* drunk the "poison".'

This man had that kind of sublime compassion celebrated here and there in the world which gave him no rest in the presence of desperate need. He tried where he could to help particular cases known to him – and he wrote his book in order to help those he couldn't.

His friend John Whitelock says 'he would never watch anyone go without if he had anything, and would help workmates laid off or having a rough time'. Kathleen says 'He was the kind of man who would give away the clothes off his back' and, herself a devout Christian, 'He was the most truly Christian man I have ever known.'

Of Chapter Four – 'The Placard' – where Owen walks across the town saturated on a wet night to tell the old Tory, Linden, sacked for smoking, of a job he has heard about, Gower says that the incident is typical of Robert himself and indeed the whole scene in Linden's

*Mark 16: 17–18.

house in Chapter Five – 'The Clock-case' has the detailed observation which could only result from actual experience.

Kathleen describes another example of his generosity, unmindful of self.

> The Doctor ordered him an alcoholic drink – in my mind it is gin, yet I can't think why the doctor should give him gin, and there was a young workman, a curly-headed chap who I think was called 'Charlie', married and with a young baby and he was an awful drinker and Dad told the man that he himself would give up his gin if the man would give up drinking and did so but found that the man hadn't. He felt he must help people whatever the cost. But he didn't lecture. He was always doing things for people.

He makes many references to drinking and drunkenness in his book, some of them comic.

It is said to be at Kite's Nest, a big house in St Helens Woods, at the time it was a hotel, that he witnessed a drunken orgy which gave him some of the material for the scenes of abandon induced by drink which he depicts in the book.

The men were redecorating the interior while the proprietor was away and the hotel empty, with a barman only left as caretaker. Unable to endure the thought of so much lonely beer lying around in the cellars, the men broached a thirty-six-gallon barrel, and for the rest of the day every man except Robert worked with a pint-pot at his elbow. For a time the work went with a good will under the influence but as the hours and the pints went by the atmosphere of work gave way to an atmosphere of festivity – singing, shouting of jokes and jigging alternated with increasingly feeble attempts at the redecorating. The weaker spirits at last gave up work altogether and sat about the floors or strolled over the hotel, so far as their legs would carry them, to see how their betters lived, coming to rest wherever they happened to be. The stronger spirits carried on emptying the thirty-six-gallon barrel while continuing their valiant efforts with the redecorating, until they, too, had to admit that work *was* 'the curse of the drinking classes' as the man said, and applied themselves in earnest to the bacchanalia.

When most of them, except Robert they say, were safely drunk and the uproar had reached a pitch when it disturbed the surrounding gentility and even the birds in the trees, the boss put his head in at the front door.

This unofficial beano cost the firm the services of all hands on that job (except one) but I believe that some were taken back on for another go. I don't know what happened to the barman.

Robert wasn't a teetotaller and we know the names of some of the pubs where friends occasionally had a drink with him; the Imperial, Queen's Road, which he decorated; the Bodega at the Memorial; the Clarence, Station Road, where the Trades Council of his day met; the Golden Cross, Havelock Road, near the Station, where he sometimes went for a drink with Mr Green's father; the Cambridge, Cambridge Road, where the Trades Council meets today; the North Star, Clarence Road; The Nag's Head, Gensing Road, where, said Poynton, one of the meetings took place to organize the 'Annual Beano'; the Fountain at the end of Grosvenor Crescent on the Bexhill Road; and the Cricketers, South Terrace, where the SDF met and where he got the prototypes for the 'Semi-drunk' and the 'Besotted Wretch'.

At Kite's Nest, too, he nearly fell off the roof. He was painting an airshaft when someone from below shouted up a remark about a 'bloody Irishman'. Robert started to descend in too great a hurry, slipped and knocked a kettle of green paint over the red tiling. Luckily he managed to retain a grip of the ladder laid up the sloping roof.

Kathleen tells of a curious episode when he was working in one house and 'the lady sent him tea, not just a cup but on a tray with a silver set, and buttered scones and when he came home he said it was just like being at his old home again; she treated him like a civilized being instead of one of the lower animals'.

Another anecdote he recounted to Poynton and Poynton to me. One morning when working for Adams and Jarrett's, Robert walked to work as usual, arriving at 6 a.m. at a large house in St Leonards, at the back door, of course. The door was opened to him by a child about sixteen years of age – the servant-girl. She wasn't, said Robert, looking her best at that time in the morning. Her eyes were heavy and lustreless, she was unkempt and looked about double her age. After a while Robert was struck by the fact that she appeared to be the only servant in this sizeable villa and he therefore observed her at work more than he might otherwise have done.

He saw her clean the grates, light the fires and wash up supper things, after which she washed herself, did her hair and put on clean cap and apron. Then she made a cup of tea. After that she cleaned three pairs of shoes and Robert understood that there were three ladies resident – three middle-aged ladies. After cleaning the shoes the girl boiled several gallons of water, there being no bathroom, and at eight o'clock she made three journeys upstairs with a large jug. Back once more in the kitchen she made preparations for breakfast and at eight-thirty made three more journeys upstairs with three breakfast-trays. After that she made Robert a cup of tea and he had his breakfast half-hour and the girl herself sat down to eat. Her breakfast, of course, was interrupted every now and again as three ladies rang three bells for something or other.

At nine o'clock she made three journeys upstairs to collect three breakfast-trays and began washing-up. During this, Robert, busy at work, heard a door upstairs open and one of the unseen ladies apparently entered the lavatory. A little later the lady returned to her room and Robert's attention to his work. Presently he heard the door open again and another lady entered the lavatory. And a little while after her return the third lady was heard there. Robert, who had only the social historian's interest in the women was nevertheless struck by the close relationship between assimilation and evacuation. He wondered what interesting and valuable work these ladies did.

In the meantime, the servant-girl was busy on the stairs and eventually the three ladies, after more ringing of bells, were safely settled in their rooms with books and knitting. The morning wore away, during which the girl did all the work and ran several times over the house to fetch and carry as bells rang. Then came lunch prepared by the same girl, and after lunch, Robert, who was expecting it, heard a door open and a lady enter the lavatory. And, of course, when she returned the second lady, after a discreet interval, entered in her turn, and finally the third. Once, the servant-girl entered, but the bell rang.

At four-thirty she took up tea for the ladies and a while later Robert, still at work, heard the lavatory door open again – three times – at intervals. Robert drew the conclusion that the servant-girl was born into the world to keep these three ladies alive. *Their* function appeared to be to eat and evacuate – only he didn't describe it quite so to Poynton.

It was about this time that he painted the huge advertisement for Adams and Jarrett's on the blind end wall of the right-hand side of

Perth Road, looking up, an elaborate piece of signwriting, I suppose twenty-five feet long by thirty feet high. It incorporates two insets; one a painting of the old Hollington Church-in-the-Wood in a little landscape, and a smaller one of a heron in its natural haunts.

This piece stood for nearly sixty years and was obliterated only when the firm changed hands a few years ago.

And I believe he decorated about this time the Moorish room, mentioned in the book. He gives, besides his usual sardonic picture of the boss's attitude, 'You're a bit of a hartist, ain't yer?', hints of how he had been taken on for special jobs and how he was paid, which bears out his friends' opinions that he got no fees but only extra rate, overtime, etc. and, according to Sellens, perhaps not that at Adams and Jarrett's.

The boss in broaching the subject of this particular job refers to Owen's (Robert's) samples 'what's hanging up there' from which it is evident that Robert submitted samples of his work when applying for a job with a firm.

'At first,' says the boss, 'Mr Sweater thought of getting a firm from London to do it, but 'e give up the idear on account of the expense; but if you can do it so that it doesn't cost too much, I think I can persuade 'im to go in for it.'

He shows Owen a photograph which he says is a 'sort of Japanese fashion'.

It was Moorish, says Robert. The boss hummed and hawed wishing to give the impression that he wasn't particular whether it was done or not in case Owen asked for extra money.

Owen, says Robert, and he is speaking of himself, began to feel an intense desire to do the work and suggested that he make a water-colour sketch – a design – 'and if you think it good enough,' he says, 'of course, I can reproduce it on the ceiling and the walls, and I can let you know, within a little, how long it will take.'

The boss shook his head dubiously. 'If I let you spend a lot of time over the sketches and then Mr Sweater does not approve of your design, where do I come in?' 'Well, suppose we put it like this,' says Owen, 'I'll draw the design at home ... in my own time. If it's accepted, I'll charge you for the time I've spent upon it. If it's not suitable, I won't charge the time at all.' The boss accepts this but tells him not to 'pile it on too thick'.

It was Monday and the boss wanted the drawing by Wednesday

but Owen says Friday, resolving that he would stay up all night if necessary to get it done, but the boss couldn't wait.

'I can't get them done any quicker in my spare time. . . . If you like to let me stay home tomorrow and charge the time the same as if I had gone to work at the house, I could . . . let you have the drawings on Thursday morning.'

The boss agrees to this and Robert says that long after his family was asleep Owen worked in the sitting-room searching through old numbers of the *Decorators' Journal* and other books for examples of Moorish work.

Kathleen says that he always worked in the sitting-room and not in his tiny bedroom where the bed was under the sloping attic roof. The Hastings Borough Library, then a reference library and known as the 'Free Library', still possesses volumes of *The Practical Decorator and Ornamentist* and *The Manual of Ornament* which he must certainly have consulted and which contain in gold and colour many styles of interior decoration, including his Japanese and Moorish. In his own description he gives complete technical details of his ideas and the methods of working in those days.

The question of what personal advantage he would gain didn't occur to him, he says; he simply wanted to do the work but he couldn't help making the point that personal advantage was the only consideration for the boss and that this was what is meant by the oft-quoted saying 'The men work with their hands – the master works with his brains.'

His chapter is headed 'Hands and Brains', and I came across an article in the *Hastings and St Leonards Weekly Mail and Times* for 26 August 1906 headed 'Hands and Brains' and it is possible that he got his heading from this.

Both Gower and Kathleen remember him working late into the night and Poynton, himself an amateur artist, said that Robert was quick and bold in his designing and that the 'Moorish room' was a magnificent piece of work executed by Robert 'almost alone' for a house in Hollington Park Road, and still remembered a few years ago.

In his *Builder's History* (1923) Raymond Postgate confirms that Robert was 'an artist of great abilities, not only with his pen as his book shows, but with his brush as well and specimens of his work are still shown around Hastings'.

Examples of his work survived for many years after this but with the pulling down of St Andrew's Church, Queen's Road, recently, the only specimen remaining is a fragment of an advertisement for the firm on the wall of their old workshop in Alfred Street, St Leonards.

He assisted the unemployed, says Walsh, by painting banners for their processions. He took part in marches of unemployed, carrying a collecting-box although himself in work, and went on various deputations to the Mayor and the Borough Council on their behalf.

There is a story from Mr Boreham, another workmate, that Robert painted a scenic wall for the Buchanan Hospital without pay.

Len Green says that Robert spent Christmas 1907 with his friends the Greens.

> He visited my father three or four times a week. I lived with my father and four sisters at 17 Mann Street and Louie, the eldest girl, said to Robert, 'Dolphus' (they used to call him that,) 'would you like to spend Christmas with us and Robert accepted.' We knew he had nowhere to go.
>
> He danced with my sisters while the youngest, who became blind later on, played the piano for them and he played with the other children there and danced their dances with them and sometimes called himself 'Ole Wun Lung the Chinaman' which he wrote down for them in the 'chinese' fashion. He always saw the funny side of things and was a jolly little chap always laughing and singing.

On Boxing Day, Kathleen made an entry in Rose Cruttenden's new autograph-book:

> Flag of Freedom rise resplendent
> From the ashes and the gloom
> Like the martyr's spirit flashing,
> From the grave and dungeon tomb.
> K.Noonan. 17/9/92.   26/12/07.

These words appear on Robert's membership card for the Transvaal '98 Centenary Association where they begin, 'Flag of Ireland'.

The photograph of a beach meeting by the *Albertine* in which both Robert and Kathleen can be seen seems to have been taken this summer of 1907 when Harry Quelch addressed the crowd on the subject, 'Eighteen months of Liberal Government.'

16

A new home

Sometime in late 1907 or early 1908 Robert and Kathleen made yet another move, without Adelaide and Arthur, to 241 London Road, St Leonards. Perhaps brother and sister had at last decided to part company.

Poynton and others said that the relationship between them was not brotherly and sisterly, and this seems borne out by Kathleen. Their differences were, perhaps, brought to a head by his work in the SDP, but there was in any case little feeling between the brother and any of his sisters. Ellie from Liverpool had visited in 1901 but never since; and Kathleen never saw her again and says that Adelaide never visited Robert after they parted nor did she ever visit her sister Mary Jane. Kathleen says,

> Adelaide like the rest of the family did not approve of Robert's social 'descent' and possibly she came to the end of her tether and may have returned to the family.
>
> I don't remember them after Warrior Square except for seeing Arthur walking in crocodile with the choir boys on the way to Church – all the boys in Eton suits and mortar-boards. I don't remember missing either of them or how the break came. I was always shy and retiring and with my nose in a book most of the time – I do not even remember many friends of my own age. There was a difference of age between Arthur and myself. I think Robert treated us both the same. Arthur called Dad 'Uncle Robert'. I think Arthur looked upon him as a father and that would be the relationship between them.

One wonders whether man and boy missed this relationship. It seems incredible that Arthur shouldn't visit at London Road, although, of course, he was only about nine years old when he left. This parting adds another dimension to the portrait of Frankie in the book.

Kathleen, although apparently friendly to Arthur, makes no mention of the deeper feelings of brother and sister, and Adelaide never took the place of a mother to her. Says Kathleen: 'She never forgave me for that first meeting at Cape Town, which was very foolish for a grown woman, and every now and again she would throw it up at me. But she was very good in lots of ways. I was always well dressed as she used to make most of my clothes but apparently she used to spank me because I can remember the children saying to me: "Your Aunt beats you, doesn't she?"'

The flat at 241 London Road, was over a cycle-shop – the Adna Cycle Depot – owned and run by Charles Alfred Beney, who, as owner of the whole house, became their new landlord.

Robert had rooms, not a self-contained flat as before, at the top of this five-storey house – four flights from the front door on London Road – and Kathleen gives a little description of them and of the tenants.

First there was a landing with a bathroom and then four or five stairs to the next floor where we had a kitchen-dining-room and Gypsy had a room. On the top floor was a big front room which was Dad's and where he did his writing, and a little room which was my bedroom and another room at the back. 'Gypsy' was a friend of Mrs Beney's. Her name was Kitty Saunders and she was very nice. Mr and Mrs Beney were very nice people, too; she was about twelve years older than I was and we became friends. Mr Beney was about ten years older than his wife and they were a very devoted couple.

Mrs Beney told me how they came to be married. When she was ten or eleven years old she was taken ill and Mr Beney, who was a young man, used to visit her and after one of his visits he told her mother that he was going to marry the girl when she grew up. The mother told him not to be silly but he waited, even through the time when the girl grew older and had a crush on his brother, and at last his fidelity was rewarded and they were married.

The Beneys' little boy was about five years old and used to be in and out of our rooms. At one time I was 'engaged' to him – with a rubber ring out of a pop bottle, one of those that used to have marbles in the top. There was also a baby who I used to take out.

Dad liked the Beneys and it was Mrs Beney who cooked the dinner on the occasion Dad asked my cousin Paul round and we all ate in the Beneys' living-room.

I used to like to read in bed and would go on reading late and Dad would call up to me.

'Katie, is your light out?'

'No Dad.'

'Put it out at once.'

'Oh, can't I finish this chapter?'

'Put your light out.'

'All right.'

And I put out my light, but darn it all it was such an exciting book that I couldn't sleep and I put on the light again and he came up and found me and thought I had lied to him before and there were ructions.

This year too, Kathleen received a bursary to St Helen's Pupil Teacher Centre, later St Helen's High School for Girls. It seems very likely that after only a couple of years in England Robert had already exhausted what resources he had and was unable to keep up the payments for St Ethelburga's.

After returning from St Ethelburga's in Deal at about twelve years of age, Kathleen was sent to St Andrew's Church of England Elementary School, at the bottom of the very steps in Stonefield Road which her father walked to and from work. She tells a little story about her first term.

'In the middle of term,' she says, 'they moved me up to the form above and at examination time I came top of the class and dashed home with pride and told Dad: "I beat them all!", only to be snubbed with the remark that so I should have done as I'd had so many more advantages.'

Kathleen's bursary was repeated and her education was following the lines her father had desired for her. He told Ward that he hoped she would become a teacher of some kind. She had had youthful ambitions to become a nun and later an actress, but says that her father would never have allowed her to go on the stage, which suggests, with other evidence, that he had reservations about the emancipation of women and of his daughter in particular.

According to Mr Cruttenden, a new friend he made this year,

'Robert had just enough goods and chattels to enable him and his little girl to get along', but through it all, says Kathleen, he had tried to give her as good an education as possible, augmented with the use of his library which included besides the usual classics, Plutarch's *Lives*, Pliny, Plato, *Poetics* of Aristotle, Josephus, Gibbon. 'He read', she adds, 'everything except rubbish', and she surprised him by her own ability to absorb 'the utmost trash as well as what was worth while'.

But, as Gower says, Robert himself could enjoy the thrillers of the day, Conan Doyle's *Sherlock Holmes* stories, Bram Stoker's *Dracula*, Eugene Sue's *Mysteries of Paris* and others. He seemed to be living a full and vivid mental life and had now broken his isolation. His health too seems to have been 'fair' at this time.

Kathleen tells a little anecdote which illustrates another side of her father's character. When she slipped on the pavement outside a police station which stood on a sloping corner, her father went along and complained that several people had fallen in the same spot and something should be done about it. 'Perhaps he got mad', says Kathleen, 'like he did about Bert working in the cold paint-shop, and created a scene, but whatever he did or said, the pavement there was scored and so made safer for poor pedestrians.'

Robert did his best to rear Kathleen as a civilized human being, even if this meant a handicap in life for her, and insisted on a good education to enable her to fend for herself, for he feared deeply for her future in an uncaring world. In any case he believed education to be as necessary for women as for men – both men and women need enlightenment and women bring up the next generation. He well knew that the heaviest burdens fell upon the mothers.

He encouraged her to work hard at school and to study in her spare time; he had made great sacrifices to equip her, and Kathleen certainly *did* study. Friends say that she was always busy when they visited the Noonans and even on picnics and outings she always took a book. Rose Cruttenden tells of a blackberrying trip during which Kathleen sat reading and allowed her friend to gather the blackberries.

Kathleen mentions an incident of their life at Milward Road through which again we get a glimpse of her father's strange reticence: 'When I wanted to learn the piano Robert would not let me and my aunt told me my mother had played and it made him sad to see a woman at the piano.'

I find it difficult to understand why, if his wife meant so much to him, he didn't celebrate her memory with her daughter, but the fact is he told Kathleen little.

The National *Clarion* Van, 1914 – a travelling headquarters of a growing socialist movement.

Vote Again for Our Daddy. A Tory exercise in public relations by the children of Arthur Du Cros, MP, in Hastings during the 1910 General Election.

The unmarked site of Tressell's pauper's grave.

Memorial stone erected on Tressell's grave by subscription sponsored by the Liverpool & Hastings Trades Councils, Mr George Smith of UCATT, Mr Jack Jones of TGWU and Fred Ball, through a committee comprising Mr Eric Heffer, MP, Mr Hugh Dalton, UCATT, Mr John Nettleton, TGWU, Mr Bill Kelly, TGWU, Mr Alan O'Toole, NUPE, and Mr Eric Pye, FTAT. In keeping with the spirit of Tressell it was decided to record also the names of the other twelve paupers buried in the same unmarked grave.

ROBERT NOONAN
18TH APRIL 1870 — 3RD FEBRUARY 1911
AUTHOR AS ROBERT TRESSELL OF
"THE RAGGED TROUSERED PHILANTHROPISTS"

"THROUGH SQUALID LIFE THEY LABOURED
IN SORDID GRIEF THEY DIED
THOSE SONS OF A MIGHTY MOTHER,
THOSE PROPS OF ENGLAND'S PRIDE.
THEY ARE GONE, THERE IS NONE
CAN UNDO IT, NOR SAVE OUR SOULS
FROM THE CURSE,
BUT MANY A MILLION COMETH,
AND SHALL THEY BE BETTER OR WORSE?

"IT IS WE MUST ANSWER AND HASTEN
AND OPEN WIDE THE DOOR,
FOR THE RICH MAN'S HURRYING TERROR,
AND THE SLOW FOOT HOPE OF THE POOR"

ALSO
ELIZABETH MARY DAVIES
ANNA BROWN
MARGARET BETHELL
JAMES GRIBB
WILLIAM ASH
MAY JAMES
ANN ASHTON
WILLIAM DUCKSBERRY
WILLIAM BARNES
MARY DAVIDSON
LILLY HARRISON
RICHARD DONALD

17

Work with the local socialists

Robert had some very useful ideas for advertising socialism.

His earliest, even before he joined the SDF, was a penny-a-week lending library of selected books from his own bookshelves for his workmates who could not get much of a selection in the town's small privately donated 'Free Library'. He tried to counter the pernicious teaching they had been brought up on and the influence of the growing yellow press and of the religious tract which had often been the only literature used in their education in Victorian England. Was it Cobbett who said a century earlier that when he went to America, English working-men were discussing the vital political questions of this world and that when he returned they were in chapels discussing life in the next?

Nevertheless at this period, because the Liberal Party, unlike the Labour Party today, had its own press, both national and local, the people were better served in some ways than they are now. There was a growing rise in literacy of the younger generations due principally to the Education Acts of the previous quarter-century, and consequently a great demand for reading matter, including newspapers, and the turn of the century saw the introduction of the popular Press.

While Robert was here, apart from the national papers, Hastings had no less than eight local ones. Published weekly on Saturdays were the *South Weekly News*, at one penny; the Liberal *Hastings and St Leonards Weekly Mail and Times*, at one penny; the Conservative *Hastings and St Leonards Observer*, at one penny; on Wednesdays the *Hastings and St Leonards Chronicle* at one halfpenny; and on Thursdays the *Hastings and St Leonards Advertiser* at twopence.

For daily locals there were the *Sussex Daily News*, at one penny; and the *Morning Argus* and the *Evening Argus*, at one halfpenny. And in October 1911 the local branch of the SDP produced the first number of a socialist 'monthly journal for working people'.

Besides these locals there was a wide national range of special circulation papers and journals representing minority opinions and, of course, a great range of socialist papers.

So Robert had a wider range of political opinion and coverage before 1910 than we have in 1973, and he made good use of it.

He was generally more conscious than the other socialists of cultural and intellectual starvation among the workers, yet like the others, he believed that culture should be founded upon an understanding of their own lives, and a 'cultured' man in his view would automatically be concerned for the welfare of the common people. He also gives many sardonic examples of the cultural poverty of other sections of society – witness the portraits of his employers and members of the Town Council.

'I went to the Paris Exhibition myself,' said Grinder ... 'I remember 'avin' a look at the moon through that big telescope. I was never so surprised in me life; you can see it quite plain, and it's round!'

'Round?' said Didlum with a puzzled look. 'Round? of course it's round! You didn't used to think it was square did yer?'

'No, of course not, but I always used to think it was, flat – like a plate, but it's round like a football.'

'Another thing that gets over me,' continued Rushton' 'is this: according to science, the earth turns round on its axle at the rate of twenty miles a minit. Well, what about when a lark goes up in the sky and stays there about a quarter of an hour? Why, if it was true the earth was turnin' round at that rate all the time, when the bird came down it would find itself 'undreds of miles away from the place where it went up from! But that doesn't 'appen at all; the bird always comes down in the same spot.'

'Yes, and the same thing applies to balloons and flyin' machines,' said Grinder. 'If it was true that the earth is spinnin' round on its axle so quick as that, if a man started out from Calais to fly to Dover, by the time he got to England he'd find 'imself in North America, or p'r'aps farther off still.'

'And if it was true that the world goes round the sun at the rate they make out, when a balloon went up, the earth would run away from it! They'd never be able to get back again!' remarked Rushton. ...

'Talking about science,' said Grinder, as the holy man relapsed into silence. . . . 'Talking about science reminds me of a conversation I 'ad with Dr Weakling the other day. You know, he believes we're hall descended from monkeys.'

Everyone laughed; the thing was so absurd: the idea of placing intellectual beings on a level with animals!

'But just wait till you hear how nicely I flattened 'im out,' continued Grinder. 'After we'd been arguin' a long time about wot 'e called everlution or some sich name, and a lot more tommy-rot that I couldn't make no 'ead or tail of – and to tell you the truth I don't believe 'e understood 'arf of it 'imself – I ses to 'im: "Well," I ses, "if it's true that we're hall descended from monkeys," I ses, "I think your famly must 'ave left orf where mine begun." '

And his picture of the rich businessman, Sweater, and the aristocrat Sir Graball shows them exclusively preoccupied with narrow self-interest and the mere pomp of social position. How could such 'educated' men be said to be any more enlightened than the most benighted labourer? Enlightenment depended more upon humanitarianism, common sense and wisdom than this kind of 'education'.

Robert always used diagrams to illustrate his own 'lectures' and his discussions. The 'Professor's' lectures in the book are good examples but in real life they were delivered in much more direct and homely language.

In summer he liked to sit on the beach with friends and, says Gower, always chose to sit near a patch of dry sand. Before long, if he hadn't something with him for the purpose, he would be searching for a stray stick and then would draw in the sand.

He had ideas too for advertising the SDP and its meetings. Once, for a visit of Hyndman, he suggested that a huge streamer be hung high across the street but this was turned down so he proposed that he should make a large box-kite inscribed with the slogan 'Hyndman is coming', to be flown high over the town. This too was ruled out and Robert finally made a four-sided box of sandwich-boards illuminated from inside to show off the same slogan. This was duly carried through the main streets by a regular sandwich-board man and Robert insisted that he be paid a full craft-union rate for the job.

It seems that during his tour the man was accosted by a local Colonel Blimp who indignantly 'ticked him off' for advertising a socialist meeting, to which the poor man replied that it was indeed against his principles to advertise socialism, but that he had never been so well paid for any other job! Robert was delighted with the logic of this reply.

A more ambitious proposal was that boats should be hired, rigged up with coloured lights and hung with red banners, to carry streamers announcing national speakers, the famous names of the Socialist Movement. These should then be sailed just offshore along the length of the sea-front. This proposal too was turned down.

But one idea took on. The branch acquired its own Socialist Van, and this was fitted up with a screen across the back. Inside, Gower fixed up his lantern and slides and the van was taken round the town, pulling up in convenient back streets. The inhabitants would be treated to an instructive entertainment, and Cobb's caustic commentaries are said to have been vastly entertaining.

Cobb is never known to have obtained a neutral reaction from his audiences at any meeting. The apathetic, the placid, the partisan soon responded one way or another to his prickly style, and by the use of this van people were reached in their own homes, especially the women, and Gower remarks upon the great popularity of the Socialist Van with people who were starved of both entertainment and instruction.

Gower's magic lantern was often used at meetings at 11 Priory Street and Robert undoubtedly derived his scene 'The Pandorama' from Gower's magic lantern and the SDP commentaries.

Robert is said to have written leaflets, manifestoes, election addresses, etc. but unhappily none survive. He also made posters for the SDP and Gower who was then working at the Gaiety Theatre, now the Classic Cinema opposite the Town Hall, mentions that many times after the performance he went along to Robert's and they were up till two and three o'clock in the morning making these posters, and drinking coffee between times. Robert also painted banners and bannerettes. One of them was in existence until 1940 and may still be somewhere in Britain. This, known now as the 'Robert Tressell Banner', was painted at the house of J.H.Poynton, of 139 Marina, St Leonards, in 1910.

'We worked on it on Saturday and Sunday afternoons. It was hung for painting on a large wall in a room at the top of the house and Bob had frequently to rest on the stairs going up as he suffered from chronic asthma.' And Mrs Poynton, who also suffered from it, would take a breather with him, and Poynton describes how the two would sit and grumble about their common shortness of breath.

But much earlier than this Robert painted a far more beautiful banner for the SDP, but it doesn't survive.*

The SDP held its open-air meetings near the Fishmarket and opposite the Queen's Hotel and at these meetings he would distribute handbills and sell literature and if the poorer people couldn't buy it, he gave it to them. He would often be arguing the point on the out-skirts of the crowd, and he used to see red when people passed in-sulting remarks about the socialists.

At one meeting someone called out 'an insult about the red flag flying over the rostrum and Robert chased him across the beach to remonstrate until he was restrained by other socialists.

Often the meetings were very rowdy and it wasn't long before Cobb had stones thrown through his windows, too.

In Chapter Forty-three – 'The Good Old Summer-time', Robert describes an attack on a Socialist van. In various parts of the country there must have been many such scenes, such as even off-beat religious groups had suffered, witness the history of Nonconformism and the Salvation Army, and often the police were in no hurry to intervene. Newspaper and official propaganda incited such mobs and violent anti-socialist propaganda in Robert's day gave a kind of sanction to violence.

The veteran trade union organizer, with Ben Tillett, of the dockers' strikes and others, Tom Mann, himself an old SDF man, once displayed his head to an audience of which I was one and the scars and bumps on it not only gave evidence of attentions received from mobs, and thugs hired by employers, but would have delighted any phrenologist.

I believe Tom had also on more than one occasion been thrown into people's rivers and harbours, not to mention his various arrests for 'incitement', 'sedition' and other crimes invented by clever Govern-ment lawyers. And he was only one of thousands.

Says Robert of a visit by the Socialist Van – in fact one of the famous *Clarion* Vans:

As soon as the crowd saw it, they gave an exultant cheer, or, rather, yell . . . and in a few minutes it was surrounded by a howling

*And talking of 'slogans' I wonder whether Prime Minister Harold MacMillan in more recent years ever discovered that under the wallpaper in one of his bedrooms was the slogan 'Vote for Labour' painted, I believe, in red paint.

mob. . . . [The speaker's] voice was inaudible in the din of howls, catcalls, hooting and obscene curses. . . . the crowd began pushing against the van and trying to overturn it, the terrified horses commenced to get restive and uncontrollable . . . then someone threw the first stone, which by a strange chance happened to strike one of the cyclists whose head was already bandaged . . . the man on the platform was the next to be struck. He got it right on the mouth, and as he put up his handkerchief to staunch the blood another struck him on the forehead just above the temple, and he dropped forward on his face on to the platform as if he had been shot. . . .

'We'll give the b—rs Socialism!' shouted Crass, who was literally foaming at the mouth. . . .

. . . the victory being complete, the upholders of the present system returned to the piece of waste ground . . . where a gentleman in a silk hat and frock-coat . . . made a speech. He said nothing about the Distress Committee or the Soup Kitchen or the children who went to school without proper clothes or food. . . . But he said a good deal about the Glorious Empire! and the Flag! and the Royal Family. The things he said were received with rapturous applause; and at the conclusion of his address, the crowd sang the National Anthem. . . .

This scene, I am told, was a composite picture of local events, and scenes during the so-called 'Tenterden Riots' at Tenterden in Kent.

There are other ways of closing the mouths of leaders, the best known being promotion in the hierarchy. Cobb was offered jobs. One was as talleyman with a guaranteed wage of five pounds per week subscribed by twenty businessmen at five shillings each, and another job at eighteen shillings per week. When Cobb protested he was told 'but it's regular!' But Cobb always stood for Council as a socialist, disdaining any lesser label and when one man said to him 'I never see you praised in the papers, Mr Cobb', he replied, 'On the day you do I'll expect you to come and punch me on the nose!'

Despite the opposition of hooligans the visits of the *Clarion* Van were put to good use. The little group of stalwarts helped to push it about the town, and there are some steep hills in Mugsborough! On one Sunday they hired a horse and took it over to Bexhill, themselves helping to draw it. When a tour was made of surrounding villages they were warned that if they went into Rye (another Cinque Port) they would be stoned. Of course the van duly arrived in Rye and a meeting was held under the historic Landgate.

The speakers were heard without hostile demonstration – the Rye champions were nowhere to be seen. After the meeting the van and its escort of cyclists, among them Noonan and Gower, were heading out of the town for Hastings, about eleven miles away, when they were suddenly under heavy fire from street doorways. Luckily the ammunition consisted of turf and the aim being unmilitary, no one was hurt.

It was before the First World War. As they rode off unscathed, members of the *Clarion* party called back congratulations upon the prowess of the ambushers. It's more than likely that some who later became socialists themselves threw mud that day at Robert Noonan. Rye has had stalwarts of its own.

Kathleen herself became an ardent socialist with her father and used to attend the beach meetings and says, 'I would have a socialist pamphlet in my hand and by the time the meeting was over it would be all screwed up while I listened and nobody would have read it. We used to sing the "Red Flag" and the "Internationale".'

After the evening meetings on the beach a few people usually remained behind in discussion and would often stay very late. On one occasion Gower remembers seeing Robert at twelve o'clock at night surrounded by a little group, still going strong, the sea pounding up the beach a few yards back and the dark waters of the English Channel stretching away behind them.

18

Danger: men at work

Adams and Jarrett's showrooms were in the lower part of Norman Road, near Warrior Square and the workshops and yard in Saxon Street, behind, with another workshop in Alfred Street at the top of the steps leading from London Road near Christ Church, and to these workshops he would walk down London Road from his flat at 241, the 'Long Hill', iti s believed, of the book.

Robert was on an hourly basis at the painters' rate of 7d. an hour, although rates varied in different parts of the country and even in the same town, from firm to firm. Cradduck and others tell me that some paid only 6½d. and others as low as 6d. and 5½d. Robert gives an example of 5d.

Hours were from 6 a.m. to 5.30 p.m. 'and 2d. per week', says Sellens, 'was stopped from our wages to ensure the firm against our meeting with accidents. If men objected they received the 2d. and the sack.'

'There were no such things as holidays or even Bank Holidays,' says Cradduck. 'I remember if you had a day off you had to ask for your job back to start again and men often lost their job through it.'

Here, too, Robert did signwriting, graining and gilding, but a large part of his time was spent as a 'plain-layer-on' as it was described, that is a semi-skilled painter but here, too, he was given special jobs of interior decoration when there were any. He may have received a higher rate per hour for this but Sellens, who was there, comments:

The trade union rate was 7d. per hour and if Bob got 8d. per hour he was a very lucky man. If there was a big prize for guessing the right answer I should say that he received the top painters' rate of 7d. per hour, but for his extra skill was given a *regular* job with washing off and stripping and plain painting to fill in his time. Adams and Jarretts would not permit any fancy prices [wages]. In 1906, at 19, I went on the firm as Painters Improver for 4d. an hour.

In the book, however, Robert says of Owen that he always got an extra penny per hour.

Anecdotes about Robert's working life on this firm are sparse but it was here that he met the other half of his chief foreman Misery, or Nimrod, who had come to the firm from the ironmongery trade, and apparently filled much the same position as Misery in the book, having the dirty work to do, that is, supervising the jobs and specifications. He was therefore liable to be scapegoat in any trouble, exactly as in the relationship between Rushton and Misery in the book.

Mr Noakes, who worked there, says,

> This man, like Misery, was a Chapel-man, and always wanted to rush everything. There was a no-smoking rule on the firm and he would go around sniffing for smokers and would instantly dismiss anyone he caught. Men used to lie down on the floor in empty houses and smoke up the chimney.
>
> At the Convent in Magdalen Road one day he comes in suddenly and a chap smothered the cigarette he was smoking by putting the lighted end into his mouth. I have seen men burn their mouths doing this. Men were not even allowed to smoke when pushing a hand-truck.

Much of the material in the book is based on Robert's experience with this firm. Misery's snooping is recorded almost as an occupational disease.

> Mr Hunter was ... executing [on his cycle] a kind of strategical movement in the direction of the house where ... [the men] were working. He kept to one side of the road because by so doing he could not be perceived by those within the house until the instant of his arrival. When he was within about a hundred yards of the gate he dismounted ... there being a sharp rise in the road just there. ... three yards from the gate he noiselessly laid his machine against the garden fence. The high evergreens that grew inside still concealed him ... from ... anyone ... looking out of the windows. ... Then he carefully crept along until he came to the gate post, and bending down, he cautiously peeped round to see if he could detect anyone idling, or talking, or smoking.

One may imagine Robert's feelings upon discovering that he had fallen under just such a man as he had endured before, and many actual incidents with this new Misery are recorded in the book, but I have few direct records. Sellens was there only a short while and Noakes and Cradduck were youngsters and were emphatic that Robert was a quiet gentle man with them and of a whimsical turn of humour.

Noakes remembers working with him at the Presbyterian Church of St Columbia* when he was painting the walls and a series of panels and shields. Robert working on high steps, asked his mate, Noakes, for the signwriter's straight-edge and as Noakes stood under Robert on the steps Robert began swinging the straight-edge like a pendulum until, says Noakes, 'I was nearly hypnotized and would have fallen off the steps but Bob put out a hand and stopped me.'

The men used to eat their food and make their tea exactly as described by Robert, all dipping their mugs, jars or condensed-milk tins into the same pail or dixie and often the poorer eating bread and butter 'disinfected', as they described it, with pickled cabbage.

'Their operations extended all over the town,' he says, 'at all hours of the day they could be seen ... carrying ladders, planks, pots of paint, pails of whitewash, earthenware chimney pots, drainpipes, lengths of guttering, closet pans, grates, bundles of wallpaper, buckets of paste, sacks of cement, and loads of bricks and mortar' and all of it on hand-trucks. There were no vans, and Hastings and St Leonards is a very hilly town, and, of course, Robert Tressell was often with one of these gangs struggling up the hills or along the long sea-front, and from references in the book to supercilious or amused bystanders watching them, he appears at times to have been a shade self-conscious.

He gives a description of the painter's boy Bert White struggling up the Long Hill with a hand-truck and tacking from side to side of the street with the heavy load, and being caught 'resting' by the boss who is driving past with a gentleman and who admonishes Bert with the words 'The idear! Sitting down in my time!'

The conditions under which these lads worked filled Robert with fury. On one occasion he told Kathleen, 'I nearly got the sack today.' He describes the incident in the book.

He had occasion to return to the paint-shop where he found the boy alone cleaning out dirty paint-pots and stood watching the lad who hadn't heard him arrive. The stone floor of the paint-shop was damp and shiny and the whole place, he says, as chilly as a tomb. The

*Destroyed during the Second World War.

boy was trembling with cold and looked pitifully undersized. Robert asked him why he didn't light a fire, there was plenty of old wood lying about the yard. Bert replied that the boss had kicked up an awful row when he had a fire the previous winter and had told him to get some work done and he wouldn't feel the cold.

'Oh, he said that, did he,' Robert replied. 'We'll see about that,' and himself collected some wood, poured some old paint over it and soon produced a roaring fire. He waited around for half an hour to see whether the boss came in and told Bert that if anything was said he was to say that Robert had lit the fire. On the way out he told one of the men not to dare to interfere and to tell the boss that if he, Robert, found the boy like it again he would report it to the Society for the Prevention of Cruelty to Children.

Then he went on to the boss's office and was in such a fury that he didn't bother to knock but flung the door open. What with his weak lungs and his anger he was out of breath and panting violently.

'I've come,' he gasped, 'here – to tell – you – that – if I find young – Bert White – working – down in that shop – without a fire – I'll have you prosecuted. The place is not good enough for a stable. . . . I give you fair warning – I know – enough – about you – to put you – where you deserve to be. . . .'

The scene is written out in full in the book and Robert describes his own fears of the consequences of his action as he walked home through the snow. Undoubtedly, but for his special skills and the fact that there must have been a real basis for his threats, he would have lost his job. Employers regarded it as a divine right to treat employees how they liked and had finally to be restrained by laws forced upon them by working-class organizations, and still not fully operative for every kind of worker.

Robert gives many instances of the men's attitudes to his independent spirit and unorthodox ideas and sums them up in this passage.

'For the man himself most of the men . . . had a certain amount of liking, especially the ordinary hands because it was known that he was not a "master's man" and that he had declined to "take charge" of jobs which Misery had offered to him.'

He himself said that he turned down offers of foremanship because, he said, he didn't want to become deeply involved in 'business' nor to have to act as spy upon the men.

To some of the more demoralized men, he appeared, of course, as a crackpot, although (and he makes this point well in the book) they had to admit he *seemed* as if he was all there.

Gower says that in any company he gave an impression of intellectual superiority. 'In conversation at work,' said Gower, 'Robert was usually affable and friendly but if roused could launch a stream of bitter invective sometimes against social evils or, if called for, against an antagonist personally.'

There was always a note of eagerness and enthusiasm in his manner and always this friendliness towards people even in argument, unless they showed hostility or contempt. He would often ask pointed questions in a very low and quiet voice: 'You agree then that your children are not good enough for a better standard of living?' 'Do you agree that your children are not fit to be properly educated?' 'Can you tell me *why* your children should have shoes on their feet?' And, 'What makes you think you are *entitled* to food and clothing?'

If he found himself in argument with an educated or supposedly educated man he adapted his questions accordingly, often with great effect as in his encounter with the Conservative Party candidate Du Cros.

In this way he was able to expose pretension and ignorant prejudice to the person concerned, in so far as pretension and ignorance may be rendered self-conscious. Intellectual dishonesty he dealt with summarily by the use of invective, such as 'You're a bloody hypocrite' or 'Don't try that damned rubbish on me!'

With working-men who showed any interest in reading and improving their knowledge he would discuss at length all kinds of subjects, always treating knowledge as belonging to all by right, and trying to instil that sense of human dignity and social consciousness which he so passionately pleads for in his book.

The best among those of his acquaintance were deeply influenced and the strange thing is that in general the men recognized his superior education and accepted him without any self-consciousness. This is more extraordinary than those who don't know their working classes and who imagine they are uncritically impressed by superior education realize, for they, especially the Tory or apolitical working-men, are normally impressed *only* when the educated mouth the conventional platitudes, and, preferably, speak with educated accents.

And so some of Robert's mates would cheerfully argue vehemently with, and ridicule, him sure of their own (because socially acceptable) platitudes. Were not Press, Pulpit, Employer, Politicians and School-masters mouthing them daily?

His mates were all familar with his opinions and he was known as 'the Professor' for years among them in Hastings. Where he was employed for a number of years and got to know the men better he used, in fact, to give impromptu lectures when he was set on fire by argument at 'dinner-times' and he is, of course, something of the professor in his own book.

Noakes gives another side of his character. Noakes was in the old Volunteers, in the Artillery (my father too was a member) who drilled at Hatherley Road, St Leonards, and he described the scene, which must have been quite a spectacle, of the parades with the guns being drawn along the sea-front by cart-horses led by farm-labourers in their traditional smocks. Some of his workmates would rag Noakes, some were sarcastic about belonging to 'such a crowd', others expressed mock disapproval about learning to kill, but Robert, he says, always asked him interesting questions about how the men were treated, what they did in camp, and showed a general interest although he hated war and militarism.

One of the main themes of *The Ragged Trousered Philanthropists* is the demoralization of people by the 'Capitalist System', employers and men and their womenfolk alike, and how many rise above this demoralization and refuse to accept the morality of capitalism. At work, among the more demoralized of the men, this sometimes led to strange capers.

If a man were disliked he might find himself haunted by invisible enemies. Mysterious smears and defects would appear in his work; he might find his jacket nailed to the door, or the sleeves painted inside, or his boots nailed to the floor if he brought a change of footwear to work in. Various unpalatable seasonings would go into his tea and sometimes attempts would even be made to arrange an accident for him, especially if some felt threatened by him or he was a tale-teller. Robert gives instances in the case of Misery and Slyme and of the way many men slandered their mates.

Sellens gives an example of how fear of unemployment could demoralize men:

> I did not last there long on Adams and Jarretts. The painters tried to make it appear that I was of little use, afraid I might work

one of them out of their job. One of the Foremen put me on a job, let Jarrett see me on it, then when he was gone took me off it, but arranged for me to be back on it just before Jarrett came back. Jarrett, of course, thought I was on that one job all the time. The painters were all fighting each other and not the boss.

Among the results of these conditions were fear, apathy, often poor workmanship, backbiting, tale-telling, crawling and petty fiddling. The bosses themselves set the example. Robert hated the spectacle of men fighting among themselves like this instead of organizing to fight for better pay and conditions.

Kathleen said, 'He would get exasperated when he could make no impression on the workmen when trying to get them to better their conditions. He would say they deserved to suffer, but that it was their children who would have to suffer, which was so terribly frustrating to him.'

This frustration was undoubtedly more the result of his attempts to explain class society and socialism to his mates, arguments upon fundamentals which, as the book illustrates, the men neither understood nor related to their own experience, rather than to attempts to organize them industrially in the Painters' Society. Although he talks of the Society in the book and makes Owen secretary of the local branch, I can find no evidence that he was himself a union member and neither could Sellens and Philcox, both in their time secretaries of the local branch, and who both had correspondence on the subject with the Society's Head Office. Cruttenden said that at the time he knew Robert the union here had 'fizzled out' but there was in fact a small branch affiliated to the Trades Council and George Hicks, in the 1927 edition of the book, says, 'He was a member of the Painters' Union in London and subsequently on the South Coast.'

There would seem to be some reason to believe that he had in fact been a member in the short period he was in London before coming to Hastings, for Raymond Postgate, probably on the word of union members, says in *The Builders' History* that in Hastings 'the deadness of the union so depressed him that he did not re-enrol [in Hastings] as a member but put all his strength into agitating for the SDF'. And I am obliged to record that after several requests I am told that the headquarters of the Society have neither the time nor the staff to search the records and cannot allow me to do it myself.

There was a serious recess in the trade and many small firms were in desperate straits and could not face the fierce competition. The more conscientious they were the more difficult was survival. As Robert says, the competition demoralized employers as well as men.

The employers were mainly small or smallish firms engaged in cut-throat competition among themselves and at the same time at the mercy of the big manufacturers of materials. The slump in building, the introduction of 'labour-saving' methods, the skimping and decline in standards produced by the competition, the increased production of inferior mass-produced materials, all of which are savagely or humor-ously criticized in the book, led to increased insecurity which meant greater risk of unemployment. Then there was the seasonal laying-off – an occupational hazard in the trade, which particularly affected painters. As the old rhyme goes:

> The carpenter he gets bread and meat
> The bricklayer bread and cheese,
> But pity the poor old painter
> When the leaves fall off the trees.

From 1905 to 1908 between 50 and 70 per cent of all unemployed who applied for aid in the Greater London area registered themselves as building-workers.

Jobs were as scarce and the tradition of trade unionism weaker in the non-industrial South Coast regions, at that time much behind the industrial centres. Mr W.W.Wood, Labour Councillor and Parlia-mentary Candidate in Hastings for many years gave me an example – 'When I was in the Boot and Shoe Operatives TU. I used to collect the men's dues and had to go round the factory picking up the money the men had left under pieces of paper and tools. We would have lost our jobs had the Management known what was going on.'

Sellens says, 'There was nothing I can recall as direct struggle. We had unemployment demonstrations and waited upon the Corporation demanding work which to a small extent was successful. They intro-duced what we called "Linger and Die" – three days' work once a fortnight, three days this week but not next, and then three days again.' Incidentally, in meetings and demonstrations 'white-collar' workers sometimes wore masks to prevent victimization.

It was hardly surprising that trade union organization could not appear to the men to offer a solution in places like Hastings. Hence the insistence of socialists in those days upon a fundamental change, and to a man like Robert it would appear that he must use his energies to fight for what must have seemed the only real and lasting remedy.

Sellens says, 'I remember no fights for better conditions until after the 1914–18 War, when I was Secretary of the Painters' Society and also the first Secretary here of the National Federation of Building Trades Operatives.' And it is true that it was after the war that trade unions began to gain strength. Mr Walsh, in the *Painter's Journal*, December 1922, already quoted, says that the union was in process of organizing a campaign in the South of England.

> The Master Builders' Associations are still determined to enforce a lower status upon painters in these districts, that is Southern, South Western and Eastern England and in support of their claim are asserting that enormous numbers of 'rough' painters are working below the standard rates and that these men are chiefly employed by non-federated employers. It is even claimed that some members of our own society are offering themselves below the rates and are clamouring to work more than the recognized hours.

Walsh finishes by saying that unless every union member became a missionary for trade unions, there was every prospect of the South of England '*retaining* the unenviable reputation of being a drag on the forward Movement'. He then gave, as a spur to the campaign, a short account of Robert's life and extracts from what he called 'this wonderful book' and expressed the wish that every painter in the three regions 'could be persuaded to risk half-a-crown in the purchase of a copy', and 'that in view of all the circumstances (including our failure to appreciate the man's spirit and devoted service while he was living) the best way to keep his memory green is to devote our energies towards abolishing root and branch the wretched conditions which he depicts'.

Perhaps it is no accident but symbolic of the society round him, that Robert chose as the setting for his men at work, the renovating of an old house rather than the building of a new.

19

Political music-hall: the 1908 by-election

Sometime in 1908 Cobb took over the secretaryship of the Social Democratic Party branch. Cobb was the son of a London docker and came to Mugsborough from Walthamstow when a young man, round about the time of the Boer War. As secretary he was in a position to make himself felt in Mugsborough and the branch became a real force.

It conducted street meetings all over the town and put up candidates in local wards. Cobb soon brought a touch of glee, and irreverence for the 'bigwigs' (as he called them), into the arena and used to delight many and outrage others with his sallies. After all, it was hardly respectful to refer to the Workhouse Master (whom Cobb was opposing in a Council election) as 'that retired skilly-server', or to the Chief Constable's Sword of Office on a ceremonial occasion as 'that cheese-cutter', or to advise the public that if they visited the gardens of certain officials they could view plants and flowers which had got mislaid on their way to the Alexandra Park and beautiful drives surfaced with Corporation asphalt.

Some of the jiggery-pokery uncovered by Cobb went into Robert's book and I'm sure Cobb's uncompromising, sardonic and fearless style helped to fire Robert to speak his mind.

Cobb had his slogan, too: 'Many are called – but few get up.' And there was a crying need for some to get up.

This very Easter of 1908 the National Union of Teachers, here for their Annual Conference, actually placed a fund at the disposal of the Local Education Authority, an act, one would think, which should have shamed a town of 61,000 inhabitants, many of them very wealthy. This fund was the result of a special collection prompted by the delegates 'having seen in their wanderings about the town so many children entirely shoeless and stockingless running about in several inches of snow'.

This fund, still in existence, was later incorporated and administered with other charities. Yet Hastings had only that March returned again a Conservative Member in a Parliamentary by-election.

Arthur Du Cros, son of Harvey, and Chairman of Dunlop Rubber, friend of the financier Ernest Terah Hooley and a founder of the Junior Imperial League, was the new MP in place of his father. The campaign followed the familiar and tried pattern and scenes from it are recorded by Robert, who was there, but in any case he couldn't have improved on the Press accounts of the actual events.

The *Hastings and St Leonards Weekly Mail and Times* for 3 March 1908, records for history the candidates at work.

> The speaker for Arthur Du Cros, Conservative candidate, called to the crowd: 'Who kept the unemployed from starving through the winter?'
>
> 'Harvey Du Cros' shouted back some women in the crowd.
>
> 'Did Freeman Thomas [ex-Liberal Member] do that?' asked the orator.
>
> 'No!' came the chorus.
>
> 'Will Mr Harcourt [Liberal Candidate] do that?'
>
> 'No!'
>
> 'And who found boots for the poor little children in the cold weather?'
>
> And the crowd, having got the cue, rejoined:
>
> 'Harvey Du Cros, God Bless him!'

The Liberals responded with poetry:

> Lloydie Georgie bent his bow,
> Aimed at a pigeon and killed Du Cros.

But this was wishful thinking; the old Crow wasn't dead.

Reports of scenes of fighting in the streets between Tory and Liberal described by Robert may be found in the local newspapers.

It was during this by-election that the candidate himself was canvassing and called at Robert's lodgings in 241 London Road, St Leonards. Robert was entertaining Gower and Turner his school-teacher friend, a Tory, or an ex-Tory, then in a fluid state of mind.

Mrs Beney knocked on the door and announced that the candidate, Mr Du Cros, would like a word with Mr Noonan. 'Show him in!' said Robert, his hair beginning to curl.

The candidate entered briskly, as if he were half-way to a vote. Robert kicked a chair into place by the fire* and asked Du Cros to sit. The poor candidate started off full of hot air, until Robert, sitting facing him, and watching him with a quizzical expression, asked a quiet question. The candidate stopped in mid-air for a moment and then hit the floor. He had never been asked such a question by a working-man in the whole of his life. The trouble was that Du Cros was of Irish origin and Robert didn't like Tory Irishmen. He went on asking pointed questions upon, of all topics, Irish history, in which subject he soon had the candidate confounded. Says Gower,

> Bob went back hundreds of years into the history of Ireland and that's where the candidate obviously wished himself at that moment. Hard words began to flow. Du Cros's agent stood at the door rattling the handle to indicate that he should break off the engagement, and Robert rose to his feet, two hectic spots glowing on his cheeks, the sign that I got to know so well.

Burning with contempt and indignation, he bade the candidate 'Good day', calling him an Irish traitor and renegade as the agent hurried him through the door. His daughter Kathleen remembers him saying that the problems of Ireland would not be solved until the Irish 'got rid of the priests and the whiskey'.

'I never met any man, however well educated and high up,' says Gower, 'who didn't appear intellectually inferior to Bob, even in ordinary conversation. Bob was completely at ease in any company and never addressed a "superior" as other working-men did, but as an equal. He gave the impression of lowering a man's intellectual stature.' He confounded more than one person who was deceived into condescension by his workman's dress. The man who condescended to Bob was in for a few home-truths.

Cruttenden confirms this episode and corroborates Robert's scenes of the socialists in Chapter Forty-eight – 'The Wise Men of the East'. The SDP carried on their meetings during the election in the manner described and Cruttenden mentions an occasion outside the Royal Oak (not there any longer) in Castle Street near what is now Woolworth's, when the little group was surrounded by a hostile mob laughing and jeering which finally broke up the meeting, the members

---

*This seems a little out of character for the kind-hearted Robert but he wanted to bring Du Cros down to man to man.

having to make a getaway as best they could, some being manhandled in the process.

According to Sellens Robert wrote a leaflet for this by-election headed 'Under The Red Flag'. Kathleen says he made up rhymes for her and remembers this one but didn't know whether or not it was her father's.

> There was a man lived down our street
> Who was full of aches and pains.
> He fell out of the window one day
> And dashed out all his brains.
> And when he found he had no brains
> What do you think he did?
> He became a member of Parliament
> Where brains he did not need!

On polling day while the count was proceeding, Gower and Robert toured the booths through streets full of people eagerly awaiting the result. Robert amused himself by going up to groups of Tory supporters at the booths and asking in a troubled voice, as one who had heard bad news, whether they knew that if all the votes still to be counted went to Du Cros, nevertheless the Liberal was already elected. And then he continued his journey knowing as much about the result as they did, but leaving them to worry about it. But Hastings made no mistake. The Conservative was again elected.

Mr Cradduck, then an apprentice signwriter with Robert, remembers a job they had to do, painting a top hat with Conservative colours and the election result for a hired man to walk the streets in, a job Robert must have found very interesting. And Len Green remembered for sixty years seeing three little men, all about the same size and in black Homburgs or trilby hats, walking along Robertson Street deep in conversation – Ben Tillett (who had been addressing a meeting at the Market Hall, George Street), Alf Cobb and Robert Noonan, three redoubtable little men each of whom made a dent in the shell of the old crustacean.

20

Recreations

Gower says that he spent a good deal of time on walking and cycling outings with Robert and together they seem to have explored half of east Sussex. The countryside, he says, delighted and restored Robert. There he could relax, and the outings provided him with long opportunities to air his favourite topics and 'educate' his younger friend.

Besides his favourite politics, economics, socialism, his conversation ranged over all kinds of other subjects and out-of-the-way information, to Gower mind-opening, and made marvellous by the enthusiasm and spirit of the little man. Gower learned vastly more about his own country than he ever learned at school.

The open air released Robert; he seemed, says Gower, to have a weight lifted from his shoulders when in the country and his underlying love of life and enthusiastic temperament would come to the top.

'This is better than washing off ceilings!' he said once when they were cycling down Westfield Lane. At Brede on this day they went into the church, at which Dean Swift's cradle is preserved.

'This should be in Ireland,' said Robert – and off he went on the subject of Dean Swift and Ireland.

One Sunday morning on a walk in the district known as 'Old Roar' on the outskirts of town, Gower took the photograph which is featured in the Lawrence and Wishart and Panther Classics editions of *The Ragged Trousered Philanthropists*. It catches Robert in quizzical mood or with the sun in his eyes I don't know which, for each picture of him seems to me to portray a different person. The date of this photograph which is a bust taken from a full-length of him sitting on the stile at the top of Old Roar, I put at about the summer of 1908.

While it was being taken Robert said to Gower, 'Look out or you'll finish up being hung in the Tate Gallery.'*

'About this time he conceived the project,' as Gower puts it, 'of carrying entertainment and enlightenment to the people of Brede,

*I think Gower meant to say National Portrait Gallery.

Westfield and country districts around. I had a lecture lantern and we hired a set of slides called "A Trip Round The World", including scenes from the Great San Francisco Earthquake of 1906.'

Gower was to operate the lantern and Robert was to supply the 'lecture'. They would be known as 'The South Coast Amusement Company'. They wrote to Mr Harvey the village schoolmaster at Brede and he allowed them to hire the schoolroom for their opening. Then they had handbills printed and Gower, he says, 'billed' the village and waited outside the village school to hand bills to the children as they came out. Robert stayed at home preparing the 'lecture'. They next arranged with half a dozen local firms that advertisement slides would be shown to help defray expenses and with a music-seller to supply a phonograph and records in exchange for a free advertisement.

These and the lantern were to go out by carrier and Gower and Robert would cycle out.

On the afternoon of the day, Gower cycled over from Hastings to 241 London Road. It was pouring with rain and when Gower arrived, already wet through, Robert was standing at his window gazing out in deep depression.

'Look at that lot!' he said, 'I don't think we can go!'

'But we *must* go,' Gower replied. 'We can't back out now.'

Robert was thinking of what a soaking would mean with his weak lungs but he finally consented to risk it. They set off in the early afternoon. It was midwinter and one of those days of incessant rain.

'We were wet through when we arrived,' Gower said. 'The schoolmaster gave us some tea and we dried out a little and then got ready for the lecture.'

In rigging up the show at the school they discovered that the carrier had delivered everything but the phonograph needles! The music people had forgotten to include them.

'We had a full house,' said Gower, 'and two prices for seats.' These were threepence and sixpence and it wasn't long before the hall was full up, some people tramping through the terrible weather from places outside the village. In 1907 there wasn't a lot of entertainment in a small village.

Gower took the money at the door and the audience had to wait without the introductory music which the Company had planned. At last Robert decided they had got everyone who was coming and decided to begin. Gower left his place at the door to operate the lantern,

Robert took up his stand by the screen with a pointer, borrowed from the schoolmaster, in his hand, and with his saturated boots squelching at every movement took his audience for a Trip Round The World. Says Gower, 'Certainly if the audience were not entertained they were instructed that evening.'

The lecturer apparently took the opportunity to introduce his audience to a little socialist theory which Gower says they took wonderfully well. Perhaps the lecturer's success was due to the originality of his commentary to people used to being entertained by the vicar and well-intentioned ladies back from holidaying in Baden or Broadstairs. Perhaps it was because at Brede during the land labourers' revolt, the famous Captain Swing period, the farm-labourers had trundled the Parish Poor Law Overseer down the hill in a wheelbarrow and thrown him into a pond, probably in the hope of saving him from growing prematurely old.

At any rate, said Gower, the lecture held the attention so that there wasn't a sound beyond the lecturer's voice and the squelching of his boots.

It was eleven o'clock at night before the Company packed up and started for home, several miles away, on its cycles. Progress was very slow and Robert frequently had to ask his younger partner to stop, as the speed was too much for him. There is a lot of 'up-hill' between Brede and Hastings. It was after midnight when they arrived home and Robert was exhausted.

'That journey nearly killed me,' he said.

'Next day,' said Gower, 'poor Robert was laid up and the South Coast Amusement Company ceased to exist. We didn't make any profit anyhow.'

A little later the country people were to get entertainment and instruction of a slightly different kind; says Rose Cruttenden – 'We also belonged to the Clarion Fellowship and the Clarion Cycling Scouts round about 1908 and onwards and held Sunday meetings in the rural areas, having previously chalked the roads advertising the meetings.'

'Robert was "obsessed" by his poverty,' said Gower, 'and on another occasion he called on me in a state of great enthusiasm. "Bill," he said, "I've got an idea. Let's hire the St Leonards Pier Hall and show Moving Pictures!"'

Moving pictures of course were in their early days and there was no organized and regular showing of them in Hastings at this time.

'No,' Gower replied. 'I couldn't entertain that.'

'*You* couldn't entertain it!' exploded Robert, and a tiff arose, until eventually he calmed down. But he kept talking about the idea. I believe that by this time he was completely disillusioned with England and the hope of getting a fair living in his own trade, and this scheme marked one more step towards his final 'idea' for making his fortune and his final self-realization. And I don't think there is any inconsistency between such ideas and his hatred of 'business' – only a pathetic casting about for any kind of lifeline out of the morass.

Afterwards, Gower admits, he realized that Robert had a good idea and later on he had the chagrin of watching someone else open the pier for films.

Kathleen talks of visits to the cinema. 'I don't remember where, or the names of films – a St Bernard dog racing all over the countryside after a stolen baby – that type of thing,' she says.

Kathleen also remembers being taken by her father to see *The Bohemian Girl*, *Les Cloches de Corneville*, and *Madame Butterfly*, and the D'Oyly Carte Opera Company 'did' a week in Hastings every year, so they had *some* kind of musical fare beyond his Irish songs.

And then she offered a glimpse into the influence of the morality of the time upon Robert, or was it some kind of personal inhibition, or a reminder of something to do with his marriage?

'I was singing one day the song "Teasing, teasing, I was only teasing you", and Dad called out "Stop! you don't sing that!" I don't know why. It must have been risqué.' But she didn't fear her father.

Entries in her autograph-book are a comment upon the times.

> Self reverence, self knowledge, self control,
> These three alone lead life to sovereign power.
> Yet not *for* power, power of herself would come
> uncalled for,
> But to live by law acting the law we live by without
> fear,
> And because right is right, to follow right
> Were wisdom in the scorn of consequence.
>
> ———
>
> To thine own self be true and it shall follow
> As the night the day thou canst not
> then be false to any man.

Their schoolmaster friend, who apparently was being converted from Toryism by Robert added his:

The Golliwog Rhyme

A Golliwog was she of powder, paint and scent
Who spake sweet words to all and none were meant,
She praised her sister's dress; said 'twas a lovely style
And then behind her back smiled a sarcastic smile.
God save us from all such; speed the day when we
False Gods dethrone, no more to reign,
Our own true selves may be.

'My father had a great love of truth and truthfulness,' said Kathleen. ' "A lie is a cowardly thing," he would say. "Never lie to get yourself out of trouble." '

'In his hard and lonely life,' said Gower, 'he hadn't the consolations of religion. He did not attend church. He once called me to his front window to observe a man going to church, a business-man with whom he was acquainted, the Bible carried ostentatiously under the arm, umbrella and tall hat complete, and wearing an air of devout respectability. The sight was too much for Noonan. He rolled up with merriment.'

'That'll be the time,' he once remarked, 'when you can go to the station and take a ticket to Jerusalem – the heavenly one.'

In 1908 Robert's circumstances must still have been fair, for he was supporting Kathleen at the St Helen's Pupil Teacher Centre, precursor of the Girls' High School, and she was sixteen years old. In fact her father had Mr Beney, over whose cycle-shop they lived, make her a bicycle for travelling to school which was a long way from London Road. Kathleen was frequently in trouble with her father and others for her dare-devil riding.

'One time,' she said,

coming home from school the wheel of my bike got caught in the tram-lines on a hill not far from home. I was thrown and my handle-bars bent and I had to wheel it home. I don't think I was hurt but when I took it into the shop and told him what had happened, Mr Beney said, 'You know they say that there's a special providence that looks after children and fools and you're not a child Katie!' I think I always went in to see Mrs Beney when I came home before going upstairs.

Both she and Robert were on good terms with the Beneys and this eased many of the problems of this lonely father and his motherless daughter. These problems were to increase later on but Kathleen in the meantime tried to be of some domestic use. One of the problems was father's evening meal. Kathleen knew nothing of cooking but this didn't deter her from trying sometimes to give him a treat. On one occasion this treat was a ground-rice pudding which, Kathleen decided, needed a little flavouring added, but the only flavouring available was oil of cloves which father had purchased as balm for a toothache. She put in a drop about the size of a teaspoon. 'It was so awful,' she said, 'that I couldn't even eat it to save my face.' She doesn't give her father's opinion. She was so shy of strangers that when her father told her to return a tin of bad meat she was unable to face the shopkeeper. 'I couldn't do things like that,' she said.

I remember until I was seventeen meeting Dad in a small restaurant for our evening meal. I suppose I must have made sandwiches for me to take for lunch to school and him for his lunch at work. I shiver when I think what kind of lunch he had. After I was seventeen I cooked our meals during the holidays and these were not very successful. I remember making a stew one time and thinking it very successful, but when I suggested making it again Dad said "Oh no", and I said, 'Well I thought you liked it', and he said 'Well I didn't want to hurt your feelings.'

The restaurant could have been Pallett's 'eating-house' at 97 Bohemia Road, which is the nearest I can locate, and Kathleen says that it was 'a very small place'.

Why didn't this lonely man ever remarry? In fact none of his friends ever remember him having any women friends, the company of women, or any hint of sexual relationship.

Kathleen says that he may not have felt the necessity for a woman's company, that he worked hard and was not very fit. His book treats sex in a rather romantically honourable way but nevertheless with sympathy and understanding of the married state as 'natural'. It is possible that being the man he was and believing that he was tubercular he may have determined not to remarry or even to run the risk of infecting a woman friend.

On the other hand he may have had other scruples or simply, in his circumstances, lack of much opportunity and no desire for promis-

cuity.* That he was not unsusceptible to women is borne out by
Kathleen. He had apparently thought of marrying a few years after
his wife's death:

> When I was little, before I was six, apparently, in Africa there was
> somebody I think he was thinking of marrying but she wanted him
> to get rid of me and so he didn't accept her.
>
> And then there was another time when he came home, he started
> talking about this girl he saw in the tram and all of a sudden he
> didn't talk about her any more. At the time I thought I was going
> to have a stepmother. And then I asked him about her and apparently
> he had heard her talk and that finished him.

This was when he was living at London Road. Kathleen gives her
own version of this abrupt change of mind. 'It was probably her voice.
I have the same trait – I can listen to the most absolute drivel if the
voice producing it is lovely in tone and expression, whereas if a voice
is unpleasant or strident I just cannot hear what is said, from listening
to the voice, no matter how interesting or informative the subject may
be.'

He may have continued, as many people do, to live in the aura of his
first marriage. Kathleen seemed to think this possible. 'There was never
any question of my mother being impossible; on the contrary. I was
brought up a Roman Catholic probably in accordance with my
mother's wishes. Once when I asked Robert what she looked like he·
said I was very like her. Was that why he was so fond of me? I think
he never spoke of her because his feelings were too deep.'

He kept alive the memory of his father, she says, and the only other
person he had to love was herself.

Gower's account of their country trip is further evidence of the
delicacy of his health but his friends don't seem to have thought it
serious. Poynton talks of Robert's asthma and Kathleen of his 'bronchial chest', but neither thought of his coughing as serious. I believe he
was secretly living with his old and constant fear and the book bears
this out. He seems to have been to a doctor for Kathleen says the
diagnosis was 'bronchitis' and that he was given 'medicine', 'but', she
says, 'he would never measure it out in doses, but used to drink straight
from the bottle'.

*In Chapter Twenty-five – 'The Oblong' he speaks of the 'unnatural' unmarried life
of the bachelor.

Again, she says, she doesn't remember any other treatment apart from rubbing his chest with Elliman's Embrocation and his remarking once that 'he should perhaps get the kind for horses'. But there are little telling remarks by friends. Gower mentions in passing the 'two hectic spots' glowing in Robert's cheeks when he was excited and Green when telling me that Robert was always ready for a bit of fun says 'but I always noticed that after a good laugh he would put his hand to his side as though it was a strain'.

21

The writer

There is no doubt that having a motherless daughter had a profound influence upon Robert's outlook. He was in an extremely vulnerable situation and he knew it and must have been filled with fear of the future, a fear which forms one of the themes of the book.

Yet he seems to have kept the worst from Kathleen although there were times when he couldn't contain himself.

Both were strong-willed and Kathleen needed as much forbearance as her father.

> I remember doing an awful thing once. I was usually a good girl with him, obedient, and that because I loved him very much, but I don't know what I had done this time but I was really mad. I can't remember whether I had left a note but I made up my mind that I wasn't coming back when I left home to go to school, and of course by the time I came out of school I didn't know where to go and I hung around here and there and probably went into the park. Anyway, it was getting dark and I don't know how late it was and I decided I had better go home and I met him just on his way to the police station. I can imagine the hell he went through. I used to have a terrible temper.

He did his best to make Kathleen happy but she inevitably lived much in herself. Yet she seems to have thoroughly enjoyed life nevertheless and this is a tribute to how much Robert had achieved.

Perhaps his forbidding her to sing a popular song because it was 'risqué' is understandable in a man feeling a heavy weight of responsibility for bringing up a daughter alone. She says of his attitude to sex:

'Perhaps he wasn't ahead of his time in moral attitudes, perhaps not more than the man in the street, but he was more compassionate. If he came across an immoral person he wouldn't brush them off but take their real worth in themselves without condoning immorality.'

He makes a derogatory reference in Chapter Twenty-seven – 'The

March of the Imperialists', to women 'coating their faces with powder and paint', but as he is describing the gluttonous rich this may not in fact represent his real attitude to make-up.

He had in his time lived something of a social life himself, says Kathleen,

> because one time when I was going to a dance he was shocked at the price I'd paid for my shoes – according to his explanation it was a lot to pay for 'one night's wear.' If he wore out a pair of shoes in a night he must have danced more than I ever would! We used to play cricket and hockey at St Helen's, Robert liked cricket – and I played tennis at various places.
>
> I remember a group of us, possibly part of our class, going to Battle, I don't remember how, and we were met there. I'm not sure of all the conveyances but a couple of girls and myself drove off in a dog-cart. I don't know whether it was Telham or not but I think it was a large white house two storeys high, I would think, with lovely grounds. It was a garden-party. Sometimes the girls used to cycle out to play tennis there and to walk round the gardens.

The account of this trip, brief as it is, brought to mind my own childhood at Telham, near Battle, where in 1908 my father moved his family out of Hastings to become gardener at Telham Hill House, a 'large, white, two-storeyed house in lovely grounds' where Mrs Basil-Woodd used to entertain schools and various young women's and children's homes and give the Sunday School children of Telham and Battle an annual summer 'treat', and where ten years later I became her garden- and coach-boy and often drove a horse-van and dog-cart; it could well be this same dog-cart. It seems likely that this is the house where Kathleen played tennis and in 1909–10 she would inevitably have seen my father.

Noakes describes Robert in 1908 as not very robust but not looking a sick man. He was, however, losing some time through sickness. On one occasion the boss himself was in the shop when Robert didn't turn up till after breakfast-time after a bad night of coughing.

'I do wish you would get here at six o'clock,' he said. To which Robert replied, 'But you don't have to pay me for the lost time, do you?' At which, I am told, the boss turned on his heel and walked away without a word.

People have often asked why he did not use his knowledge to obtain a different kind of employment, as a teacher or instructor of some kind, for instance to teach languages, but there could have been few openings for a man without academic qualifications. In my opinion he had also no wish for it, or he would have made the effort; teaching was not for a man of his views and creative ability. Teaching was prescribed, in most cases rigidly, and he was temperamentally unsuited for the paternalistic atmosphere of an institution. There may well have been an element of truth in his niece's assertion that he 'became' a working-man as a kind of crusader, but I believe the real answer is that he set out to find a job which would give his talent for painting some scope but which would not make too heavy demands on his imagination and energy and leave his mind free to develop its bent and what that was he gradually discovered in a different manner.

In his workmates he saw men like himself for whom there was no escape. Yet they had a way of coming to terms with their situation without becoming wholly contaminated. And they had a strange ability not to become so dispirited as they ought. This gave him a deeper understanding of the working classes, opened his eyes to their deep roots and their resilience which he almost unconsciously portrays all through the book, even when most exasperated about them, indeed perhaps in that very exasperation itself. And gradually his own circumstances made him realize that he had little more chance of 'escape' than they had and this gave him a feeling of total involvement. He was hardly any longer a man outside looking in although this feeling he never completely overcame because this is not a matter of will but of nurture. He was not quite of them but was wholly with them.

He found only partial fulfilment in his work for the SDP branch, although this was vital to him in many ways, but his were not the talents of the public leader and organizer such as Cobb, and he could not fully express himself or work to his capacity simply as a party member. He had to do more.

But he didn't waver in his basic socialist convictions. He says hopefully in the words of the renegade socialist in the book that when a man has once acquired knowledge he cannot relinquish it. Far from wavering, he was to make that affirmation, and the reasons for it, the chief work of his life. His socialism was a belief in a greater conception of man's nature, and in his ability to find his way out of the morass so that as Robert says:

No man shall profit from another's loss and we shall no longer be masters and servants but brothers, free men and friends. A state wherein it will be possible to put into practice the teachings of Him whom so many now pretend to follow. A society which shall have justice and co-operation for its foundation and International Brotherhood and love for its law.

And because of his own need to live like this, to him this age-old dream was a matter of pure common sense, and it was as much a matter of affirming this to himself as to other men in the jungle. Mankind literally could not afford capitalism – or any society based upon the sheer materialism of property and money values.

It almost seems as if his realization that writing was his true calling was a sudden one. And even then his impulse was uncertain. The tone of his own description of his motives in his preface and the limited objectives he says he assigned himself are at variance with the tone of the book, which has far greater range and intimately concerns his own personal search for identity.

'He finally gave up talking to the workers,' says Kathleen, 'and set about his book. Maybe *that* would wake them up and others like them.'

But the motive wasn't as simple as that. He was a writer.

He said to Gower one day: 'I'll have to make some money or I'll die in the workhouse!' And these words have more than their surface significance.

He was really saying, 'I'll *have* to do *something* with my life or I'll die a defeated man.' All through these years, said Gower, he seemed to be searching and restless yet expressed no desire to continue his wanderings. Perhaps another impulse that got him launched was his concern for his health – a feeling that he must make a decisive effort of the only kind open to him.

Judging from the evidence in the book, he had to face the thought of dying before Kathleen grew up. He was always conscious of that South African diagnosis even if everyone believed it was 'asthma'. But I think the greatest impulse was the realization of his true talent and the joy in using it and finding this medium to express himself in full, to live like a complete man.

Edward and Phoebe Cruttenden, Social Democratic Federation members, and friends of the Noonans.

Kathleen Lynne, *nee* Noonan, in 1970, at the time of the BBC television production of *The Ragged Trousered Philanthropists.*

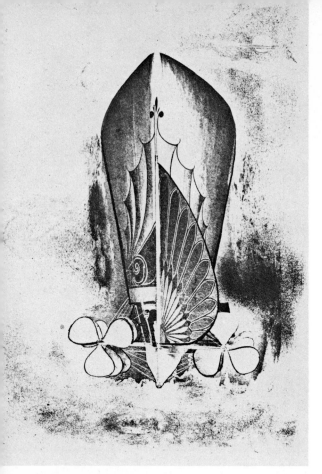

Two views of a six
foot model airship,
designed, constructed
and painted by Robert
Tressell.

22

The Ragged Trousered
Philanthropists

Exactly when or even in what year he began serious work on organizing his book or made a decision to write it remains a mystery, for although he was writing for years not even Kathleen knew when he had actually begun *The Ragged Trousered Philanthropists*. Incidents in the book itself are known to cover many years of actual fact and personal experience and were almost certainly kept in note form; and friends and Kathleen herself speak of his writings over a long period.

Neither can Kathleen remember when it was finished and her account puts it at any time from late 1908 to early 1910 before a fair copy was finally ready for a publisher, and she believes that he spent five years' work on it.

This could put its commencement as early as 1903 and at the latest 1905 when he was living at Milward Road, but she believes it was entirely written at 241 London Road, to which of course they didn't move till late 1906, but Gower was emphatic that Robert was often writing at Milward Road as well as at London Road.

At Milward Road he may well have been working on other writings which were not completed, or as Kathleen said possibly articles of which there is no surviving evidence and if published I have found no trace of, and which were perhaps published under an unknown pseudonym.

I think it more likely that the writings were notes from reading – he was a voracious reader and student – notes of events from the Press, from work, and from tales told him by friends, notes for a book of some kind he had always projected according to Ogilvy, all of which were the raw material which became *The Ragged Trousered Philanthropists*. He may well have been organizing the book at Milward Road.

My own opinion is that he projected a book as early as Kathleen says, 1903/4 and possibly earlier, that the new life in a new scene, England, and his new experiences fired him and he undoubtedly began to keep notes; but that the process of assimilation of this new experience and re-orientation made for a long period of gestation. From the dates of his experiences in the Socialist Movement and of the election scenes alone, and the time of his encounter with the other half of the character of Misery, and Philpot, I would say that he began to organize the book in 1907 from notes written earlier.

There is further evidence that he was preparing the material for a number of years before writing it.

The whole aura is that of the period before the various social service measures of the Liberal Government: the Old Age Pensions Act which came into force on 1 January 1909, the Labour Exchanges established the same year, medical inspection in schools in 1907 and the regulation of child employment outside school hours in 1908. The main argument – Free Trade versus Protection, the Big and Little loaf argument – was at its height in 1904, 1905, and temporarily culminated in the 1906 General Election and his election scenes relate mainly to that event. I would think 1907–9 was the main period of organizing and writing-out because in Chapter Seven – 'The Exterminating Machines', he quotes the *Daily Mail Year Book* for 1907 and this chapter is in the first fifth of the book.

In Chapter Twenty-five – 'The Oblong', also, Crass refers to 'them there Labour members of Parliament'.

Certainly the book wasn't finished before 1 April 1908 because in Chapter Forty-five – 'The Great Oration', he mentions the Territorial Force (in 1921 it became the Territorial Army) and this Force was only established on that date.

He probably finished a main draft in 1909 but then spent many months in making a fair copy entailing still further emendations. The actual manuscript surviving is carefully written out.

Cruttenden's story indicates that this finalization was still in process as late as April 1910 or at least that the manuscript was still in Robert's hands.

In my opinion Kathleen's estimate of five years' work on the book is near the mark and one has to remember that he was working a fifty-six and a half hour week and often longer until the last year or so and that he was active in the SDP for two or three years of it.

And about the book he was as secretive as in other matters and this gave rise to various stories. Close friends had known he was writing for some years and occasionally he mentioned a book but gave no one any details. Poynton, who didn't meet him till after 1906, says, 'Few of his comrades or friends knew he was writing; indeed I know he was very shy about it. The book was written over many months and was made up of a collection of real incidents and talks that had taken place on the various jobs.'

The statement that the book took 'many months' to write can hardly be taken seriously in Robert's circumstances and for a complicated book of 250,000 words.

Gower says, 'I did not know he was writing a book, he didn't tell me what he was writing but he did refer again to this "work which must be done or he would die in the Workhouse".'

To Cruttenden Robert had said that he was 'working on something important'. And Green told me that 'Dan Pankhurst, who was the Joe Philpot in the book, said that Robert used to come to his house and do a lot of writing.' Others believed Dan to be the original of Philpot and strangely enough the only Daniel Pankhurst in the Directories of the time lived at 10 Tower Road, just round the corner from 241 London Road, near enough for Robert to call round when he wanted to refresh his memory or draw on someone else's experience, which he would note.

Dan apparently became a convert to the SDP.

In the later stages of the book, and this appears from Cruttenden's memory to have been late 1909 or early 1910, Robert attended SDP meetings less frequently. Cruttenden says that when he once asked Kathleen 'where her father had got to, she replied that as he was always busy writing he should be left alone to pursue his work'.

Later he asked to have his membership cancelled on the grounds that if he couldn't be active he felt it wasn't right that he should call himself a member, but I couldn't confirm this. In any case he painted a banner for the branch in 1910 according to Poynton's story.

Gower said that some fellow members were a little put out over his absences and mystified about what could be more important than 'political' work.

This sectarian prejudice against the arts, 'wasting one's time with imaginative writing or painting', has always been strong in the working-class movement although not by any means confined to it.

Consequently we have little literature based on working-class life and written by working-class writers and as little of working-class history.

The history of trades and crafts, and of the domestic lives of those who work in them, have been almost entirely neglected and the workers as human beings have received scant recognition in our literature. Robert recognized the importance of correcting this, and of giving the worker a sense of identity and a perspective on his position in society without which he was literally 'unconscious'.

There is another story about the making of *The Ragged Trousered Philanthropists* which needs some explanation.

In the course of my correspondence with Edward Cruttenden, before I wrote *Tressell of Mugsborough*, he told me:

> I lent George Meek's book, 'George Meek, Bath Chairman' to Bob. When he returned it he said it was too Meek and Mild and that he could do something better and stronger and after that he did not attend our meetings very regularly, said he had something important on hand and we should know later on what it was. His daughter said her father was always writing so we let him get on with it.

This letter, in my ignorance as an amateur biographer, I accepted at its face value in my first book and must now set the record straight and, incidentally, do George Meek justice.

In *Tressell of Mugsborough* I described how Meek on reaching Sandgate in Kent on his tour of SDF branches had called on H. G. Wells and had suggested a book to Wells who in turn had proposed that Meek write the book and he, Wells, would write a preface for it and that the outcome was *George Meek, Bath Chairman*.

I said that copies of this went round the socialist branches and that Cruttenden lent one to Robert whose verdict was 'too Meek and Mild' (Cruttenden's words) and that this was sometime in 1906/7. I myself, without having read Meek, or checking facts, dilated at his expense on Robert's verdict saying that I was told George had turned out an innocuous piece of work in 'good taste' evidently with his clients in mind – a feeble piece of work and that this had fired Robert to write his own book. And there I left it.

And then in March 1953, eighteen months after the publication of my book, I received a letter from Mr R. A. H. Barltrop of Chingford, Essex, in which he said:

... Meek refers to an interview with H.G.Wells in November 1909 to settle certain details [of the book, F.C.B.] and another chapter was written after the interview; it is therefore scarcely possible that the book was published before the end of 1909. This obviously conflicts with your information that Noonan, after finding the bath-chairman's book 'too Meek and Mild' in 1906/7 began three or four years' work on *The Ragged Trousered Philanthropists* and completed it about 1910. From the evidence of Meek's book alone it could be taken that Robert Noonan did not in fact derive his stimulus from that source, and began work long before Meek called on Wells.

I thought, pity the horse has bolted, and I left the matter for fifteen years. For *this* book I decided to find out the details and also to read George Meek for myself.

The stories about Meek's visits to the branches, his tour of south-east England (on foot!), his visit to H.G.Wells, in the year 1906/7 as stated by Cruttenden, are fact.

And his book was written with Wells's encouragement and, with a preface by Wells, finally published by Constable in April 1910. Robert knew of Meek, of course, and he read Meek's book in 1910, but there is the discrepancy.

It couldn't have been Meek's *book* which fired Robert because his own book was by all accounts then completed, but he would have known of Meek's book in the making; Meek was well acquainted with Robert's friend Cruttenden and I'm sure that when Cruttenden told me that Meek's *book* fired Robert he meant that when Robert heard that a man he knew and a man in extremely humble circumstances, a bath chairman, was actually writing a book and was talking of getting a man as famous as Wells to write a preface he *was* fired – by this knowledge.

And *that* even if he had already begun on his own.

Further, when he finally read Meek's book, written in a much less passionate manner than his own and autobiographical, he *did* express the opinion, as Cruttenden stated, that it was 'too Meek and Mild' – for a socialist.

Cruttenden admits that he knew little about it and when I met him twenty years ago he was a man of very advanced age and got his facts a little mixed.

And as for my remarks about Meek's efforts, taking Robert's word, all I can say is that it is a much better book than I expected to read, it contains a damning indictment of social conditions and much social history of his life period, much of it very sad, and is completely honest, if perhaps a little self-centred.

It was one of the first genuine accounts of working-class life written by a genuine worker, one of the lowest in the social scale at that. In this Meek is more 'genuine' than Robert himself who had the advantage of some education and of not coming quite from off the floor. Eastbourne should make something of Meek.

Well's preface says, 'so far as this book goes I put him high among the writers of our time', but this is a gross overstatement. In fact the preface is not worthy of the book in many other ways, having touches of cleverness and facetiousness, and showing little appreciation of the poignancy in many of Meek's anecdotes – such as the one about Mike and his mother:

> About this period [about the 1850s, F.C.B.] the countryside was frequented by a 'natural' named Mike. When his mother died (under I presume some hedgerow) the overseers of the parish in which it happened gave him half-a-crown to carry her body into the next parish, and when she was buried, he laid her shawl on her grave 'to keep her warm'.

You have probably spent holidays at Mugsborough and admired the splendid promenade (not there in Robert's time) and walked in Bottle Alley under it, where the walls, decorated by Italian craftsmen with the coloured glass of broken bottles, sparkle in the light reflected from the sea. If you were there between 1902 and 1910 and are a very old man, you might have rubbed shoulders with or borrowed a light from Bob Noonan.

You may even have been the possessor of some physical characteristic which went into one of the little notebooks kept in the capacious pocket of a painter's apron or a paint-stained waistcoat.

There are glimpses of Robert writing. Both Gower and Cruttenden give the same picture, with one slight difference. Gower tells of finding him in the middle of the room, surrounded by books and writing on an improvised table, a 'box' Gower called it, and seated on a pile of books.

Cruttenden says, 'I could always find him on Sunday morning

seated on a pile of books at a desk busy with his classic. He never told me the title but he assured me it was to be something better than *George Meek, Bath Chairman*, which I had lent him.'

This was obviously after April 1910 and either Robert was on the last stages of his manuscript or was revising or writing out fair copy, but both Gower and Cruttenden refer to this pile of books for a seat. Kathleen, too, describes her father at work:

> The only details I really remember were of him writing the book at London Road and he had this large table and papers all over it and sometimes he would be writing and didn't like what he had written and he'd just screw it up and throw it aside, but you daren't go and pick it up again because it was quite possible that if you cleared up those papers and threw them out he'd want them back again. So I had to leave him to clear up his mess. I can still see the screwed-up papers lying around the floor.
>
> I can see that room. As you went in, right opposite the door was his bed and at the head of that on the side where the fireplace was, there were books up to the ceiling and then opposite that was quite a big table.
>
> I can remember Robert drinking tea – tea was his drink. He had said at one time that he could understand how difficult it was for men to give up drinking beer and stuff because if he had to give up drinking *tea*, he didn't know whether he could do it. He used to smoke but he never bought packages of cigarettes but used to buy them loose.

When finally finished his manuscript was huge, as we shall see, and could hardly have been written in Poynton's 'few months' by a man who had a living to earn and was beginning to suffer increasing periods of ill-health. In fact, of course, it was written in his 'spare time' – evenings, Sundays, and sometimes in the nights when his illness kept him awake. According to Gower he was beginning to cough blood before he reached the end, but Kathleen does not confirm this.

He had other problems. The book was based upon life in Hastings, upon public figures, private employers, friends, acquaintances many of whom were treated very critically and satirically and it featured many public and private scandals – and he had to live in the town, and what was more, work there. He could be prosecuted or blacklisted and find himself unemployable as other socialists and trade unionists had done. So he had to disguise everything.

Then he had to decide what to call the book and what name to give its author.

For the book he chose 'The Ragged Trousered Philanthropists', and of this title Poynton in his *Daily Worker* article of 10 May 1936 says: 'I think the reason he gave the book such an unusual title was that the local press at that time was boosting up a gentleman who had given large sums to the hospital. Bob used to say that the workers were the real Philanthropists but didn't know it.'

Whether this is so or not the title neatly expresses his fundamental attitude to labour. He refers to the workers all through the text as 'philanthropists' – as spending their lives and work to make not themselves but others rich. I like to think also that he had read Wordsworth, who, in his youth planned to produce a 'Republican but not revolutionary' journal to be known as 'The Philanthropist'.

And why 'Ragged Trousered'? Working-men normally don't use the expression 'ragged trousered' and Tressell I'm sure didn't affect such a prissy phrase when with his workmates. The men said 'ragged arsed', and so did Tressell. The expression is an ancient colloquialism. It was always used about the old Militia which was often made up of the dregs, the unemployable and the gaol-birds, and labourers who saw no hope but to take the 'King's Shilling', and the old expression became a working-class joke, and then an affectionate byword – the 'Ragged-arsed Militia'. It was current in Robert's time and mine. But he could never in that day call his book 'The Ragged-arsed Philanthropists' (I have heard locals shorten the title so) so it had to be 'The Ragged *Trousered* Philanthropists'. And out of the same necessity for disguise the author became 'Robert Tressell'.

Trestles are part of the basic equipment of house-painters and sign-writers, and Poynton in the article already cited says, 'It was because he was so often seen at some shop-front working on trestles that he signed himself Robert Tressall.'

This 'Tressall' of Poynton's was a misspelling which for some reason had been adopted by the publisher and used in all Grant Richards's editions. And curiously, Tressell himself when using the word 'trestles' in the book spells it 'tressels' and sometimes 'tressells'.*

*For quick reference see Chapter Forty-seven – 'The Ghouls'.

Some friends tell me that he told them he was writing his 'diary' and in fact the description is not inapt. And Kathleen even hints that we might have had an illustrated *Ragged Trousered Philanthropists*: 'I wish he had lived to illustrate The Ragged Trousered Philanthropists – his line-drawings, judging by those I have seen, would have added vastly to the text even though his verbal pictures are so good.'

It had become a book, and a novel, it would seem almost by accident. Said Grant Richards in a Press handout: 'It seems that when the work was started the author had no intention of writing a book but had in mind the writing of a series of pamphlets. It was only when the book was begun that he found it turning into a novel under his hand.'

He had finally found the right way. Perhaps with George Meek's book in mind he told Whitelock that he was going to try and get H.M. Hyndman to write a preface but evidently nothing came of it and I haven't been able to examine any Hyndman correspondence although I made inquiries. In the end Robert wrote his own preface, which, however, he left unfinished.

'Then,' says Kathleen, 'he had someone make a tin box with a handle in which to keep the manuscript for sending to publishers. So far as I know it was just packed consecutively. I don't know whether it was in chapters or not – my memory is just of a box of loose paper.'

Into this manuscript he had put all the honesty and fervour he had. He had written a unique book, the only one of its kind. Perhaps it would make history. Perhaps now he could emancipate himself from drudgery, poverty and perhaps even from ill-health and give Kathleen a new life. They discussed what they would do with the money the book earned, says Kathleen. 'First they would travel round the world together, and not on a luxury liner but perhaps as the only passengers on one of those little tramp steamers that would stop at all the out-of-the-way little ports which most ships never called at. And afterwards they would see.'

Knowing so well her father's views Kathleen had to know what this new property entailed.

'Once when we were talking about investments and interest,' she says, 'I said to him, "Supposing something happened to you and I got the money for the book, aren't I entitled to have that?", and he said, "Yes, you are, but if you wanted to invest it, before you could touch the interest you'd have to make sure that the workers who were providing that interest were being properly paid".'

These rather pathetic discussions show that Robert had little experience or knowledge of the publishing or book world; but they also show that he believed in his book and was full of hope despite the increasing bouts of sickness which in 1910 were reducing him to real poverty. And perhaps his spirits were raised by the success of Blatchford's *Merrie England* and other socialist works and by the growing working-class movement and, of course, by his joy in his own achievement.

The two sent off the huge handwritten manuscript, nicely written out on quarto sheets, nearly seventeen hundred of them, in its 12 × 9 × 9 inch tin box to a firm of publishers.

And we may imagine with what feelings they watched the postman bringing it back very soon after, and unread, because, said the publisher, it was too long and must be in typescript.

It is said that he sent it to Robert Blatchford as the most logical man to send it to, but according to the Central Library in Manchester to which I was directed, there is no reference to Tressell or to a Robert Noonan in the Blatchford Papers in their possession.

This doesn't, of course, rule out the possibility. It may well be, also, that he sent it to Hyndman or wrote and told him of it.

It also went to Constable's but no one would have it and I shall deal with this later.

As his preface is unfinished, it is possible that he wrote it as an attempt to explain the book to publishers and to answer doubts about its authenticity, but gave it up. A passage in which he asserts its authenticity is strongly reminiscent of a passage in Fielding's preface to *Joseph Andrews*.

I have given some examples of the factual authenticity of the events and characters in the book and many locals between them corroborated others. I must however mention one more scene which might otherwise be thought pure fiction.

This is the episode of the Electric Light Works, the Gas Company and the Town Council which is in fact based upon actual events which took place just before Robert came to Hastings and he must either have been told the story or have made notes from newspapers in the Library. A history of the Gas Company written by the founder's son many years after Robert and preserved in the Library gives a discreet but telling account of the transactions which confirms Robert's story in its main facts – the war between Gas and Electricity, the imposition on the Gas Company of a duty on coal, their building of a new Gas-works just outside the town boundary to escape this duty, the proposal that the failing Electric Light Works should be purchased by the Town Council, the hiring of an expert to value it, and its eventual purchase at a price, says the author of the history, which was considered very excessive.

'When the book had been returned from some three publishers with the same comments,' said Kathleen, 'Robert did not even try and read it again, overcome by its faults and lack of typescript. It would have probably have had the same fate as the model of the airship if I hadn't rescued it.'

23

Give us this day

Not the least of his difficulties when writing the book, particularly in the later stages, had been the worsening of his health.

Gower has mentioned the effect on him of their trip to Brede in the rain and by 1909 his friends and workmates were beginning to notice a marked decline. In the winter of 1909/10 he was having serious attacks and spending more time at home than at work, though in better weather his health would improve. Cradduck says:

> When I joined Adams and Jarrett's ... Bob was very thin and looked a sick man. He used to come to work for about two days and then he would be away for two or three weeks. He always looked cold and pinched-looked as if he needed a good meal. I was only seventeen and offered myself for 2*d*. or 3*d*. an hour less than the rate and I said to Bob, 'Don't think I've come to cut you out of your job,' and he said 'Don't you worry about that at all, son.'

Noakes, on the same firm, confirms this: 'By this time he was a very sick man and couldn't do a full week and was losing a lot of time.'

And Gower said that he noticed Robert 'getting thinner and thinner'.

According to Kathleen 'he would have recurrent attacks of bronchitis and would cough and cough. He had blamed his condition on the rides over the open veld in South Africa. It would be very cold and the men would drink whisky to warm themselves and then would get chilled again.'

Yet, as he says of Owen, 'Although he was often seized with a kind of terror of the future – of being unable to work – he fought against these feelings and tried to believe that when the weather became warmer he would be alright once more.'

Like Goldsmith, Robert seems to have had 'a wonderful knack of hoping' yet between the lines of this passage he recognizes the truth. But he still kept the worst from Kathleen.

It is difficult to get a clear picture of how he lived during these last years, especially in 1910. 'In winter those out of work often had to live on credit at the local grocer's or pawn belongings, or apply to the vicarage for Parish Funds,' he says.

Unemployed painters used to be given the job of painting the town's lamp-posts, but Robert never had to suffer this (in public opinion) public indignity, although he was often perilously near it.

Many went to the soup-kitchens where, with a ticket, you could get free soup, or if you had a penny you could buy a pennyworth, and many of the poorer would send their children to collect it but as Robert says, some people slunk through the back streets to avoid being seen coming from the place and many would rather go without.

Kathleen believes he did odd jobs outside of his work for the firm. He certainly had letter-heads printed:

R.P.Noonan
Signwriter and Decorator
Blueprinting.
241 London Road, St Leonards.

'When we were at 241,' she says, 'every now and again he would give me some money for "riotous living" as he called it. I don't remember how much it could be – two shillings? five? This makes me think that he must occasionally have sold articles or short stories for he would not have been able to do that out of his wages and it must have been spasmodic and not a fund he could draw on at will or he could have used it when unemployed.'

But she doubts whether he would have written anything else at London Road as 'he was too busy with the book', but says that he sometimes did illuminated addresses.

Gower speaks of him writing showcards for shopkeepers as Owen does. He may also have pawned or sold some of his possessions. He speaks of Owen wearing a pair of three-shilling second-hand boots and pawning his overcoat.

'One time when we were hard up,' says Kathleen,

we were having some soup. There was only enough soup for him so I dirtied a soup-plate and put it in the sink and saved the soup for him and when he came in he said I might have waited and had my supper with him and I said, 'Well, I was too hungry to wait', and I

don't know now which would have hurt him most, the fact that I
had not waited for him or the fact that I had gone without and he'd
eaten it. That's the only time I can remember being short of
food.

It's a mystery how he managed to keep going because he certainly
doesn't seem to have had any reserves and it wasn't as if he were one
of the able-bodied unemployed. His unemployment was due to
sickness and he could have done little work privately, even if it were
available.

Sometimes he wrote coffin-plates. Adams and Jarrett's had a contract
for writing the coffin-plates for all Poor Law funerals, that is for all
people on Relief buried as paupers whether in workhouses or not and
Robert being the signwriter had the job of writing them – apparently
the name and age only of the deceased.

During these long absences from work Noakes had the job of
delivering the plates to the flat on his way home from the shop at
half past five, and he describes how Robert would often be in bed
and when Noakes had sometimes to wait Robert would be propped
up with pillows writing the plate fixed up in front of him.

He always took extra pains with these for the paupers out of fellow-
feeling and to accord them a respect as people which the world didn't.
He was by now not far from pauperdom himself.

He had told Noakes that he had 'thought what a wonderful place
England was and that was why he came'. He had suffered ten years of
disillusionment and it must have seemed to him now that he was going
to die a broken man. England had nothing to offer him even when in
work but the status, as he described it, of a beast of burden compelled
to live from hand to mouth for a lifetime in order to keep alive long
enough to die. He had written his book in rejection of this way of life.
And his book was lying in its tin box rejected in its turn. But it was
not in him to give up hope while he was on his feet and he made what
seems an extraordinary decision. He decided to emigrate.

Here again there were conflicting or perhaps complementary
accounts of his reasons.

Raymond Postgate in *The Builders' History* says, 'Ill health, tyranny,
poverty, and disgust at the work, he, an admirer of William Morris
was forced to do, made him decide to try and work his way to
America.'

Poynton says, 'His asthma was getting worse. He had been advised to go to Canada as the climate was more likely to suit him.'

And Kathleen says, 'I think he was sometimes tempted to give up his crusade and set out in business on his own as he finally decided when he made up his mind to go to Canada.' And again, 'Before leaving St Helen's I took the Oxford Locals and got five honours, English, French, History, Geography and Maths. We made enquiries about Whitelands College and they would have accepted me but it was not financially possible. I think this is what started the Canada project.' And again:

> Since the book was no good, and we couldn't go round the world, we'd go to Canada and make a fresh start, this time forgetting his ragged trousered philanthropists who would not listen to sense and for whom he had written the book. He would make some money to leave me in more comfortable circumstances. He was sure he would be able to get his own kind of decorative work with good wages and a good home for both of us.

This doesn't sound as if he intended to change his course and go into business as an employer but would work as a private craftsman.

Having made his decision he made arrangements to go to Liverpool where health permitting, he was going to get work to help pay for his passage. Kathleen was to go to her Aunt Mary Jane who in 1910 kept a school at 48 Kenilworth Road, the only special school in England at the time, she says, for blind and sighted mentally handicapped children, and her father would send for her when he had been able to book passage.

'I only expected to be at my Aunt's a few weeks,' she says.

Not one of his friends seems to have heard a word of his intentions. Perhaps he was diffident about telling them of what must have appeared to them a forlorn hope in his condition.

In Canada he would have needed his health above all to stand any chance of settling. Perhaps he thought there might be better opportunities for Kathleen there, though I am more inclined to believe that he could no longer stomach the suffocating class structure and snobbery of England and longed to get to somewhere where a man was a man, in the greater freedom of the dominion.

But could he really have believed he would ever get to Canada? Why leave Kathleen when he knew his health was so precarious? Had he given up all hope for his book? Why the secrecy of his departure? Did he fear that he was going to die, and feel that he couldn't die slowly in his lodgings? Kathleen couldn't be kept at home indefinitely to nurse him, and he and his sisters were not on such terms that he would care to be upon their hands. And perhaps he shrank from the idea of being forced to seek relief or of creeping to the workhouse under the eyes of those to whom he had so savagely denounced such institutions. But Kathleen said, 'I do not think he had any dread of ending up in the workhouse. He would often say "Well, this won't buy the baby a new coat", or he would probably say, "If I don't get something soon we'll end up in the workhouse." '

And his niece confirmed that his spirit was not yet broken. 'We knew he would suffer anything to be independent of others and follow his inclinations.'

He had no stable place in the world, he possessed nothing, the world was again gone from under his feet and perhaps he really believed he could make another start.

There are passages at the end of the book which seem to me symbolic.

The family are looking out of the window of their high flat into the darkness waiting to see the train carrying their friend Barrington away pass over the bridge (a scene Robert and Kathleen saw every day from their flat in Milward Road) and presently the rails are illuminated by the train headlights and they can see a white handkerchief fluttering from one of its windows. They wave back until 'there remained nothing visible of the train except the lights at the rear of the guard's van' and soon these too 'vanished into the surrounding darkness.'

To me this expresses something of Robert's own feeling for what might have been in his life, for the destruction of his prospects and hopes of fulfilment, the thought of leaving Kathleen.

No one had ever come over that bridge on a visit to Robert – no one he loved deeply – except Kathleen returning from school at holiday time as a child.

In the story, Barrington had left them a farewell note enclosing ten pounds as a kind of pledge to Owen that he is not alone, that life has a destination with a happy ending.

So, as in his boyhood, he was to set off again into the unknown. In periods of feeling better his spirits must have risen and he must have

felt capable of undertaking the journey. To Kathleen, his bouts of
ill-health had become a normal feature of their lives and she was not
seriously worried. 'He was always up and down,' she says, 'and was
seemingly "well" at this time and full of hope that it would not be
long before we were on the high seas to Canada.'

There seem to have been few problems about moving. He had few
worldly goods. Kathleen says:

> I think the rooms at London Road were furnished. Our books,
> pictures and other properties were packed in packing-cases and I
> don't think Robert sold anything when we left except perhaps
> some of his books. More probably he gave things away.
>
> The manuscript was left with me. There was too much looking
> forward to the plans he would make for us to go to Canada to think
> about the manuscript.

Her father never gave her any instructions or advice about it.

This contradicts Poynton's article which said 'He gave his only
daughter, a girl of sixteen* the manuscript, and told her he had no
money to give her but perhaps his writing would be worth something
one day.' But Robert may have said some such thing to Poynton about
his book or more probably the tale arose out of discussion with
friends after Robert had gone.

Kathleen remembers 'Dad sending me down to the station to get
his ticket and me coming back without it because it was a man at the
ticket-office. That will show you what I was like. My life must have
been too sheltered and home-bound. I don't remember him scolding
me for it.'

In the end he got the ticket himself.

*She was eighteen – (F. C. B.)

24

A pauper's death

He left Hastings sometime in August 1910 and Kathleen saw him off from Warrior Square Station watching the train until it went into the tunnel out of sight.

It was the last time she was to see her father. Even Cruttenden and Gower, probably his closest friends, didn't know he was gone.

Said Cruttenden, 'He just slipped away unbeknown to anybody.' And Whitlock, 'He just faded out overnight.'

'He took with him,' says Kathleen,

a lot of art things and drawings, originals by William Morris, his pounces and designs to use in any work he might get to earn the money for our sea-fares, and his clothes.

We were quiet and sad at parting but looking forward to soon meeting again for our journey. After seeing Robert off I went back to see Mrs Beney and be comforted before I started off for my aunt's at Kenilworth Road.

There are one or two unconfirmed stories about Robert's journey. He is believed to have stayed briefly in London. I had heard rumours in Hastings that Robert had been assisted by painters in London on his journey but could discover no details.

Jack Mitchell in his book *Robert Tressell and The Ragged Trousered Philanthropists* says that Mr Frank Jackson, a building-worker – an old SDF member and trade union organizer – told him that he was present at a meeting in a London pub where a collection was made to help Noonan on his way. It was still customary for union members on the tramp for work to receive some little help from branches to get them on to the next town. This was known as the 'tramping system', and was still going on in Robert's time, although Postgate in his *Builders' History* says that it was dying out a hundred years earlier.

But such help was almost certainly confined to union members and

I cannot establish that Robert was holding a union card. And further it is very doubtful whether he would seek assistance.

This story ties up with a rumour that assistance was given to 'a comrade from Hastings', but Mr Jackson wrote in a letter to me, 'I cannot remember whether this was for Noonan or someone else.'

Then there is the story, whose source I cannot now trace, from Mr C. Jones of Egerton Street, Wrexham, that Tressell had passed through there on his way to Liverpool and had said he intended emigrating to Canada. But howsoever he travelled he was in Liverpool in August, the month he had left Hastings.

According to Gower, in Liverpool Robert got lodgings at 35 Erskine Street and got himself a job there but Kathleen has no information of this period. He had a sister, Ellie, in Liverpool and may have lodged with her but without her married name I have been unable to trace her although I advertised in Liverpool newspapers.

In 1910 35 Erskine Street was tenanted by a James Johnson but whether this was Robert's brother-in-law is not known. Robert wrote a few letters to Kathleen and to Gower and possibly to others but only a fragment of one letter survives and a few remarks remembered by Gower and this is all that is known of his stay there. He had in any case just three months of freedom and then suddenly there was news that he had been admitted on 26 November to what was then the Royal Liverpool Infirmary, infirmary being the new name for workhouses, and was officially registered in the General Ward of the hospital. I quote from the United Liverpool Hospital Authorities that: 'It was quite common to nurse tubercular patients in a side ward off the general ward. This would be counted as admission to a general ward as opposed to a private ward where the patient would pay for the treatment.'

On this very day, 26 November 1910, at Manchester, two hundred delegates representing seventy groups, sixteen Trades Councils and sixty thousand workers formed the Manchester Syndicalist Education League, a piece of news I'm sure must have given him satisfaction even in his hospital bed.

So despite his assurance to Kathleen about not fearing dying in the workhouse, here he was at last in that very institution which looms so ominously over the elderly workers in his book. And he always knew this – that without means and unable to work it would be inevitable. There was nowhere else to go.

There had been some slight improvement in workhouses since the eighteenth and nineteenth centuries but they were still a disgrace to the nation, to the Christian Churches and to the medical profession.

Throughout the history of the Poor Laws, medical treatment for inmates was neglected and even scandalous, the paupers themselves being used as nurses with often no separate wards for the sick.

In many, lunatics roamed unrestrained among the other inmates – expectant mothers and lunatics were housed on the same floor in Hastings in Robert's time with 'small children running among the totally unattended idiots'.

Sidney Webb in vol. 2 of his *English Poor Law History* says that 'in the whole reign of the Poor Law Commission, no women sat with that body nor, it seems, not even a doctor'.

It was in Liverpool Brownlow Street Workhouse, in the early days of the new policy of medical attention for workhouses, that the philanthropist William Rathbone provided at his own expense a trained superintendent nurse, twelve trained nurses and eighteen paid probationers for three years, and the fifty-four paupers who had been doing the job, including nursing a fever epidemic, were sent back to the ordinary wards as confirmed drunkards. There was still no doctor. The Superintendent was Agness Elizabeth Jones, 'the Florence Nightingale of the Poor Law', who herself died four years later of typhus contracted in the institute. That was in 1864, and in 1909 the Commission, as Webb states, 'still found between two and three thousand paupers acting as nurses'.

Conditions were somewhat better when Robert was a patient and he wrote to Gower saying the nurses had been very kind to him.

The story of his stay in hospital, however, continues the story of his loneliness. It was as if he had been abandoned. No one from Hastings or, as far as is known, from anywhere else, visited him, not even when the weeks began to turn into months.

Kathleen gives one explanation:

> When he became ill and was taken to hospital I was not unduly worried. When a person is ill on and off for years, one does not expect them to become suddenly worse and not recover. I had no money of my own, I was working in the school teaching handwork and helping with the care of the children, dressing and washing them, but I got no salary. I just lived in my own dream-world

thinking of what we would do when we got to Canada. I'd get a job as teacher and Dad would paint and write. He wrote cheerfully from hospital about decorating the ward for Christmas.

But he seems to have been sparing Kathleen's feelings. Perhaps he thought it would be too distressing for her, yet one would think he would have asked her to visit him. Perhaps he still hoped he would recover as he had so often done before, though I think he had always known the truth about his condition. Kathleen believed that he never suffered from lung haemorrhage but Gower told me that the incident in the book about Owen's haemorrhages was true of Robert and quite recently I received a press-cutting, unfortunately with the date missing, from Mr H.J.Brierce of Prenton, Birkenhead, of a letter written to the *Daily Herald* by Gower probably following the 1927 edition of *The Ragged Trousered Philanthropists* in which he says: '. . . the chapter in which Owen is stricken with haemorrhage is literally true; he told me of the occurrence and of his fears for the future of the children.'

I don't know why Gower should refer to 'children' but I'm quite sure he wasn't making a wild statement and Robert may well have concealed his true condition from Kathleen when in hospital. And in the light of her behaviour in not visiting him nor sending Kathleen, perhaps Mary Jane knew the end had come and played her part in concealing it in accordance with his wishes. Whether Adelaide even knew of it is not known.

'Robert never gave me any idea of finality about his illness,' says Kathleen, 'had he done so I'm sure my aunt would have helped me to go to him. One of the symptoms of TB is optimism and after all his other illness he probably expected to recover as he had then.' But to Gower he wrote that 'his health had gone all to pieces and that he wouldn't mind much when the end came'.

'And then early in February,' says Kathleen,

I received a telegram saying 'Your father died at 10.15 last night'. The bottom fell out of my world and I do not remember much of the days immediately following. I was absolutely shocked and stunned. It *really* took my breath away. All I remember was just sitting on my bed for about three days, no getting undressed or doing my hair or anything. I suppose they must have brought me food but I do not remember any trays.

The hospital wrote and asked what arrangements should be made and my aunt told me to tell them to make the 'usual arrangements'. They must have wondered what kind of a creature I was. I don't remember writing the reply. I was completely dependent on my aunt.

The date was Friday, 3 February 1911. No indication of the seriousness of his condition had been sent from hospital to Kathleen or his relations, as far as she knew, yet it seems to me the authorities must have known he was a dying man. At the same time no inquiries, to Kathleen's knowledge, were made to the Hospital Authorities from Hastings. Perhaps again, the aunts knew and it was Robert's wish. It would account for their seeming callousness.

No one from Hastings or, as far as I know, from Liverpool attended the funeral or even knew the official cause of death. It was believed he had died of 'bronchial pneumonia'.

According to Kathleen he was uninsured and this meant that he would be buried as a pauper. The instruction from Hastings to 'proceed in the usual way' with the funeral was the last communication in the matter. No one even knew where he was buried – and no one knew for another sixty years.

Kathleen says she thinks her aunt didn't bother to get in touch. Something had divided this family. Robert never mentioned his brothers or his sister Ellie, and his relations with Adelaide were not 'brotherly and sisterly' in affection, but still Kathleen says, 'I think Mary Jane was the only one who was hostile, probably because she didn't want to be linked to a working-man, especially in her own town. She resented his choice of life and also possibly there was a guilt complex as she may have had most of the family fortune though most of it was tied up in Chancery.' But I believe Adelaide had grown hostile too.

Robert would have appreciated in that age of charity the sentiments quoted in the *Liverpool Hospitals' Report* of 1911.

> We can all do more than we have done
> And be not a whit the worse.
> It never was loving that emptied the heart
> Nor giving that emptied the purse.

I found no notices of his death in the Hastings papers. His memorial was still buried in the tin box. And Kathleen was now, at eighteen, virtually alone in the world, with no one who cared particularly about her. It had all, apparently, turned out just as he feared.

None of his effects were returned to Hastings or heard of again; perhaps his landlady sold them for rent – perhaps he had arranged for her to do so. Kathleen's letters, Gower's and other correspondence, together with his tools, his William Morris and other designs, with his own were lost, and only the fact that he couldn't take his heavy manuscript with him prevented that too from being lost for ever.

He was always remembered with affection by his friends and by many of his workmates as a true man, an incorruptible, though by authority and the purblind he was treated with neglect and even hatred. And many people referred to him thirty, forty and fifty years after his death as 'dear little' or 'dear old' Bob. Kathleen says:

> I wouldn't have had him any different except that I wish he had not had so much physical suffering – filled with a burning zeal for justice and the betterment of mankind no matter what the personal cost. He was an agnostic but surely lived the most Christian life I have ever come into contact with, who hated sham and hypocrisy and who loved children and all weak and helpless creatures and who suffered agonies when he contemplated their probable futures and his inability to alter them.

And she follows this with a curious remark: 'When he gave way after finishing *The Ragged Trousered Philanthropists* he died.' And I say 'curious' because when he left for Liverpool he was looking forward to a new life according to Kathleen and this seems borne out by a letter to her.

His niece said:

> I have told you quite truthfully that Robert was not born into the working class. He would have had a very much happier life, no doubt, had he been.
>
> He felt that the working class had been grievously wronged beyond all measure and he also believed that before he formed any judgement or expressed opinions he would find out the smallest details and the innermost secrets from his own practical experience and life, and therefore he took upon himself and became the class he so earnestly desired to help.

And finally the following fragment of a letter, the rest of which is lost, from her father to Kathleen some time in August 1910 – the only surviving piece of his correspondence known and one of the most extraordinary letters from father to daughter that I ever read. It is at once revealing a special element in his feeling for Kathleen, and pregnant with long years of unspoken spiritual loneliness, a loneliness deeper than the merely personal and which I can only describe as a deep human social need.

He wrote to her:

I feel so unhappy at being away from you and miss you more than I can say. It makes me very miserable to think of all you used to do for me and of how unkind and irritable I often was in return and although I know that you always made allowances for the worry that caused me to be like that, I cannot forgive myself and try in vain to comfort myself with the thought that you know I never meant to be unkind and that you know I love you more than anything else in the world.

I have thought of nothing but you since I lost sight of you on the platform and the world seems a dreary place to me because you are not here. I cannot write down here all that I feel and want to say to you but if it were true that circumstances compelled us to live apart from each other permanently – then I would much prefer not to continue to live at all. . . .

Je vous aime toujours
Dad

25

Kathleen and the manuscript

Aunt Mary Jane's special school to which Kathleen went when her father left for Liverpool comprised two houses situated back to back with gardens linking them – 48 Kenilworth Road and 37 Carisbrooke Road, St Leonards. Here Kathleen stayed until her aunt moved to 12 Upper Maze Hill, St Leonards, which was some time in 1911 as she appears at that address in the 1912 directory. Mary Jane had three daughters, Alice, Olive and Ruby, and three sons, of whom Paul figures in this story.

Alice was the niece I interviewed twenty-five years ago and as far as I knew then was the only surviving member of the family in Hastings. Here Kathleen was given board and lodging and a little pocket-money, but no wages, and her cousins were treated in the same manner.

Presumably Robert accepted these arrangements probably thinking it would be only for a short while.

'What puzzles me,' says Kathleen, 'is, with their attitude towards my father, why should he leave me with them except that they were the most well off of the family and perhaps for shame's sake she would treat me well and I would be fed and clothed and perhaps after a while she might have paid me a salary. Alice never liked me and possibly, too, she didn't like Dad.'

She tells a little story of Mary Jane which well illustrates both that lady and the attitudes of the times.

'Olive went to Johns Hopkins Hospital somewhere in the United States to train as a nurse because it was *infra dig.* to train in England. It wasn't an honourable profession, so she had to go to the States. And Aunt Jane was very upset when her son Percy, visiting from Canada, married beneath him to a girl in the laundry business!'

Says Kathleen, 'I can't understand why my aunt who was the wife of a linen-draper should have been so upset. She said to me she wouldn't have cared how poor the girl was if only she had been a lady.'

Mary Jane's husband was described in her marriage certificate as a

'Draper' and in her death certificate as a 'House Furnisher's Salesman'.

The husband, John Bean Meiklejon, lived in London and only visited Hastings for occasional week-ends. Paul was also living in London and visited more frequently. Of him Kathleen says:

> Paul was delicate and a cripple, having suffered a fractured leg in childhood which, not being properly re-set, had necessitated amputation below the knee and he had to have a 'peg-leg'.
>
> His second name was Alexander and his mother used to say: 'Paul was born to command.' He was waited on by mother and servants. I was with my aunt for over two years until my cousins convinced me that if I had to work for my living it was better to work for strangers and be properly paid than to remain at home for practically nothing. Olive and Ruby had left home for the same reason although Ruby had returned to England after years in Canada.

So she decided to go to London and her cousins helped her to find a position and provided references for her. In the meantime she and Paul fell in love and came to an understanding to marry and emigrate to Canada when that was possible. In her own words:

> Paul came for a visit from London just after the girl he had been courting died. It was a case of misery loves company. Paul said nothing of our understanding until after I had told my aunt that I was leaving and going to London. She was very upset at my leaving her, said I was ungrateful after all she had done for me. I couldn't reply or I would have broken down, so I just sat in silence and she afterwards told Ruby that I'd just sat like a stone!
>
> Ruby and Olive had left home possibly because, being family, they were expected to work without salary and after Robert died my aunt treated me in the same way and perhaps instead of being a niece she regarded me as a daughter and *that* was why I was so ungrateful in leaving. I never saw it in that light before.
>
> I went to London in the spring of 1913 to become nurse-governess to one child. I don't remember whether my aunt gave me any extra clothes – she had given me some while I was living with her and I didn't need anything special for my first job. I think Ruby and Paul possibly paid for my fare.
>
> I don't really remember much about this job but they were very

nice people and I wish I could remember what caused me to say 'If you're not satisfied perhaps you should get someone else.' The mistress replied 'Oh, but I am satisfied, Miss Noonan.' It was my first experience of being on my own out in the world and perhaps I was a bit touchy.

However, I decided to leave, and got a job with a Mr and Mrs Mackinlay and their five children in North Finchley.

The first job had lasted only a few months at the most because Kathleen was at the Mackinlays before August. 'Mrs Mackinlay was very nice and so was her mother who lived in another suburb and I used to cycle over there and she came to North Devon with us when we went there for our holidays.'

In the meantime Paul had already gone to Canada.

'Mrs Mackinlay knew I would only be with them until Paul sent for me. He used to write every week.'

This account of Kathleen's whereabouts contradicts Poynton's story in the newspaper article where he says that when her father died 'a local comrade took the girl to a woman who is still alive [1936] in Tunbridge [this refers to the Cruttendens who were then living in Tonbridge (not Tunbridge), Kent – F.C.B.] and eventually she got a job in London as a General Servant'.

This article with other garbled accounts was responsible for many errors in my first book.

The move to Mrs Mackinlay's was a fateful one in Robert's story, in Kathleen's, and in literary history.

In *Tressell of Mugsborough* I told the story as it had come to me via various friends of Robert's, of how Kathleen still kept the manuscript tied up in pink ribbon in her tin trunk under her bed, of the visit from a 'literary Lady' to tea with Mrs Mackinlay, and of how Kathleen had told her mistress of her father's book, of how the mistress showed it to her literary friend and she took it to Grant Richards.

This is Kathleen's own account:

> The manuscript was never tied up with pink ribbon [another legend] but was in the deed-box Robert had had made for it. One day Mrs Mackinlay saw the box when I was at my trunk and asked me if it was full of treasure and I told her about it.
>
> One day Miss Jessie Pope and her friend, who lived next door to the Mackinlays, were having afternoon tea with Mrs Mackinlay

and I took the two young boys in to them and was introduced. Mrs Mackinlay had evidently told Miss Pope about the manuscript and she asked to see it and took it away with her.

As another example of the extraordinary rumours that have cropped up about Robert and his book and made his story so difficult to get at I mention here that I was told by Mr Cruttenden, hardly the man to tell lies, that Kathleen had given the manuscript to a Mrs Pope of St Leonards who had sent it on to Grant Richards and sure enough at the address given there was a Mrs Pope, but when I wrote to her in 1943, thinking I had found Jessie, the reply was that she had had nothing to do with Tressell and his book and that she was Mrs *Marion* Pope. And as late as 1953 the letter from Mr Barltrop already quoted concluded by saying, 'It has been suggested to me that Jessie Pope was not a woman at all and that the circumstances under which the manuscript was obtained and published may not have been those which are commonly described.'

The real Jessie Pope tells in her preface how she first came to read the manuscript.

A few months ago a friend asked me to look at the manuscript of a novel, 'The Ragged Trousered Philanthropists,' the work of a socialistic house-painter, who wrote his book and died. I consented without enthusiasm, expecting to be neither interested nor amused – and found I had chanced upon a remarkable human document.

Kathleen continues, 'Miss Pope read it and suggested to me that she should show it to Grant Richards.'

This is Grant Richards's own account taken from his book *Author Hunting* which I quoted in *Tressell of Mugsborough*.

It was from a friend that I first heard of that mountainous manuscript 'The Ragged Trousered Philanthropists! ... My secretary Miss Hemmerde had a cousin Miss Jessie Pope. One day I heard that Miss Pope had heard from a neighbour that her children's nurse ... had confessed that her own father had written a book – well not exactly a book since it wasn't in print, but a story in the sense that it was a novel, the novel of his own life that wanted to get itself into print and to be a book. Politeness and curiosity made Miss Pope promise to read the book and it was brought to her.

It *was* a manuscript! It must have been as long as *A Traveller at Forty* [by Theodore Dreiser]. Miss Pope told me of it. 'Bring it along,' I said. 'Have you read it?' Miss Pope had read it. She thought it was ever and ever so much too long; full of repetition. It would have to be cut down. Ultimately she did bring it along.

'I'll publish this,' I told her, after examination, 'if you will cut it down, say, to a hundred thousand words.'

She discussed the matter with its owner. She told her what she and I must have sincerely believed, that its chances of success were very slight. But the opportunity of publication appealed to Miss Tressall – I will call her so for her father had taken 'Robert Tressall' as his pen-name.

The book was damnably subversive, but it was extraordinarily real, and rather than let it go I was willing to drop a few score pounds on it.

Kathleen continues:

This resulted in an interview with Mr Richards, when he told me that he had sat up all night reading it, that he had never been so impressed by a book and was willing to publish it, but that it would have to be cut down a lot as there was a lot of repetition in it. I explained the reason for the repetition – that my father felt that he had to hammer home his message to get the workers to see it – but that made no difference to Grant Richards.

He also wanted to change the title but I held out for that and would not consent. He explained that publication was a gamble – it might be successful or a complete flop. He would pay me twenty-five pounds for all rights including dramatic rights and if it was a success would pay me more but would not bind the firm to that. I was getting twelve pounds a year at Mrs Mackinlay's and twenty-five pounds outright seemed a fortune. It was explained to me that it was going to be costly cutting it down to make it possible to publish. Miss Pope probably got more for her work than I did for the manuscript.

This 'work' of Jessie Pope's, a writer of children's books and pro-fessional journalist, a regular contributor to *Punch*, and I believe, a member of the Fabian Society, was to be the editing of the manuscript. Grant Richards's own book *Author Hunting*, plus rumour, were my only sources of information about publication for *Tressell of Mugsborough*, although I had been in correspondence with Grant Richards about any letters relating to publication which might be in his possession, but he made no mention of any, nor gave any other particulars. But in 1956 through the courtesy of Mr Martin Secker correspondence between Grant Richards and Jessie Pope was passed on to me by Messrs Lawrence & Wishart.

The first letter discloses that the book had already been to another publisher before it was sent on to Grant Richards.

19th August, 1913

Dear Mr Richards,

I have been looking for Constable's letters, and now remember I passed them on to the nurse to read and told her I did not want them back. The gist of them was this – They impressed their indebtedness to me for bringing the MS. to their notice and said they had read it with very great interest, but feared in its present form it was too unwieldy for them to handle. They asked if I would make any suggestion in the matter. I offered to discuss the matter with them and saw Mr Meredith who was enthusiastic over the book, but did not seem to know who to get to edit it. I said I was not inclined to undertake it but advised him to look about for someone else, he said he would, and the matter was left at that. After some long time I advised the nurse to write to know what they were doing in the matter and they wrote back to her saying they understood that I was going to make the next move – which of course was exactly what I said I could not do.

So we had the MS. back and sent it on to you. There is no doubt Mr Meredith realized that it was good stuff, though I don't think he had read very much of it, or perhaps he would not have let it go. Of course it is always open to question if the biggest stuff commands the biggest public.

Yours sincerely,

JESSIE POPE

It is a coincidence that she sent the book to Constable's, the firm that had published George Meek – or had Jessie read Meek?

'Mr Meredith' was the son of George Meredith the novelist.

Frank Swinnerton in his *The Adventures of a Manuscript* fills in the story: 'Jessie Pope discussed the ms with various friends one of whom was a remarkable woman named Pauline Hemmerde, sister of Edward G.Hemmerde, K.C., Recorder of Liverpool, the innocently adoring and too often unpaid secretary of Grant Richards. "Why not let Mr Richards see it?" suggested Miss Hemmerde. "It couldn't do any harm." '

Grant Richards evidently soon made his decision to publish, for Kathleen's interview with him was on 22 August and the same day he wrote confirming his offer, adding that publication date was to be not later than June 1914. He also made the stipulation that, if he wished, he should be at liberty to alter the title. He advised her to talk the matter over with Miss Pope and if Kathleen decided to accept, to acknowledge by letter and he would then get to work. He offered nothing in the way of a royalty contract, that is, payment according to sales.

He remarked in this letter: 'I will tell you now, before you have formally accepted this offer, that I do not remember reading any manuscript which affected me more deeply than this work of your father's. I should like to have known him.'

On 28 August Jessie wrote to Richards:

... I have advised her to accept your offer and have told her I consider it a very generous one, and she certainly feels she is being very well treated.

Personally I don't think anybody could read that MS. and treat the daughter of the man who wrote it, badly.

Now that her part of the business is satisfactorily settled, I feel I can entertain the idea of editing the book without injuring her prospects.

It is going to be a big job, and I should like to know what terms you feel inclined to offer me if I undertake the work.

As regards the time it will take I should think your estimate of 100 hours (at 3 hours a day) is a fair one. That would run into about 6 weeks of working days.

I certainly think the title will have to be altered. In my opinion it is neither effective nor applicable.

Yours sincerely,
JESSIE POPE

And here we must pay a tribute to Miss Pope who had sent the book to a number of publishers and acted as unpaid agent all through for Kathleen.

There followed negotiations about her fee. On 2 September she wrote, 'I do not see how I can undertake to edit the book for less than £24. I only want to charge you what I should be making by my ordinary work. I don't think it can possibly be less than 200,000 words – I think it is probably more and it must be judicially and sympathetically cut down to half its length to make it marketable.'

Evidently there had been suggestions from someone, but not apparently Richards, about changing the names of some of the characters, probably because Robert's habit (Old English) of personifying attributes – Sweater, Didlum, Grinder – was thought to be a little overdone, for Jessie goes on to say that she thinks they are best left as they are, though 'we could think of a better title. In any case I wish the book the very greatest success for . . . I keenly and enthusiastically appreciate what really big stuff it is.'

By 24 October she is sending the first instalment and by 3 November has finished the editing, sends the preface and is still not happy with the title. 'It has been suggested to me that "The Ragged Philanthropists" makes a tidier title.' Six weeks later, on 9 December, she offers 'The Tattered Philanthropists' as 'less of a mouthful,' or 'The Threadbare Philanthropists'.

Her letter of 3 November also shows that there were doubts as to whether Robert really had worked in the trade.

> You will remember I raised the question when I saw you . . . and from what his daughter told you, you were quite satisfied about the matter. However, to make quite sure I sent her a message by Mrs Mackinlay and she came round to see me yesterday. . . . Anyhow she satisfied me that her father was the character Owen in the book, that he followed the same trade – endured even greater privations – until his death three years ago. She said perhaps he had greater advantages than other workmen in the matter of education but as he started his apprenticeship at 16 and worked as a house-painter and decorator for various firms from that time till his death without any outside support I think his advantages must have been natural ones. In any case the book is the book of a working man pure and simple – there is nothing whatsoever scholarly about it – the work of a man who knows nothing really about the better classes – but a great deal about his own.

It was to be one of the main selling points, that the book was the work of a house-painter and signwriter and therefore completely authentic.

There were reasons for this doubt on the part of both Richards and Jessie as we shall see later. This meant that publicity had to be carefully controlled and on 14 April 1914 when the book was nearing publication date Richards wrote to Kathleen, 'It is very important for the sake of the book that you should not see any writers from newspapers about it.'

I am not entirely sure of Richards's motives. Did he also fear that journalists might discover that he hadn't offered Kathleen a royalty contract as was normal practice, but had bought all rights for twenty-five pounds?

It was this correspondence that furnished the answer to all the rumours of the amount actually paid for the rights. Mr Ward gave me a figure of thirty pounds; Poynton in his article had said it was twenty pounds; and Mr Cruttenden ten pounds.

However 'generous' (as Jessie called it) this might have appeared at the time, it was fundamentally unjust to Kathleen and has cast its shadow over the history of *The Ragged Trousered Philanthropists*. And furthermore not only did Richards buy all rights of publication for his money but he kept the handwritten manuscript, too, as a property.

As Kathleen said, 'Apart from my ignorance, I was only twenty and a very young twenty at that. My upbringing was far too sheltered.'

Nevertheless there were extenuating circumstances. As Swinnerton points out in *The Adventures of a Manuscript*, copyrights were often sold for less in those days and even an author destined to become a bestseller might have been pleased to begin so well. And, of course, while publishers will often gamble on a young writer hoping for reward in the success of his later work, few will invest in one who being dead can produce no more. Even then a publisher could easily lose as many as two or three hundred pounds on a book and half a dozen failures for an under-capitalized but adventurous publisher like Richards might have been very serious.

Jessie perhaps expressed both her own and Grant Richards's genuine opinion when she wrote on 2 April, 'I do hope it will be a success and that the English publisher may be well repaid for a sporting risk in the matter.'

26

Publication and reactions

The book appeared on 23 April 1914 price six shillings, 'London Grant Richards Ltd, Printed at Mercat Press, Edinburgh. Author Robert Tressall.'

Kathleen was given the usual six copies and Grant Richards gave her a few other books including J. R. Green's *A Short History of the English People* which, says Kathleen, she 'had already seen enough of at school'.

A second print was issued a month later, in May.

Richards certainly didn't let the grass grow under his feet and in his book *Author Hunting*, he explains how the book was accepted by an American publisher. 'Then Maynard Dominick appeared on the scene from New York. Dominick had a nose. He read the subversive story and in spite of the fact that the conditions with which it dealt were English and had not even a superficial likeness to the conditions then obtaining in America, he arranged to publish it.'

This American edition, published in New York by Frederick A. Stokes and Co., came out later the same year.

Richards evidently took some trouble to maintain his secrecy about Robert and Kathleen. On 27 April, four days after the book appeared, he wrote to Kathleen, 'I enclose a sheet that shows all I am proposing to say about your father. But unless I am asked for further information I see no particular reasons in the circumstances for giving it.'

This statement said:

> Robert Tressall was born in Ireland in 1871, and died in 1911. He was a Roman Catholic until his own reading of books on religious matters convinced him that neither Roman Catholicism in particular nor Christianity in general had any sound basis. For a little while he worked in Johannesburg, but most of his work was in England.
>
> His book was finished in 1909 and was offered to three publishers. The first seems to have returned it without reading it, frightened, it would seem, by its length and by the fact that it was not typed.

The second did not have the actual manuscript but on being written to replied that his list was too full. The third had the manuscript and returned it. It seems that when the work was started the author had no intention of writing a book but had in mind the writing of a series of pamphlets.

It was only when the book was begun that he found it turning into a novel under his hand.

Outside his work as a house-painter and signwriter he was particularly interested in Aeronautics. He worked for some time on an airship and had hopes that the War Office would take it up; but as he could not provide a full-sized working model, not having the money, the result of his work did not get proper consideration.

He learnt Dutch in South Africa, and he also taught himself French and, to a lesser degree, Spanish and German; and he also worked at Geology and Astronomy.

Kathleen commented, 'Grant Richards only told the public that Robert was self-educated, that it was a working-man who wrote the book. Had they been told it was an educated man it would have taken away from its value.'

In the event Grant Richards actually described the author to the Press as 'a builder's labourer' as many of the reviews testify.

Publicity and the preface itself made no reference to Tressell's identity nor to where he had lived, nor to the setting for his 'Mugsborough'. Grant Richards knew he had a book which might become famous or be damned out of hand.

It was widely reviewed and on the whole sympathetically.

Apart from the Labour and Socialist Press, the main national dailies and Sundays – *The Times*, *Observer*, *Daily Sketch*, *Daily Telegraph* – reviewed it, with the *Daily Mail*, the *Manchester Guardian* and the two 'Labour' papers, the *Daily Herald* and *Reynolds News*, the most notable exceptions. So did many provincial papers including the *Glasgow Evening News* and the *Dundee Advertiser*; the weeklies; and literary periodicals such as *Review of Reviews*, *Books and Bookmen*, *Men and Books*, and the *Athenaeum*.

In *Books and Bookmen*, James Douglas saw the book's publication as a portent, a sign that 'the long silence of the poor is about to be broken'. 'Slowly the workers are becoming articulate,' he wrote. 'The new workman is a rebel ... not willing to put up with the hardships and privations ... which the old workman accepted as necessary evils.'

Under the headlines: 'A Remarkable Human Document.' 'A Painter's Philosophy.' 'Noble Task of Making Money – For Others', the *Daily Sketch* said, 'It is a wonderful book, and Robert Tressall must have been a wonderful man, for he was but a house-painter himself. Formless and without a connected story, it can hardly be called a novel. It is rather a series of character studies, conversations and incidents depicted with the minute exactitude that Tolstoy employed.'

The reviewer went on to comment on the bad language. 'The conversation is transcribed with brutal frankness. You will find the word that we supply with —— on nearly every page, but there is justification for its use, for without it the rude philosophy of the men could hardly be rendered.'

Thus, according to the *Daily Sketch*, 'bloody' is a technical term of working-class philosophy.

The *Daily Telegraph* on 24 April published a long review referring to it as

> ... one of the most extraordinary revelations that have ever been made in the guise of fiction. Fiction is, however, a wholly inadequate term ... it is about as much fiction as is Defoe's 'Journal of the Plague Year;' had that master of impression been a modern house-painter, even thus might he have fixed the lives of his fellows in words. Beside such work as this the pessimism of a Gissing, the 'realism' of a Masefield are self-conscious essays in a literary genre. It is unpleasant, but fascinating; terrible, but convincing; unbelievedly sad, but suggestive.

The *Daily Telegraph*, however, thought it proper to say that the bosses were not really so bad as Tressell painted them.

The Times, in its weekly Literary Supplement, reviewed the book at some length on 23 April.

> The book lives by its minute fidelity, its convincing air of fact, and by the writer's passion for his subject. He had a remarkable gift for the suggestion of character. Before the tale is over, we know every one of these working men so well that we should recognize them in the street. ...
> Are things really so bad as he makes out in this terrible story?

That is a question which can only be answered by those who know the facts 'from the inside' as well as Robert Tressall knew them, but no graver indictment of an industry has ever been written.

The Liberal *Daily News and Leader* recommended the novel as one

which everybody should read. . . . The book is really a tract in favour of Socialism, and it has some of the faults of a tract. . . . It is a true indictment of the worst sort of employer, but it misses the effect of reality, much as Dickens's 'Hard Times' does, through over-statement. . . . But these faults cannot be found with the picture we are given of the precarious lives of the house-painters, who are the true characters of the story. We know no book in which the anguish of the man with wife and children at the chance of getting 'the sack' . . . have been more faithfully and harrowingly portrayed. . . .

The *New Witness* said: 'There is no one, no one at all, who will be, after reading it, quite the same man as he was before. No commendation of this book can be exaggerated.'

Forward said: 'It bites, it leaves a permanent impression, it sears the mind. If we could get the clergy to start reading chapters out of this book each Sunday morning, the Capitalist system would end in a month.'

Ironically the *Clarion* was one of the few that were lukewarm, and Winifred Blatchford, who reviewed it, begins, 'Reading *The Ragged Trousered Philanthropists* I was continually distracted by the wish that the author had been a genius.'

She mentions this point about lack of genius no less than four times, and sums up: 'It is not without skill . . . the chapters on economics and politics are high above the rest in power and craftsmanship. It is full of sympathy and understanding of the lives the workers lead. It is a terrible accusation against the men he used to work for. To our "Clarion" Vanners I recommend a day's reading of *The Ragged Trousered Philanthropists*. It would prove invaluable read aloud from the platform.'

She also discusses whether the 'lack of skill in storytelling and construction is Robert's fault or Jessie Pope's'.

Jessie herself commented to Grant Richards on this review: 'I don't take the writer's views very seriously. They are rather contradictory. . . . It seems to me that the original manuscript must have been in her hands at some time. Do you know if his daughter sent it to Robert Blatchford or The Clarion? It is comforting to find that other papers do not curse at Robert Tressall's "lack of genius".'

Jessie also had a go at the *Athenaeum* which, she said, had 'expressed the pious hope that people of leisure could employ it to better advantage than by reading such rubbish', though she added that 'it was quite refreshing after the monotonous enthusiasm of the others'.

Justice, H.M.Hyndman's paper, said:

> Nothing as significant as this book has been published for a long time. It has come right out of the ranks of the workers themselves. . . . Amateur though the author is, his very instinct for form and proportion gives his writing a literary quality approaching the technique of the conscious artist. An imperishable impression. The fiery vengeance of a man whom Reality has put to the most exquisite torture.

I could find no mention of it in the local press but it had made a remarkable start, if only its author had been there to see it, and Kathleen must have profoundly wished he were. His friends were conscious of the perversity of fate but at least, they thought, his work would live. Or so it appeared to them.

But 1914 was an ominous year and Richards describes the fate of the book's 1914 editions. 'In its first three months it sold in England one thousand seven hundred and fifty-two copies; it sold fourteen hundred copies to the colonies apart from Canada, where the sale amounted to two hundred and fifty. Then it died. In America it had the same fate.'

The whole story seemed to end suddenly in 1914.

Within a few weeks of publication and with her twenty-five pounds in her pocket Kathleen too disappeared from the scene and neither Grant Richards, Jessie Pope nor her friends and relations in England ever saw her again, with the exception of Rose Cruttenden who was to meet her in circumstances stranger than fiction. She seems to have made a visit to Hastings during which she presented the Cruttendens with a copy of her father's book and then she was gone.

For my first book on Robert I could discover little of what had happened to her, most of it from her cousin Alice (whose name I wasn't then permitted to mention), from Poynton's article in the *Daily Worker* and from friends, and all of it garbled.

Briefly this was the story as I then told it:

She and her cousin had determined to marry despite opposition and he had been packed off to Canada, I was told, 'to remove the temptation'.

After the publication of her father's book she determined to follow him and not long afterwards she took ship for Canada. There she found her lover and they were married. He was working on the stage and Kathleen got a job with him. Later a daughter was born to them and Alice told me: 'I remember at their Canadian home they used to have a large Christmas Tree at Christmas on which were presents for the children of a local institution of some kind. The children used to come to Kathleen's home for the presents and the little girl would give them out.'

So they appeared to be in good circumstances.

And then Kathleen's husband joined one of the flying services and was killed in the war and Kathleen and her baby were left as Robert had feared.

But not for long. They were themselves both killed in a motor accident just after the war ended.

The Tressells had come to an end.

27

1914-18: the book dies and is born again

The war broke out in August and the figures for book production fell immediately. From a total of 12,379 titles for 1913 – and the number was growing each year and had nearly doubled in the past ten – there was a drop of more than 3,000 titles for 1914.* But besides this, a wave of extraordinary patriotism swept the country affecting socialist and non-socialist alike and few wanted to know about socialism and books like *The Ragged Trousered Philanthropists*.

Robert had written in the last chapter of his book years before of the threat of this very war. I don't know what position he would have taken when it finally arrived but I'm certain he would have been shocked at the apparent transformation.

Much of the old Socialist and Labour Movement appeared to be finished off altogether. The Labour Party and trade unions were caught on one foot and didn't know how to act any more than did their German opposite numbers, in the end both sides deciding to support their governments. And to a realist it would be difficult to see how such a minority, as they were, however influential in industry, could have carried public opinion with them let alone the State apparatus, and they weren't ready for decisive action.

It was to be the dead who finally represented public opinion in the various European States. But he who had been an admirer and follower of Blatchford and Hyndman and a reader of their papers *Clarion* and *Justice* would have seen the *Clarion* come out in violent support of the war and its circulation drop from ninety thousand to ten thousand and the *Clarion* Movement killed; would have seen the *Daily Citizen* vanish overnight; the *Daily Herald*, started a fortnight before he died, become a weekly; the Labour Party and the TUC proclaim an 'industrial truce' and H.M.Hyndman, for whom he had painted the

*Marjorie Plant, *The English Book Trade*, second edition, London, 1965.

banners, expelled from the SDF's successor the British Socialist Party and form a new 'patriotic' violently anti-German National Socialist Party.

In the new-found 'national unity' there was hardly a demand for a book attacking the very roots of capitalism and class society.

But despite the 'industrial truce' proclaimed by the Labour Party and the TUC (but not by the employers), despite Labour Party Ministers functioning in the Government, the war was marked by increasing agitation against rising prices and profiteering, by strikes and anti-war propaganda from those left-wing groups who still clung to the ideas of international solidarity and of the power of organized labour to stop the war.

This industrial unrest and anti-war agitation was already strong in 1915, particularly on the Clyde, where following a great engineering strike the Clyde Workers' Committee was formed centred on Glasgow which in many ways became the spearhead of the national agitation.

And it was from Glasgow that there came the next development in the history of *The Ragged Trousered Philanthropists*. Grant Richards describes it briefly in his book *Author Hunting* but gives no dates. 'Then came the war,' he writes.

> A year or two later my friend, Clifford, was in Glasgow. Business brought him into connection with the Reformers Bookstall. Its manager, Mr Hardie, mentioned 'The Ragged Trousered Philanthropists'.
>
> 'Now there's a book of which I could sell any number you like.'
>
> Clifford reported the remark to me. Knowing that my Mr Dracott, in the course of his journey would arrive in Glasgow, I said nothing and awaited events.
>
> Mr Dracott sent me an order for a very large number of copies if only the book could be done at a lower price. [The first edition sold at six shillings – F.C.B.] So I set Miss Pope to work.

There he anticipates a little. For the last series of letters between Richards and Jessie Pope that I have, dated October–December 1915, concerns negotiations on a fee, Richards offering five pounds and Jessie asking for ten pounds. She wrote in November:

> The suggestion that I should receive £5 on publication and £5 later on, if the book is a success, does not appeal to me.

My work will be the same whether the book sells or not, and if it is not a success £5 would not be a sufficient return for my work. But I am willing to meet you in the matter by accepting £8 (eight pounds) on publication and a further £2 when such a measure of success is reached that my final payment can be made – when that point comes of course I must leave to you, but I hope the sale of the book will soon justify the completion of the deal.

If I do the book I think I shall cut out most of the *political* discussions (which as you may remember turn on 'The Fiscal question') and retain much of the matter referring to socialism – The Fiscal question is dead, and passionate reference to it will make the book seem a back number, and the conditions it describes possibly a little antiquated and belonging to another decade.

It seems that agreement was reached. But whether she did the work then or later I don't know for there was an interval of two and a half years before the book appeared.

There were serious developments in the war in 1916. Conscription was introduced for single men in March and for married men two months later. Industrial and anti-war agitation increased with the various Acts introducing industrial restrictions: strikes were forbidden and compulsory arbitration established in all war industries, and while labour suffered these disciplines, profits went unchecked, huge fortunes being made by profiteers.

The Defence of The Realm Act or 'Dora' as it was called by the people, permitted arrest without charge or warrant.

In March 1916, perhaps at the very time Jessie was preparing the new edition, Grant Richards's optimism about the market must have suffered a shock. A number of prominent left-wing leaders and shop stewards were deported from their districts and forbidden to return and John McLean, Willie Gallacher and others were sent to prison.

It must have seemed to Grant Richards that even if there was a public for *The Ragged Trousered Philanthropists* in Mr Dracott's 'order for a very large number of copies' it was hardly prudent to produce it in 1916.

And here I must deal with another story which bears on this edition. This, like the Grant Richards-Jessie Pope Correspondence, only came to me after *Tressell of Mugsborough* was written. As the result of an article by Gordon Schaffer in *Reynolds News* in September 1951, a letter appeared in that paper from a Mr Frank Cooper of Putney claiming that it was the London Workers' Committee that was responsible for the recompiling of the manuscript in 1917.

'The London Workers' Committee was essentially a revolutionary body with a powerful anti-war bias', he wrote to me later, and its Chairman, W.F.Watson,

> told me on several occasions that he was personally responsible for the approach to Jessie Pope for what he termed the re-compiling. He afterwards said that she had made a bloody mess-up of the work by leaving out the most important chapter of all, that on religion. I am of opinion that this happened about 1917 . . . but it is more than possible that he was referring to the 1914 edition. I remember there was quite a controversy about Jessie Pope being prejudiced and I am positive of the part Watson and the London Workers' Committee played in the republication. I cannot honestly say whether the sales were organised through the L.W.C.

Mr Cooper's uncertainty about which edition is, of course, answered by his reference to the chapter on 'religion' and the controversy about Jessie Pope's prejudice. These criticisms could only result from comparison with a previous text, that is the 1914 edition.

I think Mr Cooper's claim for the LWC has some foundation. Because of its reputation and influence among militants it may have been sounded out by Richards and/or Jessie Pope to confirm that there was a possible market. The date 1917 also makes sense, for the new edition, although canvassed by Richards in 1915, didn't appear in 1916 or 1917, and it is possible that the upsurge of the Socialist Movement in 1917 following the February (Kerensky) Russian Revolution, and the release of most of the Clydesiders from gaol, decided Richards to go ahead with his preparations for cashing in on what he was already convinced by his scouts was a hot property; and that it was in fact in 1917 that Jessie was finally asked to undertake the revision.

But in March and April 1918 the situation at the front was almost as bad as in 1914. A great German offensive had driven the Allies back almost to the 1914 lines and they seemed unable to contain it. The situation at home was extremely critical with extensions of food rationing now that German submarine warfare was having its full effect. Public opinion in general was as concerned to win the war as was the Government, and war-weariness did not ease the hostility towards 'peacemakers', 'sedition', strikes and agitation. Everyone seemed to be fighting wars within the war. In war the Establishment is the 'nation' and in this sense Richards was right when he called *The Ragged Trousered Philanthropists* 'damnably subversive'.

Yet by 1917 Grant Richards, a noted opportunist in the publishing world, must already have seen signs of the turning of the tide.

In June 1917 there had actually been a large conference in Leeds at which a resolution calling for Workers and Soldiers Councils on the model of the Russian Revolutionaries (not yet under Bolshevik control) had been passed with enthusiasm. The whole Labour and Trade Union Movement was at loggerheads over support for the war. And even more important was the tremendous militancy of the industrial workers at constant war with the Government and employers over every single issue which affected their legal and economic conditions.

Only in this climate would Richards have dared to bring out his new version of the book aimed specifically at the working-class market. The book had begun the same kind of underground history which had kept alive John Bunyan and Tom Paine.

It came out in May 1918 and sold at a shilling. He says in *Author Hunting* that it 'sold in scores of thousands at the various branches of the Reformers Bookstall and Henderson's Bomb Shop in the Charing Cross Road. The *Daily Herald* assisted its sale to the best of its ability.'

He goes on:

> Did I do harm by spreading such a book broadcast? I do not think so. It was a singularly sincere and moving story; it put a point of view very clearly and definitely before its readers; it was the truth as Robert Tressall saw it.

> It scarcely sold in ordinary bookshops and there was no parallel revival in America. In fact a book which on its first appearance and for several years after can have hardly done more than pay the expenses of production and its share of establishment charges became suddenly a great success and perhaps did something to alter the nation's history.

28

Editions and abridgements

The Abridged Edition was received with some criticism by readers of the original edition and rumour began to circulate among socialists that it had been deliberately toned down. That these rumours were persistent and widespread is proven by the fact that they reached the attention of Grant Richards and although I don't know what other means he used to counter them, there is evidence as late as 1923 that he was still concerned.

Raymond Postgate in *The Builders' History*, published that year, in a footnote to page 391, says, 'Mr Grant Richards . . . asks me to correct an impression that had arisen that this edition had been "expurgated" for political reasons. No such thing has occurred, but the first edition was 400 closely printed pages and to reprint it at low cost was impossible. It was, therefore, condensed but no political consideration was even thought of.'

Mr Postgate then himself quotes, presumably from Grant Richards, 'The work was done reverently, the editor never losing sight for a moment of the spirit that animated the dead author.'

Comparisons show that eleven chapter titles are missing:

Sunday School
The 'Open Air'
Christmas Eve
The Brigands
The New Tenants
The Brigands' Cave
The Brigands At Work
The Socialist Van
The Ghouls
The Wise Men of the East
The Widow's Son

'Sunday School' is the chapter Watson probably had in mind as the 'religious' chapter in which the operations of the Reverend Starr and Belcher are described. 'The "Open Air" ', however, a description of an evangelical street-corner meeting has been shortened and combined with the preceding 'The Reign of Terror'; 'Christmas Eve' has been summarized into one sentence, now heading 'The Pandorama'; the three chapters about the Brigands (the Municipal Council) are out; 'The New Tenants' has been shortened and combined with 'The Veteran'; 'The Socialist Van' has been shortened and combined with 'The Beano Meeting'; 'The Ghouls' describing the rival undertakers' struggle over the corpse of Philpot is out; 'The Wise Men of the East', the election scene is out; 'The Widow's Son' is shortened and combined with part of 'The End' but in the process the suicide of Hunter the foreman is omitted.

Most of the sharp and satirical comment upon Christians and employers and general social comment with its strong class feeling has been combed out and the book is centred round the themes of men at work, at home and in recreation, with Robert's case for socialism represented more by the propaganda sections than by the dramatized scenes of municipal and national politics in action.

On the whole, however, this version for all its deficiencies could be said to preserve the spirit of the dead author, though only a pale reflection of it.

The abridged edition was reprinted again before the end of the war, in October 1918, and again in 1921, 1925 and 1926.

According to Ralph Parker, correspondent of the *Daily Worker*, there was a small edition in Russian in the early 1920s produced by the All Union Council of Trade Unions and the 1958 German (German Democratic Republic) edition makes a reference to a German edition by Neuen Deutschen Verlag, Berlin, in 1925.

And then, in Britain, there was a new development.

On 15 June 1927 the *Daily Herald* advertised:

'A Book Bargain. In conjunction with Richards Press a Special Edition of The Ragged Trousered Philanthropists by Robert Tressall at 2/-. Look out for full details shortly.

This appeared in June with a foreword by George Hicks, President of the TUC and General Secretary of The Amalgamated Union of Building Trade Workers of Great Britain and Ireland: 'Robert Tressall was the Zola of the Building Trade Operatives. On reading this book

... we the workers in the building industry know that he was one of us. What he described is true to life. At the present time when our opponents are seeking to destroy our Trade Union organizations so laboriously established with incalculable struggle and sacrifice, the lessons in this book should be learned by heart by all toilers.'

The year 1926 had been the year of the General Strike in which the better classes showed their solidarity, determination and class unity in rather striking contrast to the working classes who have never had this kind of total class loyalty. The first Labour Government had just fallen and the new Conservative Government under Baldwin were spoiling for a fight. The Labour and Trade Union leaders fell apart under the storm and the strike gradually collapsed. 'The enthusiasm of the rank and file had no reflection at headquarters. Muddle and fear reigned there.' And the TUC caved in and called it off. Cole writes in *The Common People:* 'Trade Union Membership fell by half a million ... the same leaders were left at the head of these diminished battalions, but they could never call upon the same loyalty and sacrifice again.'

The strike was followed in 1927 by the Trade Disputes and Trade Union Acts which severely restricted the rights of unions, and deprived the unemployed of benefits if, in the famous phrase, they were 'not genuinely seeking work'. The Act was not repealed till 1948, by the post-war Labour Government.

Thus 1927 would seem another good year for the mass sale of the book which affirmed the class position of the workers, disillusionment with capitalism and the necessity of developing working-class understanding of the need for full-blooded socialism. Grant Richards doesn't mention this edition in his book, which only covers the period 1897–1925, but it is reputed again to have sold in scores of thousands as a circulation-raiser for the *Daily Herald.**

In 1935 Grant Richards returned with a new edition of his original, priced at half a crown. This was reprinted in 1938 and August 1943. The abridged edition had by 1932 been printed eight times and sold

---

*The sponsoring of *The Ragged Trousered Philanthropists* even in 1927 before the *Daily Herald* became a Capitalist paper (under Odhams Press) is one of the mysteries which make the British Labour Movement so difficult to understand. The TUC had taken over the paper in November 1922 after which only right-wing policies were pursued, and so far as I have been able to discover no reference to Tressell, even in news items, was ever made in the *Daily Herald* in the 30 years I have been associated with his story.

over 100,000 copies. Then in April 1940 (again a time of national crises) Penguin Books brought out a copy of the abridged version, which was reprinted in May 1940, January 1941 and May 1942 with an Australian edition in October 1942, and from 1944 to 1951 another eight abridged came from the Richards Press and, finally, the last Richards original version in 1954.

The Penguin editions were another important development in the history of the book because it was now introduced to a still wider section of the general reading public. This war-time edition carried the words: 'For The Forces. Leave this book at any Post Office when you have read it, so that men and women in the services may enjoy it too.'

John Sommerfield, in the *Daily Worker*, describes how he travelled in the army in Burma in the war with a little library in an ammunition-box among which was *The Ragged Trousered Philanthropists* – 'which didn't last long being handed round and read and re-read until it literally fell to pieces'.

And years afterwards, Alan Sillitoe wrote in an Introduction to a later edition: 'I read an abridged edition of *The Ragged Trousered Philanthropists* when I was nineteen and with the Air Force in Malaya. It was given to me by a wireless operator from Glasgow, who said: "You ought to read this. Among other things it is the book that won the '45 election for Labour." '

So the book was still going the rounds in the army forty years after Green was lent it in a military hospital during the First World War.

Yet as far as the established critics and literary historians were concerned it didn't exist, and to many it still doesn't.

The only reference to the book I have been able to discover among all the literary histories up to 1968 in our local library is one in Seymour Smith's *An English Library*. The Oxford and Cambridge historians have never heard of the book.

Bernard Shaw in reply to a letter from me was able to write as late as 1948: 'I never heard of Robert Tressell and am not interested in him.'

On the other hand, Poynton, in the 1936 *Daily Worker* article already quoted, says: 'Some time ago Upton Sinclair wrote in the English Press that it was getting about time we had another book from the able pen of Robert Tressall.... Like thousands of others', he claimed, Sinclair did not know that the author 'had passed to the Great Beyond three years before his book saw the light', an incredible statement because every edition including the American carried Jessie

Pope's preface mentioning the author's death. But almost every statement of Poynton's was inaccurate.

Cradduck remembers the book being read on Adams and Jarrett's soon after publication. 'I heard the men talking about Tressell's book and tittering amongst themselves. Bob Noonan was supposed to have written it but he had never talked about it.'

It gradually became known as 'The Painter's Bible' among socialist building-workers and others, even in Ireland, which would have gladdened Robert.

Brendan Behan says in *Borstal Boy* that the book was known among Irish painters. He too refers to it as 'the Painter's Bible' and says it was his 'family's book' and that 'on every job in Dublin you'd hear painters using the names out of it for nicknames, calling their own apprentice "The Walking Colour Shop," ' and of course, every foreman was called 'Nimrod', 'even by painters who had never read the book, nor any other book either'.

Like another book of dissent before it, *The Pilgrim's Progress*, saved and kept alive by the movement of religious dissent against the Establishment, so *The Ragged Trousered Philanthropists* was saved and kept alive by a movement of social and political dissent, the Labour Movement; and particularly the socialists and more particularly the various 'unofficial' anti-war, industrial shop-floor and rank and file movements.

Of literally hundreds of little incidents which have reminded me of Tressell's mysterious subterranean survival among the people, I select these two.

Many years ago I was walking through the Powdermill Woods (part of the old Battle Abbey estate) from the Powdermill Lane on the rather eerie footpath to the Farthing Pond, when a rather strange elderly recluse-type character came out from the trees and spoke to me, of course about the weather and the beautiful woods, while I in turn was noticing a kind of deep faraway expression in his eyes as if he had spent his life in woods and fields reflecting on nature. And I admit I was faintly startled at the sudden confrontation with this character because the newspapers are full of stories of men with staring eyes on lonely paths.

And there we were, looking at each other when without any preamble he suddenly said: 'That's a wonderful book, you know, *The Ragged Trousered Philanthropists*, you ought to read it, everybody ought to read it! It makes you think!'

And I regret to say, I merely said 'Oh yes', and another bit about the weather and as he evidently didn't want to talk but to go on with his meditations, so we parted.

The other concerns the Post Office. A Hastings friend, Harry Pike, visiting Putney, London, sent me a letter in 1954 saying: 'I thought I would see how the Postal Authorities reacted to "Mugsborough" so let me know if you receive this.'

The letter, addressed 'F. C. Ball, 140 (so and so road), Mugsborough, Sussex', reached me in normal time and on the envelope against 'Mugsborough' someone in the London sorting office who signed himself 'W.G.S.' had written 'Try Hastings'.

29

1946: Tressell's handwritten manuscript is found

Back in 1942 when I began collecting anecdotes about Robert, naturally one of the first persons I thought of asking for information was Grant Richards if he were still alive. It took me some time to obtain his address, but in November 1942 he eventually wrote to me, and promised to look through his papers. Early in 1943 I wrote again, having heard nothing, and by this time it had occurred to me to ask about the fate of Robert's original manuscript and whether it could be acquired and preserved for posterity for a modest sum. Richards wrote asking what I meant by a modest sum to which I replied 'about £50'. He wrote again on 7 March saying: 'I can only promise to *try* and get information. The manuscript is not in my possession, but I believe that it might be acquired for the purpose you suggest for something like £50. Is such a thing possible? Think it over and let me know, and in the meantime, but not quickly, I will make enquiries.'

So I went on waiting. I was, of course, thrilled that the letter implied that the manuscript was still in existence, even if he didn't say so outright.

My first thought was to save at least *that*, even if only as a museum-piece and to me the logical place seemed somewhere in the Labour Movement. Hastings wouldn't have been interested and I knew of no Labour or Trade Union historical societies who would or could buy it. In 1943 there seemed no prospect of my being able to buy it so when someone suggested that the Communist Party Museum at Marx House, Clerkenwell, might be interested, I wrote them in June 1943.

But fifty pounds was beyond their pocket too, and in one way I was greatly relieved. I wanted to have the manuscript for a good look at it myself.

Another year went by with further letters from me to Grant Richards. Then on 12 May 1944 he wrote: 'Possess your soul in patience I beg you. I have not got the manuscript or I should have sent it to you to look at. The man who has it is in the forces a month or so away. I have to wait his return, although I *have* (weeks ago) written to him about it. He is not likely to do anything about it till he sees me on his return whenever that may be.'

There was now a long interval until I received a letter dated 13 November 1945 from the RAF Station at Harwell:

Dear Mr. Ball,

Grant Richards has passed on your letter of October 29th to me because I own the manuscript and can put it in your hands if the 'modest sum' agrees with my estimate of its true value.

I'm sorry to disappoint you in this matter. I'm negotiating with an American University which is extremely anxious to secure this amazing and unique manuscript which contains a remarkable (unpublished) introduction or foreword by the author and a considerable amount of matter – deviations from the original plot which has never seen print.

I need hardly tell you that publication of the book in its entirety in serial form in some socialist organisation would be quite practical, stimulating and even remunerative.

Considering the fantastic prices that are being paid in the sale-rooms for trumpery trivialities, and considering that the *typescript* of a novel like *Lost Horizon* has changed hands in America for £250 I do not consider my figure of 300 guineas exorbitant for the manuscript of a book of such epoch-making and world-wide popularity as *The Ragged Trousered Philanthropists*.

As I dislike greatly selling to America, coupled with customs and export fees and regulations; and as I consider that the price I'm asking is extremely reasonable and will some day be regarded as fantastically and absurdly small, I would advise strongly that you 'close' on the deal immediately, before I change my mind.

Having secured the manuscript Mr. Grant Richards could probably provide you with a deal of biographical detail.

Faithfully Yours,
Robert Partridge.

This letter was followed by silence for I didn't reply to it. I couldn't compete with the USA single-handed.

I must confess that had the manuscript been available at any time then I would have been unable to buy it even for fifty pounds. I was really trying to find out whether it was still in existence and hoping that, if it were, something might turn up to enable me to get hold of it. But in 1945 and early 1946, friends of mine who had survived the war began to trickle back from the services with fortunes in Gratuities ranging from twenty to thirty pounds and to some of these I had proposed the idea of forming a small syndicate to buy the manuscript if and when it became available, and five people, four ex-service, agreed that they would put in ten pounds each if called upon. But when we heard that the price was three hundred guineas, we all agreed to shut up shop.

In the meantime something must have been happening in London to Grant Richards and Mr Partridge, for nine months later, on 29 August 1946, a letter from Mr Partridge came out of the blue, claiming that Grant Richards had 'pleaded so ably' on my behalf that he was ready to let me have the manuscript after all for fifty guineas.

Well, fifty guineas wasn't *much* more than fifty pounds.

I had to write immediately to my friends to confirm that our old arrangement would still stand and before I had time to close the deal with Mr Partridge, another letter arrived, saying that he had 'had the dealers in', since he was disposing of his 'collection', and that

> One dealer has offered me £75 for the Tressell manuscript and when I told him it was on offer to you at my first quoted figure he said I must be crazy to let it go at that price – because he wouldn't dream of selling below one hundred pounds at least – hence this offer of £75. Now what am I to do? I feel some sort of moral responsibility in your having the manuscript – since you have angled for it so long – but, unfortunately, I am not a charity institution and there seems no sense in giving money away on purely sentimental grounds.

Now I had again to consult on what price we could offer, so we agreed on sixty pounds and if necessary to raise another shareholder later.

Further, and increasingly querulous, correspondence followed, about where and when we could meet, and just when all seemed to be arranged, I received a final message to say that the price was of course sixty *guineas*.

But at long last on Sunday, 29 September 1946, I actually found myself travelling to London where I met my friend Mr Kelt, who was to meet me there with sixty-three pounds in cash in his pocket, and together we went on to the Elephant and Castle Underground Station where we were to meet Mr Partridge in the station entrance.

After a nerve-racking wait he arrived and the two parties satisfactorily identified each other. To save carrying out this momentous transaction in the street Mr Partridge suggested that we do it in a near-by tea-shop, a far from pretentious one at that, and there upon the little tea-shop table we opened the parcel and set eyes upon the actual handwritten manuscript of *The Ragged Trousered Philanthropists*. And it *was* a large MS. – about nine inches high and consisting of about seventeen hundred quarto sheets, with title-page complete.

We had no doubts of its genuineness – only a prodigiously patient and industrious forger would dream of copying such a work, and besides, there were other marks of genuineness which I shall discuss later, and Kelt and I made an enthusiastic examination of it.

After the three of us had stayed about an hour on two cups of tea each and talking at sixteen to the dozen we began to draw the attention of the proprietor and his staff. So we hurriedly packed up the manuscript and got outside feeling like small boys detected at scrumping apples.

And so in such an unbusinesslike and unceremonious manner we acquired the manuscript of *The Ragged Trousered Philanthropists*.

We had no other immediate plans, in fact we hardly knew what could be done with it, but it was understood by my friends that I needed it for a while because one day I was going to write a biography of Robert Tressell, although I had never written a book in my life. Their confidence which I couldn't tell them I didn't share, was based upon a few poems and a couple of short stories I had written.

I now had to raise the money for four shares to return to Mr and Mrs Kelt who had decided to take two shares each themselves, and these I had no difficulty in raising from among the friends who had originally offered, and for the sake of the record I give the names of the four who subscribed, Peter Blackman, George Jackson, Ernie Bevis and Gregory Gildersleeve, who with the Kelts made possible the saving of the manuscript.

The six shares, we decided, should in fact be called seven, in event of resale at any time, the seventh being allocated to me in consideration of my efforts and expenses in obtaining the manuscript and for its safe custody as it was to be left in my charge. And if this share was in value above my actual expenses, that was all right, they said, the balance could go towards the biography.

I wrote telling Grant Richards that I had acquired the manuscript and he replied to say how delighted he was and although I know nothing of his behind-the-scenes role during the four years I had been trying to find it, nor of his motives, he, too, has his share of credit. And Mr Partridge for selling us the manuscript and that, too, at a reasonable price.

30

How the original manuscript was butchered

When we discovered from examination of the manuscript that such a large part of it, some 40 per cent, or about 100,000 words, had been left out of the Grant Richards first edition and as much as 160,000 words left out of the abridged edition of 1918, we immediately thought that to do justice to Tressell every effort should be made to see whether publication in full was possible.

We also wanted to ensure that it didn't disappear out of sight when we found a permanent home for it. To this end we decided that it should only be sold to a trade union or other working-class organization or to an institution such as a museum, where it would be available for viewing by the general public; and that it must be made available for publication as Tressell wrote it. The question of sale would not, of course, arise in the case of publishers, who would only require to copy the manuscript. I was given the job of trying to find a publisher.

My first thought was that the Richards Press, with whom I supposed Grant Richards still to be connected, were the obvious choice, although why I should imagine that they would be interested when they had their version still selling steadily I really don't know.

Within a month of obtaining the manuscript I wrote to Grant Richards who replied suggesting that we meet and added: 'I should like particularly to help you in the matter of a publisher; it requires careful handling or you may fall into holes; and indeed I have an idea that you or your friends may care to follow up.'

But when we at last managed to meet some six months later he had no definite suggestions to make, and I now believe he was only exploring our intentions. His final letter, of 30 May 1947, says:

My opinion is that there is no obstacle to your using the *unpublished* parts of the book *if* you can get hold of the Tressell heir, but your book, to be effective, would have to include the published parts, which are, of course, controlled by the Richards Press. This should not be very difficult. I have seen the Richards Press – the sooner we can have a look the better.

Of course you could take the risk of no one turning up with claims as heir which would bear investigation – and I don't think there is a great risk.

I didn't understand this letter. Evidently the Richards Press were discussing what to do in the light of our possession of the manuscript and intention to attempt to get it published. But as for a Tressell 'heir', I failed to understand how this had any importance, for I learned that the Richards Press possessed the copyright and Grant Richards knew this and must also have known that this copyright covered the entire manuscript, published and unpublished sections alike.

In any case, what possible 'heir' could he have in mind? He himself had bought the manuscript outright from Kathleen – and Kathleen was dead. Whether he knew this or not (*Tressell of Mugsborough* wasn't yet published) I don't know, although there had been references to it in the Press on occasions for years, but I'm almost certain I told him this in our conversations, and, in the light of subsequent knowledge his silence about Tressell and his daughter becomes even more inexplicable. I conclude he had reasons which to him were of overriding importance. Nothing further came of our correspondence and a year later Grant Richards died.

In 1948 the Associated Society of Woodworkers briefly considered purchasing and publishing the manuscript. Then in July I received an invitation to meet representatives of Messrs Lawrence and Wishart, Birch Books Ltd, Fore Publications Ltd, and Central Books, which resulted in a request from Lawrence and Wishart to be allowed to see the manuscript, and I arranged with my brother to deliver it by hand as I wouldn't trust it to the post. On 8 November I received their verdict:

Unfortunately we have had to reach the decision not to undertake publication. With the number of editions on the market of the expurgated version and especially the number in the Penguin edition that must have been sold, the directors are of opinion that the market has been flooded as far as the ordinary reader goes.

They suggested we might organize publication by subscription or by the raising of a national fund but we would have spent the rest of our lives on this and decided that sooner or later curiosity and publicity would work.

Then in January 1949 I received a letter c/o Hastings Trades and Labour Council from the Porcupine Press Ltd, asking news of my proposed biography and for information about *The Ragged Trousered Philanthropists*. The Director, Arnold Knebel, added that his firm 'would be glad to bring out this complete edition'. But this scheme came to nothing because Knebel felt it would be unable to compete with a current edition being advertised by Secker & Warburg as 'complete and unexpurgated'. (This was in fact a reprint of Grant Richard's original of 1914.)

In the meantime, as a result of increasing publicity, things had been happening in the trade union world. Mr S. Horsfield of the National Society of Painters, as a result of a resolution from the Southern Counties No. 2 District Committee wrote saying that subject to the approval of the General Council the Society was prepared to purchase the manuscript if we could confirm that it was the original.

This was great news although I admit I was a little put out by the requirement about the authenticity of the manuscript. We had heard rumours that some people doubted this. I don't know what they thought our huge document might be.

There followed involved negotiations over the copyright between the Society's solicitors, a solicitor we had been obliged to engage, the Richards Press and others.

A lot of confusion arose because both sides were mystified as to how the Richards Press could own copyright of the unpublished sections of a manuscript of which they didn't even possess a copy, a confusion which wasn't helped by Grant Richards's letter to me already quoted and we even naïvely instructed our solicitor to waive any claim we might have on the unpublished parts when it seemed at one time that the NSP intended to publish the whole. In the end it was established yet again that Richards had purchased the complete copyright of the whole work in 1913 without any reservations and that the unpublished portions could not be published without consent of the Richards Press.

They expressed willingness to come to an arrangement with the NSP as to publication provided their ownership of copyright was recognized, but on 6 February 1950, nine months after the project was first mooted, the Society wrote that in view of the difficulties over the right to publish they had decided not to proceed any further in the matter.

31

The manuscript and the building trades unions

In the meantime in my spare time from meter-reading for the Gas Board, I was writing *Tressell of Mugsborough*, my first book on Robert, and it was finally brought out by Messrs Lawrence & Wishart in October 1951.

It was received on the whole very favourably and reviewed, I believe, in every trade union journal in the country, by the Socialist Press and by many provincial and national newspapers, including *The Times Literary Supplement*.

The publication had other results, too. I had mentioned that I had the original manuscript and facetiously said that callers could read it on my kitchen-table and in fact many scores of people from all over Britain, writers, students, teachers and workers, including a group of miners from the Scottish pits called to do just that. And *Tressell of Mugsborough* once more began to spark off attempts to get *The Ragged Trousered Philanthropists* published as Tressell wrote it.

The first intimation I had was a letter from Mr Harold Smith, a librarian, unknown to me, who wrote enclosing a letter he had written on 29 January 1952 to the Richards Press, proposing the publication of the complete manuscript, and their reply, reiterating their conviction that 'the present text, as edited by Miss Jessie Pope, was the best for general purposes', and raising the additional problem of 'largely increased costs of production which would render the venture commercially impracticable'.

Mr Smith added: 'I have written to Montague Slater with copies of my correspondence and he, I expect, will be taking up the matter from his angle.'

On 17 March 1952 followed a letter from Mr James MacGibbon of MacGibbon and Kee who asked whether he could see the manuscript, which he would arrange through Mr Slater, and either or both would come to Hastings for the purpose.

In April Mr Slater opened his public campaign, as it were, with a letter to *The Times Literary Supplement* setting out the history of *The Ragged Trousered Philanthropists*, the copyright difficulty and the decision of the Richards Press not to publish, and questioning the equity of this decision. This stimulated several published letters of support, including some from prominent trade unionists.

In the meantime on 16 April Lawrence and Wishart wrote saying that the Richards Press seemed now to have in mind bringing out a separate edition containing only the unpublished parts, a proposal which, as Mr Slater commented, would be hardly better than nothing, for the reader would have to hop back and forth between one volume and the other.

I think the idea arose because the Richards Press simply did not know how the manuscript had been edited, for instance largely combed out. They were not, of course, in possession of the full text.

On 22 April they themselves wrote to me asking my views 'as to whether it would at all help the situation if we agreed to publish as a supplement or addendum to the existing text such portion of the complete manuscript as would remove the objections of Mr Slater and others'. It was 'obviously impossible' in their opinion 'to remanufacture the book with Miss Pope's editorial excisions restored'.

To this letter I replied: 'The remainder unpublished is probably 50,000 words in bulk and has been combed out of the full manuscript which I think obviously makes impracticable its publication as an addendum. I don't think it impossible to re-constitute the original and there is surely no doubt that the book is better by far as written than as edited by Miss Pope.'

But the Richards Press had a book in print still selling after forty years, and were little inclined to scrap all their standing type and set up again a much longer book.

Early in May Mr Slater arrived in Hastings to collect the manuscript (we *never* trusted it to the post) and a few days later reported enthusiastically on its superiority. He did, however, suggest that it might be shortened. And he raised once more the question of support from the trade unions. If assured of sufficient support, MacGibbon and Kee were interested in publishing.

We had felt throughout that the Labour Movement could make all the difference to the prospects of publication, by guaranteeing support, even buying a certain number of copies. And in January I had addressed the local Trades Council and had described the manuscript and the copyright position and appealed for a trade union campaign to support publication in full.

Mr Philcox, who as Secretary of the Painters' Union in Hastings, had done so much over the past three years, now led a new agitation in the National Federation of Building Trades Operatives. He wrote to the *Journal* of the NFBTO and also to the General Secretary, Richard Coppock, whose response was discouraging. 'It would be an impossible problem,' he said, 'to try and force people to print manuscripts.'

Despite this cold water we intended to get past the leadership to the Union branch officials and the rank and file, and on 13 March 1952 the local branch obtained permission for me to be called to speak to a Federation Rally in Hastings, with Sir Luke Fawcett, CBE, President, and Sir Richard Coppock, OBE, General Secretary, on the platform as principal speakers. This meeting was a great success and my appeal raised enthusiasm among the audience, and the officials themselves appeared to be sympathetic.

Philcox next suggested that I should produce copies of a resolution to be put before delegates at the National Society of Painters District Committee Annual Conference, in June, and the Annual Conference of the National Federation of Building Trade Operatives at Teignmouth, also in June 1952.

Our resolution said: 'That this Conference welcomes the suggestion to publish the full manuscript of *The Ragged Trousered Philanthropists* as the author originally wrote it, and pledges all support in its power to ensure the success of a full edition.'

The Painters' District Conference representing all branches in Kent and Sussex on 7 June promised to undertake the distribution of an unofficial circular from us at the NFBTO Conference on 16 June.

But there the project encountered more obstacles. Philcox only reported to me that 'Dick Coppock made some startling statements which appeared to smash it', but we were not too discouraged. Over two hundred of our circulars had been distributed throughout the building trades unions of the whole of Britain, and the discussion reached into union branches and Trades Councils.

I have since read the *Report* of the 1952 Annual Conference of the NFTBO, and it is clear that the many confusions among platform and delegates arose not from lack of interest in Tressell, but from lack of familiarity with the ways of the publishing world, and a suspicion, that I have never been able completely to dispel, that I must have had some personal advantage to gain through publication.

After several years of correspondence with trade union officials, neither I nor other union members could convince them that they were *not* financing a venture of mine – I had no rights in the manuscript. Indeed far from owning any copyright in the manuscript I had myself had to pay the Richards Press, the holders of the copyright, for quotations in *Tressell of Mugsborough* even where these were from the unpublished sections.

Suspicions were voiced as to the authenticity of the 'original copy' alleged to be held, according to Sir Richard Coppock, by 'a young man named Ball', references were made to 'salesmanship', and complaints about the danger of buying 'a pig in a poke'. But the Conference was also reminded of the propaganda value of Tressell's book to the whole Trade Union Movement, and the resolution finally carried read: 'That the Executive should pursue the matter of *The Ragged Trousered Philanthropists* further and report.'

By August the NFBTO did in fact circulate branches and member unions to ask how many copies of the proposed edition they could take, and the General Secretary of the National Union of Public Employees had agreed to encourage members of that union to buy it.

But after a long interval the McGibbon and Kee project fell through. We were no nearer publishing.

As late as fifteen months after the Conference the Secretary of the East Ham Branch of the Building Trade Workers wrote to me saying (how often had I heard it?): 'It has been brought to the notice of the Branch that you are endeavouring to secure publication of the full script of *The Ragged Trousered Philanthropists*.'

I was indeed.

32

Publication in full, foreign editions and translations

Since the publication of *Tressell of Mugsborough* Messrs Lawrence and Wishart, too, had revived their interest in the manuscript, and on 30 July 1952 I received a letter from them saying that they had had a discussion about *The Ragged Trousered Philanthropists* at a Directors' meeting, and were again seriously considering the publication of the complete version.

Maurice Cornforth, James MacGibbon, Montague Slater and I met in the Lawrence and Wishart offices to discuss the whole matter, but *another year* of agitation and letter-writing passed before at last on 9 December 1953 Maurice Cornforth wrote to say that the Directors had 'decided that we proceed as quickly as possible with the full unexpurgated edition subject to your being willing to let us use the manuscript and to our reaching an agreement with the Richards Press'.

This time we really were off the floor because in the same letter Maurice arranged that he would himself collect the MS. from Hastings.

It was arranged that I should act as 'editor'. The period of 'unrestricted copyright', of twenty-five years, that is, when no one but the copyright-holder may publish, was long over, and the position now was that Lawrence and Wishart could publish without the permission of the Richards Press but would have to pay them a royalty until the full fifty-year period, which dates from first publication or the author's death, expired in 1964.

It was *another year* before the typescript was complete and checked, and in December 1954 it went to the printers. There had been many queries arising out of the original text and I had made two drafts of it, before, with the help of Maurice, we agreed on what the form of Tressell's original really was, and most of these are discussed in my account of the reconstitution.

In the meantime support was still being canvassed in the unions, particularly from Sir Richard Coppock, and many unions allowed their branches to be circularized with the fifty thousand circulars Lawrence and Wishart had printed.

The book at last appeared on 6 October 1955, nine years after we began the struggle for publication.

The full first print was five thousand, of which a library edition of fifteen hundred in hard covers was priced at thirty shillings and sold out in two months, and a 'trade union' edition of thirty-five hundred in cloth at ten shillings and sixpence sold out in less than three months.

The dust-cover was by Jim Lucas and showed on a red background a house-painter in white coat and apron, carrying a painter's kettle, with simple overprint 'The Ragged Trousered Philanthropists, Robert Tressell', in black lettering.

The foreword, unsigned, was by Jack Beeching and Maurice Cornforth based upon material supplied by me. The facing title-page carried Gower's portrait of Robert, and the list of contents was prefaced with a facsimile of Robert's own title-page, drawn by himself.

It was widely reviewed and inevitably comparisons were made with the Richards version, most reviewers agreeing that Robert's own was far superior, although a few preferred the 'tidier' and less digressive Jessie Pope abridgement.

Extracts from reviews in *The Times Literary Supplement* of editions over the next few years, give some illustration of the book's gradual acceptance in literary circles.

On 22 February 1952 it had said of the Richards version, 'It is not a book of genius but it has talent.'

On 1 March 1957 it said of Robert's original:

> Tressell was a literary artist and knew precisely what he was doing. The long half-baked speeches on politics, anti-capitalism and the hope of the workers are all moving and tell the reader more about the rise of the British Labour Party, its instincts, traditions and future, than all the fireworks of Bernard Shaw or the blueprints of the Webbs.
>
> But it is as a story and a work of art that *The Ragged Trousered Philanthropists* has lasted so far – and will continue to last. [The characters] are far too alive to be swamped by anything. It is true that it is because what Noonan recorded was sober fact that we are

still bedevilled in labour relations. Robert Noonan's book is the voice of the poor themselves.

I wrote to *The Times Literary Supplement* about this review saying that 'This is the second occasion* that the book has reached the portals of English literature, and one may hope that this time it will gain admittance.'

Again on 28 May 1964 the same paper said, 'It is one of those books which, while not great, have so inherent a toughness as to be seemingly indestructible. The secret of [its] endurance is its art and truth.'

Lawrence and Wishart have reprinted the book six times to date from the original standing type, all in hardback, in 1956, 1959, 1962, 1966, 1968 and 1971, and it is still selling steadily year after year.

In addition in 1965 Panther Books brought out a paperback edition in their Panther Classics series with an introduction by Alan Sillitoe, and this has been reprinted four times to date, in 1967, 1968, 1971 and 1973, once as a special edition for the BBC Television dramatization of the book (in 1967) using for the cover a colour still from the play. It has become one of the steadiest sellers in the Panther Classics series.

Today, the book is not only recognized in Britain, but known in many corners of the world.

Back in March 1952 the Russian popular magazine *Ogonyok* had printed in Russian Chapter Two of the Richards version – 'Nimrod: A Mighty Hunter before the Lord'–with an introduction by Ralph Parker, an account of Robert's life taken from my book, and illustrations, the first ever illustrations of *The Ragged Trousered Philanthropists*. I thought them very good re-creations from Tressell's physical descriptions, especially that of Hunter.

This must have aroused considerable interest, for in 1957 the Russian Foreign Languages Publishing House, Moscow, printed the complete Lawrence and Wishart edition in English for Russian English language students, with a foreword in Russian.

It also contains an extremely interesting not to say comical glossary of English idioms and slang, and I wished I could read Russian, for I would love to know what Russians made of 'knowed', and 'runned,' and 'bilin' ', and 'penny 'orribles', and 'hot 'un', and 'no 'ead for', and 'hinjoy', and 'gorn', and 'get that acrost yer', and 'doos', and 'wotcher', and 'middlin' sudden', and 'dead nuts', and 'flummoxed',

---

*Meaning the Richards version was the first.

and 'dror', and 'a fine to do', and 'see-ize'. and 'tuneropperty', and 'arf a mo', and 'touch 'im for an allowance', and 'it aint arf all right', and 'orf' is onion', and 'mishneries', and 'kimmicles', and 'tiddley bits' – and a hundred other home-made renderings of our mother tongue.

In 1958 the German Democratic Republic published a translation by Lore Krüger into German under the title *Die Menschenfreunde in zerlumpten Hosen*. This edition, too, carried a short glossary of names and a longish account of Robert's life and the finding and publishing of the full MS. by Günther Klotz.

In 1961 it was translated into the Czech language by Přeložila Dagmar Knittlová under the title *Lidumilove v hadrech* with a short foreword and an account (in Czech) of Tressell's place in English Literature by Ian Milner, in both of which, someone called F.C.Balla and F.C.Ballovi seems to be me in different guises.

In 1962, Monthly Review Press USA brought out a small edition – a reprint of the Lawrence and Wishart.

In 1964 it was translated into Bulgarian. And early in 1971 a translation by Mr T. Hironaka appeared in Japanese entitled (in Japanese) *Mugsborough*. Mr Hironaka, who is, I believe, a Japanese schoolmaster, had been writing to me for four years about his project.

And I have just had news that it is now being translated into Swahili, I believe in Tanzania, and M.Portal of Vincennes University, Paris, is planning to translate it into French, and Lawrence and Wishart have in mind an adaptation for schools.

Many years ago there was talk in Israel of translating it into Hebrew but there's been no further news of this, and Frank Swinnerton in *The Adventures of a Manuscript* says that the Poles have a translation but I have never heard of it. There were also rumours some years back that it was being used as an English textbook in Peking University, and Kathleen said that the book was part of the set reading for her cousin's child in her matriculation course in Australia.

In 1956 the Richards Press brought out a limited edition of a pamphlet by Frank Swinnerton called *The Adventures of a Manuscript* which quoted the Richards Correspondence (which I had not yet seen) and disclosed important information, as we shall see, which Richards had withheld from me.

The only books to date on Tressell's life are my own *Tressell of Mugsborough* published by Lawrence and Wishart in 1951, and this present book.

The Ragged Trousered Philanthropists is receiving more critical attention as time goes by from English scholars and critics, and has been the subject of studies in the German Democratic Republic, Rumania and Canada (Brian Mayne in *20th Century Literature*, 1967) to my knowledge, and a number of British university students have taken the book as the subject for a degree thesis.

The first full-length critical study in book form is Jack Mitchell's *Robert Tressell and The Ragged Trousered Philanthropists*, published in 1969 by Lawrence and Wishart.

33

How the mutilated manuscript
was reconstituted

When my wife and I began reconstituting the manuscript from its
mutilated form we first had to decide whether there were enough
indications to tell us what its original form was.

We had a mass of loose sheets in two parcels, consisting of a title-page
drawn by the author entitled:

'The Ragged Trousered Philanthropists'

and sub-titled

'Being the story of twelve months in
Hell, told by one of the damned, and
written down by Robert Tressell',

an unfinished preface of five pages, not numbered in the sequence and
left out by Jessie Pope, five pages of a list of contents, a number of
hand-drawn diagrams, a number of loose pages with chapter headings
and 1,674 pages numbered in sequence but not packed so, making a
total of some 1,700 handwritten quarto sheets.

There was some variation in the handwriting, some being small,
neat and uniform as if written carefully, some in apparently the same
hand but larger and more erratic having the appearance of being
written in haste or under strain – almost like the writing of an old man.
Some of it seemed to be in another hand, perhaps Kathleen's, as it
somewhat resembled the handwriting of her entry in Rose Cruttenden's autograph-book.

There were many differences between it and Grant Richards's
versions. The parts he published had been assembled and the remainder
parcelled separately and the whole was in a somewhat damaged condition. Some pages were cut through with scissors, a few were missing
altogether and the manuscript was liberally sprinkled with the first

editor's alterations of the text. Many pages were paraphrased or summarized on separate sheets by Jessie Pope and in some cases she had
pasted stiff card over Tressell's original. (She wrote to Grant Richards
about her work with scissors and paste-pot.)

The list of contents was undoubtedly in Tressell's hand and numbered fifty-five chapters, but one of these, entitled 'Mugsborough'
was an unfinished fragment numbered separately and as the rest,
excepting the preface, had been numbered in sequence and apparently
in his hand, it looked as though Tressell had omitted it and the unfinished preface and these probably only found their way to Grant
Richards because Robert had left them in when he had finally put away
his manuscript.

This seems to leave only fifty-four chapters but he had organized
his book into chapters pinned and titled separately and of those few
remaining untouched by Jessie Pope was one entitled Chapter 55 –
'The End', the final chapter of the full edition. If the numbering in
sequence *is* Tressell's own it would seem that he didn't renumber his
list of contents. His method of attaching separate title-sheets to chapters
instead of heading the first page of each made it almost impossible to
decide just where he intended chapters to begin and end and since most
of his title-sheets were unpinned and separated from the chapter by
Jessie in her editing we could only judge the subject-matter of each
chapter by reference to his list of contents, with very curious results.

According to this chapters varied in length from seven to ninety
pages of manuscript.

We decided that the numbering of pages in sequence was Tressell's
own and organized the chapters from the list of contents. If the numbering were not his this may not represent his final arrangement but
when finally put together it made sense and had a logical progression.
And we couldn't go merely by the loose title-sheets as some, evidently
his own, used Roman numerals with titles, as in his list of contents,
while others – which we took to be Jessie Pope's – were in Arabic and
untitled.

Having got the shape of the book we now had to restore Tressell's
original text in all those places where the editor had altered it. In some
places where she had pasted stiff card over the original we steamed
Tressell's pages off the card with the aid of the kitchen kettle. In other
cases, where we found this was damaging his original, we left the card
on and read his text from the back with the aid of a hand-mirror and

copied it out. In restoring the cut pages, many parts of which were taken out and stuck in other parts of the manuscript, we had to search many times to find exactly where the pieces had come from, and sometimes this was only possible by matching the two edges left by her scissors.

In addition there were certain irregularities in Tressell's grammar and punctuation, such as his disregard of the hyphen, which the editor had 'corrected', and in many places Jessie had rendered his dialogue more 'illiterate' by adding or omitting aitches. She also cut out a lot of the swearing.

Tressell's inconsistencies are interesting – and almost unaccountable. For instance, the abbreviation of 'perhaps' was sometimes written 'p'raps', sometimes 'praps'; 'there's' sometimes 'ther's' and sometimes 'thers'. In many places he wrote 'doesn't', 'haven't', 'mustn't', etc. as 'does'nt', 'have'nt', 'must'nt', and 'aint' as 'ain't'. He mispelled 'trestle' sometimes as 'tressel' sometimes as 'tressell'.

In the use of capitals, too, he was inconsistent, sometimes spelling words like 'poverty' and 'idlers' with capitals, sometimes not.

It was decided with the publishers to correct all these for the sake of uniformity and the reader, and even so many escaped us.

Finally, the manuscript contained passages completely blocked out with ink, generally where the men are exchanging lurid stories, and they looked very much like Tressell's own erasures, probably done when he came to the point of sending the book to publishers or perhaps after it had been rejected.

We decided that he wrote them in as an integral part of his picture of working-class life and had removed them for other than moralistic or squeamish reasons, and we would restore them in accordance with his original intention. Fortunately, although they were thickly blocked out, we were able with difficulty to read them against a strong light. Having got our manuscript back to its original form we could get a clear idea of its length and of the structural and thematic alterations made in the Richards version.

It is hardly the million words that Grant Richards estimated in his *Author Hunting* – a gross miscalculation for a publisher – or the 500,000 quoted by some reviewers, evidently from a publicity handout.

In a letter to Richards on 12 April 1914, Jessie Pope referring to an interview in the *Daily Sketch* says: 'I didn't say the book was 500,000 words originally, as I thought it was about 250,000.' About 250,000 is right.

Strangely, the handwritten alterations closely resemble the writing of Grant Richards, but I presume they must be Jessie Pope's.

Jessie mentions something of her editorial intentions in a letter to Richards on 29 October 1913, which are a little at variance with her statement in her preface where she says: 'In reducing a large mass of manuscript to the limitations of book form it has been my task to cut away superfluous matter and repetition only. The rest practically remains as it came from the pen of Robert Tressall, house-painter and sign-writer. . . .'

In the letter she says:

> On going through the m.s. again I find the last few chapters are in my opinion the weakest part of the book and with your permission I should like to cut out all that matter about Ruth's intrigue with Slyme. It is not that I think the public will be offended at the sordidness of the story – I suppose they have put up with many worse ones – but the long-drawn-out description of Ruth's misfortunes, the birth of the baby, the description of Easton's and Owen's attitude regarding the affair in fact the whole of that particular part of the narrative is written in a melancholy maudlin manner far below the standard of other parts of the book.
>
> I think the book would gain if it could all be cut out. My idea is to make Ruth resent Slyme's advances on the night when she returns from the public house, as I think she certainly would have done – all her former feeling of repulsion would return when he embraced her – and that could be sufficient reason for her leaving Easton's house – as she did shortly afterwards. Perhaps you will let me hear from you as soon as possible on the matter, as I am approaching that part of the story with scissors and paste-pot.

In the separate parcel we discovered what she had cut. The 'sordid' story of Ruth – her seduction by Slyme, her own and her husband's revulsion, their parting and Owen's defence of Ruth and blaming of the husband, Easton, the latter's resentment of Owen's home-truths, the reconciliation, the adoption of the child by the Owens, in fact the whole of the working out of this story is gone – the very part which shows, and is intended to show, a deeper humanity. What Jessie had left in was almost beside the point. And although Robert writes with the sentiments of the time, his treatment cannot be called maudlin merely because he makes men overcome personal and social prejudice and makes love and humanity triumph. I see the episode in fact as necessary to the whole intention of the book.

Another omission which interfered with the author's intentions was the cutting of the middle-class character Barrington, important artistically and politically to the author's case, particularly in showing that the working class have allies among the best sections of the educated classes.

It is Barrington who gives moral support in Owen's isolation, and in the original himself makes 'the Great Oration' or exposition of Tressell's socialism, and who is the subject of one or two delightful episodes. Barrington can speak with more authority than Owen, who is often abashed by his fellow workers' hostility (who does he think he is!), but Barrington is used to show that even an educated man and a 'gentleman' can see the need for socialism.

Barrington is part of Tressell's answer (this is brought out specifically where Barrington answers the crook Alderman Grinder at the 'Annual Beano Dinner') to the anti-socialist propaganda that only fools, cranks and illiterates could be 'taken in' by socialism.

He is also a tribute to those many educated men who, not only in the early Socialist Movement but throughout modern history, fought for the betterment of the common people. And he is an autobiographical echo of part of Robert's own character and background.

The other main structural alteration not merely altered the story but the shape and purpose of the book. This was the alteration in the ending where Jessie Pope brings forward from Chapter 34 – 'The Beginning of the End', the episode of Owen's lung haemorrhage and his horror of dying and leaving his wife and child to the merciless world of exploitation and poverty in the midst of the 'Christian Wolves', and his wild speculation about taking them with him.

This chapter is only an episode about half-way through the book, but the implied murder and suicide form the finish of Grant Richards's versions, as if this were the logical end of such idealistic socialistic misfits or of the working classes themselves. Many critics have defended her alterations of text and structural mutilations in the name of artistic and/or professional necessity, and while she did have a difficult task and may be excused textual excisions, the alteration of the ending is inexcusable. One should not for any reason alter any artist's intention and I believe she wouldn't have dared in the case of any but what she and Richards believed to be a working-class writer who had no educated family, agent or lawyers to look after his reputation.

It is little better than lying about a man, whatever one's opinion about his book. It is also lying about the nature of the record of his life and times he left behind him.

All through the book her 'scissors and paste-pot' had made subtle shifts of emphasis in Tressell's themes and in Owen's character, unintentional and not malicious, I believe, because she simply didn't understand. And her ending changes Owen's humanity and moral stature, bringing him finally to personal despair and moral cowardice (he wasn't shown by Tressell as either unbalanced or capable of murder). And it is at direct variance with the declaration in the preface, and I may be wrong about it being unintentional.

I have been told that no other publisher of the day would have published even a version of it, and certainly the Labour Movement wouldn't or couldn't even in serial form in journal or newspaper; but in my view Richards's credit rests in the long run on the fact that his publication probably saved the original manuscript – which in the light of Kathleen's subsequent history could so easily have been lost, leaving our literature the poorer.

Jessie Pope's pessimistic conclusions about the fate of man may well be correct; but we are in fact still here and still dreaming, and the artist and the humanist in Tressell (and he knew what pessimism meant) believed we would be, and for that I must claim that he was more true to life than Jessie.

Many socialists would claim that either consciously or unconsciously her ending shows a profound distrust of socialism as a social revolution, and of its chief agents, the working classes. Alternatively, and I don't discount this, she wanted to hammer home the apparently hopeless situation of large sections of the poverty-stricken and the extreme insecurity of their lives, and possibly to make no concessions to what she may have considered false hopes. She and Richards have been both criticized and defended ever since, but I think finally they must be given great credit, in the commercial publishing conditions of the day, for saving the book as they undoubtedly did.

34

The Ragged Trousered Philanthropists on stage

Books had played their part in bringing socialist propaganda to large sections of the people, particularly of course books like Blatchford's *Merrie England*, which achieved a mass sale, but these were mostly polemical non-fiction.

But before the First World War we had nothing in the novel to compare with the work of the Americans Jack London and Upton Sinclair, both of whom were widely read and had a deep influence among the rank and file of the Socialist Movement in Britain. While Tressell was writing *The Ragged Trousered Philanthropists* it could be said that they were the most borrowed novelists on the whole scene. London's *People Of The Abyss* (1903), and *The Iron Heel* (1907) for instance, and Sinclair's *The Jungle* (1906), were recognized as required reading.

It was the 1918 edition of *The Ragged Trousered Philanthropists* which for the first time brought an English novel into the field as a mass propaganda weapon. There had always been some socialists, such as William Morris, who saw the role of literature and the arts not as confined to political propaganda but as vital in eradicating the intellectual and cultural poverty in the lives of the working classes. And many had recognized that to do this socialist literature and art should be based upon the lives and experience of the working classes themselves. Some hoped to see this idea brought to the Theatre* and thus it was that Tom Thomas of the Workers' Theatre Movement was the first to bring Tressell's book to the stage.

Thomas's dramatization was, in Mark Cheney's words, 'a definite milestone in the history of the workers' theatre'. Cheney describes

*I am indebted here and in the following pages to Mr. L. A. Jones of Leipzig University for an account of the early attempts to form a Workers' Theatre, in his Thesis, 'The British Workers' Theatre 1917–1935'.

its performance by the Hackney WTM, of which he was a member.

> First produced in November 1927 in just over three weeks – the first scenes being put into rehearsal while the others were being written – it attained great popularity. . . .
>
> I shall never forget the show we did at Braintree – we rolled up to the Town Hall in a coach provided by the Labour Town Council, who gave us a right royal welcome and incidentally a high tea, and then we all paraded the town with bell, book and candle, with leaflets and posters, and the audience literally crammed the hall. . . .
>
> Although this play was direct and open propaganda, we managed to penetrate the Labour clubs and institutes round London and when one considers the significant fact that we had to compete with the usual club turns and the beer-swillers, who sometimes left hurriedly before ten to get their drinks, it is surprising the success we managed to maintain with these honest-to-God working-class audiences.
>
> It is due, no doubt, to the fact that the humour was typical working class, the homeliness of the dialogue with the fifteen 'bloodys' allowed us by the censor (which we expended in the first two scenes and sprinkled a few more for good measure) won their attention and support.
>
> We also did many shows for strikers who were particularly impressed by the 'Join the Union' appeal at the end; and at one historic show at the Hackney Manor Hall for the first Hunger Marchers, who marched into the hall to the stirring music of a drum and fife band during the first scene of the play, we cheered with the rest of the audience and started the show over again for their benefit.

The play was published in 1928 by the Labour Publishing Company. Thomas, who didn't know, of course, in 1927, that the tragic ending of the novel was Jessie Pope's distortion, 'grasped Tressell's real intentions', says Jones in his Thesis, and in his play of four acts and seven scenes he finishes with Philpot, at one of Owen's dinner-time 'lectures', putting a resolution in favour of socialism and joining the union, and a great shout of 'Aye!' goes up with the audience being appealed to as the 'body' of the meeting. This conveyed enthusiasm to the audiences, says Jones, 'badly needed after the defeat and betrayal of the General Strike'.

Jones has no information about other performances of *The Ragged Trousered Philanthropists* outside London and says that other WTM groups don't seem to have done the obvious thing and staged this success, but I'm sure that it *was* played. I have a letter from Mr Fred Spencer of Stockport, Cheshire, telling me that he produced it for the Stockport Labour Dramatic Society in February 1929.

In 1936, the Richards Press published a revised version of Thomas's play and Tom Thomas himself wrote to me in September 1948 saying that it was still being played.

Unity Theatre produced a new dramatization on 27 May 1949 and I was invited to be present with the manuscript for the first night. The play, an adaptation by Frank Rhodes, was performed in the following years all over the country by Unity's Mobile Theatre Players, who visited Hastings on a memorable evening sponsored by the Hastings Trades and Labour Council.

When the night arrived, 18 December 1953, and a bad night, a week before Christmas, 730 people who paid for admission and some pensioners and youngsters who didn't, saw the play and gave it an enthusiastic reception and bought twenty-one copies of *The Ragged Trousered Philanthropists* and twenty-nine copies of my *Tressell of Mugsborough*.

In my personal experience the greatest success of Tressell on the stage was at a great Labour Party Rally at the Dome, Brighton, organized by the Brighton, Hove and District Trades Council and the Brighton Council of Labour, on Friday evening, 1 May 1953, at which Hugh Gaitskell was the main speaker.

The Trades Council wanted to 'put over a real Trade Union message' as they described it and decided to present the scene 'The Great Money Trick' from *The Ragged Trousered Philanthropists* and possibly lead from that to the finale of the election meeting.

The Council decided to approach a local dramatic group, The Compton Theatre Club, Brighton, and asked me to write some introductory and linking material. My idea was to write in a Tory interrupter at the end of the scene as the actors took their curtain and this was agreed.

On the night there was a big audience – the Dome seats about two thousand – and after preliminaries the play was introduced and the curtain rose. The amused audience watched the 'workers' being fiddled in the 'Great Money Trick' of capitalist production and distribution of wealth, portrayed by Robert's manipulation of ha'pennies, penknives and slices of bread, and at the end singing 'For he's a jolly good fellow' to the boss and proposing that he 'would allow them to elect him to Parliament' to 'represent' them.

The first curtain came down on this scene to great applause and rose again but this time our secret interrupter, a young actor planted in the stalls, could be seen on his feet shouting and waving his arms. The audience stopped and the actors stared. What was this fellow on about? 'Rubbish!' he shouted in the voice of a theatrical aristocrat. 'Rubbish! What has all this got to do with us? It's fifty years out of date!'

Before anyone might take it into his head to throw something at the fellow, Owen, the chief character in the sketch, stepped forward and said with a slight air of aggrievement, 'Ladies and Gentlemen, actors don't usually have to argue the merits of a play besides acting it. I'm no politician but it struck me while we were rehearsing Tressell's scene that we're still having the Great Money Trick worked on us in 1953! I'll try and tell the gentleman what it means.' And he proceeded to explain what he thought it meant but the audacity of the interrupter and his supercilious upper-class English voice had proved too much for a Welsh lady in the front balcony. She suddenly jumped up, interrupting the actor's sweet reasonableness, and leaned over shaking her fist at the young gentleman. 'You don't know anything about it!' she cried, 'I come from Merthyr Tydfil and you want to go to the Rhondda Valley and you'd find out what it means!' and she proceeded to make a passionate defence of socialism and the working class and Welsh miners and after a few minutes of rapt attention the audience broke into acclamation and the young man subsided, no doubt wishing he could declare himself and join the actors on stage.

It was left to the leader himself to bring the excited audience down. 'What can be done?' he orated from the stage just vacated by Robert's damned. And he provided his own anti-climactic answer: 'Vote for us!'

35

A dramatic development and
a new search

I was quite unprepared for the next development in the Tressell story although perhaps I should not have been in view of the mystery about his origin.

It will be remembered that I was given three different accounts of this. Mr Ward had told me of a birthplace in Cleveland Street, off the Tottenham Court Road, and given me the date 1870, and I had actually obtained a certificate of baptism for a Robert Noonan, son of Timothy, born 5 December 1868 in the Parish of St James, Spanish Place.

Then, Mr Ogilvy of Johannesburg, South Africa, had told me that Robert came from Liverpool and was the son of an Inspector in the Royal Irish Constabulary. And finally, Robert's niece had produced her story that Robert was the son of a gentleman, probably an officer of high rank in the army and was born in Dublin.

None of these accounts had I been able to verify and I published *Tressell of Mugsborough* unable to say who Robert Tressell really was, even though I had found a record of the death and burial in Liverpool of a Robert Noonan whom I felt certain was the man. And then years afterwards came this new development.

In April 1956, following the conclusion between Lawrence and Wishart and the Richards Press of an agreement about the copyright of *The Ragged Trousered Philanthropists*, I received through the courtesy of Mr Martin Secker copies of the correspondence between Jessie Pope and Grant Richards, some of which I have already quoted.

One may guess my amazement when I read in the letter dated 28 August 1913, from Jessie Pope to Richards: 'I have advised Miss Croker to accept your offer.'

Miss Croker? Who was Miss Croker?

Jessie's letter dated 3 November, in which she describes the interview with Kathleen establishing that Robert really was a house-painter, explains:

> She – the nurse – came round to see me yesterday and after requesting a private interview began 'I think Miss Pope I had better tell you all about it – My great-grandfather* was Sir Samuel Croker.' I told her it didn't matter what her great-grandfather was – so long as her father earned his living as a house-painter and really lived among the scenes he described and suffered the privations of an 'out of work'. After a good deal of beating about the bush she admitted, that from the age of 16 to 43, when he died, he *had* earned his living in that way, only she was anxious to put it as sign-writing and graining as well as house-painting. Whether or no there is much foundation to the claims of a knight in the family a few generations back – I don't know – I am inclined to think that, being of rather a romantic turn of mind, the girl was anxious to impress me – though she afterwards remarked that she wished to make no claim to the relationship when I suggested that some of her relations – the Crokers – would probably acknowledge her.
>
> The literary house-painter was really named 'Noonan' or 'Croker' I can't be sure which. His daughter is 'Noonan' yet I believe you know her as 'Croker'. I suppose it doesn't matter anyhow.

'Noonan' or 'Croker?' So *this* explained perhaps why Jessie had given no clues in her preface – she herself didn't know who he was.

And then I remembered that Robert's niece had told me: 'I do not at all rule out the possibility that Robert did *not* take his father's real name. He was very secretive and entirely cut himself off from his family.'

My first reaction was a mixed one. Both Grant Richards and Robert's niece could have told me this more than ten years earlier, for both knew it, but neither said a word and allowed me to go on looking for Robert 'Noonan'. But then, of course, the author had been known as, and had called himself, Robert Noonan and his daughter had signed herself 'Kathleen Noonan' in the autograph-book so in my researches into his *life* I would have been looking for the wrong name had I asked about Robert Croker. But for my research into his *origins*, birth and family, I had been looking for the wrong man.

If anything, although I had doubted his working-class origin since his niece's story, this new disclosure that my famous working-class

---

*Kathleen believed Sir Samuel Croker was her grandfather, not great-grandfather.

writer was the son of a gentleman after all, added to my sympathy for his predicament. In particular, it threw a new light on his isolation, his sense of despair and futility which the workers as a class didn't share. And, of course, there was the new hope that at long last I should clear up the mystery of his identity. It would be simple to establish the background and family record of a titled man. That's what I thought.

But a check in *Burke* and *Debrett* only showed that no such person as Sir Samuel Croker or any other titled Croker, or for that matter Noonan, was recorded in either. I next searched at Somerset House for birth and death certificates of both Robert and his father but found nothing.

In the meantime I had written to Dublin and a little later received a birth certificate for one Robert Croker, son of Samuel Croker, 'Pensioner' and Mary Croker, *nee* Noonan, born on 18 April 1870 at Wexford Street, No. 3 South City District, Dublin. As I was at that time preparing a shortened version of *Tressell of Mugsborough*, Lawrence and Wishart kindly paid fares to Dublin for my wife and myself, where we made straight for the Genealogical Office, Dublin Castle. Here, too, preliminary searches yielded no information of a Samuel Croker and family. We paid out of our limited resources three pounds as a first instalment for further search and went on to the Customs House where are kept the registers of births, deaths and marriages.

There we checked the birth certificates for Robert and searched for those of his two reputed sisters, Alice and Adelaide. And sure enough, although we could find nothing about Alice Croker, we came upon an entry for Adelaide Anne Croker, born 20 March 1867, at 53 Lower Wellington Street, Dublin North, father, Samuel Croker, 'Military Pensioner', mother, Mary Croker.

We would now take up some of the other threads. Robert had left home, his relative said, because upon the death of his father, his mother remarried and squandered the family fortune. We could look up the entry of his father's death, and with the discovery 'Military Pensioner' the search narrowed considerably. Then, of course, if he were a man of standing, there might be an obituary in some of the newspapers of the time, and we could search Army Pensions Lists and discover his rank, regiment, service, etc. And since he was said to have been able to speak and write in Greek, we could soon find out where a gentleman of such standing had been educated.

Our first disappointment came when we failed to discover any record of Samuel's death, and a still greater, when it was confirmed for us that there had been no such person as the alleged grandfather Sir Samuel Croker, neither was there a Lord Croker.

So we concentrated on the search to identify Robert's father, Samuel, and this was a far more complicated business than we had supposed it could be. Where would one find out about a man when neither the registers at Customs House, Dublin, nor those at Somerset House, London, mentioned his name?

We turned to *Thom's Directory* for 1870, to have a look for 37 Wexford Street, where Robert was born, only to discover that in 1870 it was tenanted by a Dr Daly, and that there was no mention of the Crokers. So we looked up the names index under 'Croker' and found that a Samuel Croker, the only one shown, was living in 1870 at 1 Winslow Terrace, Rathgar, Dublin – and was described as 'Samuel Croker, R.M.'.

If this was our Samuel Croker, why should his son Robert be born at Wexford Street? Had Dr Daly some kind of nursing-home there, and had Mrs Croker gone in as a patient for the birth? There was no means of knowing. We did, however, go along to 37 Wexford Street. We took a photograph and made inquiries at one or two shops as to the history of the place and were informed that in 1870, No. 37 was most probably some kind of lodging- or boarding-house.

There for a moment we were stuck, so we went back to the job of identifying the Samuel Croker listed in the directory of householders as the Samuel Croker of the birth certificate. We had only the old clues of 'Pensioner', 'Military Pensioner', and the new clue shown in the directory, 'Samuel Croker, R.M.' To us, 'R.M.' immediately suggested 'Royal Marines', and we assumed that Samuel had been a member of the Garrison Forces in Ireland, had married an Irishwoman, and upon retirement had settled down in Dublin, where his name first appears in *Thom's Directory* in 1862. But no Samuel was to be found among the military appointments (also recorded in *Thom's*) although there was a Surgeon-Major Arthur Croker. Then someone told us that R.M. probably meant 'Resident Magistrate'; and sure enough there was our Samuel Croker, R.M., featured year by year back to 24 December 1838, when he was appointed. And a footnote revealed that he had been appointed from the position of Inspector, Royal Irish Constabulary.

It had been said that Samuel had died during Robert's childhood, and that his mother had remarried, so we began again. Samuel seemed to have had a number of changes of address in Dublin since 1862, previously to which his duties had taken him to many districts of Ireland, but in 1874 he disappeared from the directory and a Mrs I. Croker took his place at 1 Winslow Terrace, Rathgar. We concluded that Samuel died in 1873/4 and that his widow was left, but the initial 'I.' worried us. His wife's name was given as Mary Croker on Robert's birth certificate.

And when we checked the registers for Samuel's death we could find no record of it either in 1874 or in any other year and here I might add that neither could we later find it recorded at Somerset House. And to make it more baffling we could find no entry of the remarriage of Mary Croker, if indeed she had remarried, neither could we find the entry of her death.

The Crokers seemed to have vanished after 1870, so far as the registers were concerned. So we set about looking for a will. But again there was no record of a will at the Public Records Office, Dublin, and neither did we find any at Somerset House. This meant that we were without the corroborative evidence of his relationship with Robert, such as a mention of him in the will might have given us; and we still had no line at all on the 'Sir' Samuel Croker, reputed father of Samuel. Neither had we obtained any information about Robert's alleged sister, Alice.* We decided while still in Dublin to make a search of schools in the hope of finding something about Samuel's school life but we discovered that our visit coincided with the summer holidays, and although we visited a number of schools, we found them closed!

We returned to England leaving our three pounds at the Genealogical Office, Dublin Castle for a six-hour search period, and after reaching home we waited expectantly for a couple of weeks for the report. Eventually it arrived, consisting of a single document here given in full.

CROKER

The preliminary geneaological investigation which has been carried out has not revealed any conclusive evidence of the identity or parentage of Robert Noonan (or Croker) but details in two deeds would appear to merit careful consideration. By a conveyance, dated

*This Alice was in fact the niece.

August 11th, 1873, Samuel Croker, of 1 Winslow Terrace, Rathgar, demised to Mary Anne Noonan, of 38 Besborough Avenue, North Strand, Dublin, spinster, a house at No. 145 Great Britain Street, in the tenancy of Robert Johnston at an annual fee farm rent of £27. 13s. 10¼d. (reg. August 16th, 1873. 1873. 30. 78). On August 17th, 1874, a memorial of a Family Settlement, dated June 2nd, 1874, was registered. The parties to this settlement were:

Samuel Croker, retired Resident Magistrate, of London.

Jane Usher Croker, 1 Winslow Terrace, Rathgar, Dublin, his wife.

Annie Croker, 1 Winslow Terrace, his daughter.

Surgeon-Major Arthur Croker, of Queenstown, Co. Cork, his eldest son.

John Croker, 74 Berkley Street, Liverpool, his second son.

Samuel Croker, of Parsontown, King's Co., his third son.

Melian Jane Millington, wife of Richard Millington, 109 Belgrave Road, Birmingham, his daughter.

This deed is an assignment in trust and confirmation of Deeds of Annuity and conveyance and relates to Irvine Castle, premises at Great Britain Street and Winslow Terrace, household furniture and effects and pensions of £400 and £36.10s.

It also records that Samuel Croker 'granted one Mary Noonan an annuity of £100 payable out of his pension'. (1874. 33. 90.) Neither Deed contains any reference to a relationship between Samuel Croker and Mary Noonan but it is clear that Samuel Croker, the Resident Magistrate, was providing for a Mary Noonan in the first place by a grant of a house yielding a yearly rent and in the second place by an annuity of £100. It must also be noted that this latter provision is included in a settlement made on his immediate family. The coincidence of the name, the existence of this financial provision and the record of Samuel Croker's wife's name as Jane suggests that Robert and Adelaide may have been the illegitimate children of Samuel Croker, R.M., and Mary Noonan. In connection with the information supplied by the birth certificates of the two children it may be borne in mind that those records are compiled from details supplied by the Informant.

It is possible that some further investigations would prove or disprove this hypothesis. It is noted that in 1874 Samuel Croker was residing in London and it is possible that a grant of probate of his will was issued in England. If the will were traced at Somerset House, it might be found to contain helpful information. It is presumed that all details relating to Samuel Croker had been extracted from the R.I.C. records at the Public Record Office, London. It might also be advisable to have searches made in the Records of the parish which included Lwr. Wellington Quay in 1867, and Wexford Street, in 1870, for entries of the baptism of Adelaide and Robert Noonan (or Croker).

If it is established that Samuel Croker, R.M. was the father of Robert Noonan (Croker) it is not improbable that the immediate ancestry of Samuel Croker could be established if required. There is a certain amount of Croker material in the records of this office and whereas a brief preliminary examination did not reveal any reference to a Samuel Croker identifiable with Samuel Croker, R.M., it is possible that more detailed searches would do so. Even if Samuel Croker is not recorded, his father might be, and as Samuel Croker appears to have been a man of some substance it is probable that the name of his father would be ascertained from sources such as the Registry of Deeds.

It is trusted that the foregoing observations will be of some assistance, and it is regretted that the investigation has not, so far, yielded any conclusive information.

Whether or not this tentative document confirmed the parentage of Robert Tressell, I was myself in some doubt at first; but in face of the fact that no other Robert Croker with parents Samuel Croker and Mary Noonan is shown in the registers, I now took it as proof.

Robert was baptised at St Kevin's, Harrington Street, and the entry in the Baptism Register reads:

Parents: Samuel Croker,
             Maria Noon, 37 Wexford Street.

Sponsors: Michael Noon.
             Maria Hannah Croker.

Comments: 'Pater a Catholicus.'

Baptised: April 26th, 1870.

Priest: Jacobus Baxter.

In spite of the obvious discrepancies, there is surely very strong reason for assuming that the Samuel Croker and Mary Anne Noonan of the Conveyance were the Samuel Croker and Mary Noonan of the birth and Maria Noon of the baptism certificates, in which case, the suggestion made in the document from the Genealogical Office that Robert and Adelaide may have been illegitimate children of Samuel and Mary would appear to be the only conclusion to be drawn. But who is Maria Hannah (Mary Ann) Croker. If she is also Maria Noon, would an unmarried mother describe herself on the birth and the baptism certificates as Croker, implying that she was married? On the birth certificate (if this in fact *is* the birth certificate of Robert) she is given as Croker *nee* Noonan. The assumption of Robert's illegitimacy would therefore be unwarranted. It seems very unlikely that Maria Hannah was Samuel's sister.

In attempts to confirm this, further research into the identity of Samuel, his professional life and social background, resulted only in the single reference in the Registry of Deeds under Index of Grantors 1828–1849, Samuel Croker, and under Index of Lands County Galway 1845–1875 under Inverine; Inverine Castle, mortgaged to Samuel Croker, 21 November 1862.

And there for the time we left it.

36

The adventures of the manuscript

In 1956 I also learned what had happened to the manuscript after Richards had published his versions, and before I found it. This story was told by Frank Swinnerton in *The Adventures of a Manuscript*, published in December of that year, when I first received the copies of the Richards letters. 'Meanwhile', says Mr Swinnerton,

the 'large mass' of the Noonan manuscript remained in Richards' possession. His financial difficulties grew more and more complex; but before what was virtually his retirement from active publishing he thought of his secretary, who had served him with a lifetime's devotion.

He could make no provision for her, could leave her no legacy, but there was the manuscript of *The Ragged Trousered Philanthropists* to which she had first introduced him. He gave it to her. 'It may come in useful on a rainy day,' he said.

The gift was characteristic and well timed. Pauline Hemmerde, no longer young, accepted it as a rich token of gratitude; and as she could no longer work for Richards she struggled long to maintain herself in modest penury. The rainy day, as was inevitable, arrived.

In what circumstances she arranged to dispose of the manuscript I do not know; but she sold it to a stranger across the marble-topped table of a London teashop. The sum she received for it was said to be ten pounds. The purchaser remains to this day, as far as public knowledge goes, anonymous.

When I read this I was much struck by the extraordinary coincidence of the marble-topped table. I, too, had bought the manuscript across such a table and Mr Swinnerton may of course have confused the details of her sale with my purchase.

My own efforts to find a suitable permanent home for the manuscript continued. In 1948–49 I had some contact with the Associated Society

of Woodworkers about it, later with Wortley Hall Memorial College
and the National Council of Labour Colleges, but nothing came of any
of them. And in 1954 the Electrical Trade Union seemed ready to buy
it – publication was by this time assured, and it was only a question
of a home for the manuscript – but negotiations were cut short by the
death of Walter Stevens, then ETU General Secretary, in a motor
accident, and his successor did not follow the matter up. Then late in
1957, Peter Blackman, Secretary of the Sussex Federation of Trades
Councils, and one of our shareholders, sent personal letters to the
National Society of Painters, the Amalgamated Union of Building
Trade Workers of Great Britain and Ireland, and the National Federation of Building Trades Operatives.

As a result of this initiative, Sir Richard Coppock once more set the
question of *The Ragged Trousered Philanthropists* before the Executive
of the NFBTO, and a price was agreed on the basis of 70 guineas
originally subscribed by the shareholders, plus a further 20 guineas
expended over the years, and $2\frac{1}{2}$ per cent compound interest, which I
worked out as a total of £129 10s. $10\frac{1}{2}$d., which we called £130.

The Federation agreed to this figure in May 1958, an official visited
Hastings and examined the manuscript and it turned out that it wasn't
a forgery after all, and the sale was agreed.

I wrote a history of the MS. to enclose with it and on a day in August
my wife and I travelled to Federation Head Office at Clapham, with
the manuscript packed in a box marked 'Processed Peas', and there we
handed it over to Mr H. Heumann, Editor of the Federation Journal.
There was no ceremony, just a simple in and out with a couple of
minutes' chat during which Mr Heumann expressed his preference for
the Richards version of the book.

Sir Richard Coppock and the Federation had in fact purchased the
manuscript for presentation to the TUC where it would be the heritage
of the whole British Trade Union Movement and in January 1959
it was handed over in a simple ceremony, at which I was not present
at Congress House by Sir Richard to Sir Vincent Tewson, then
General Secretary of the TUC, where it now resides.

I confess I was selfishly sorry to lose sight of these historic handwritten pages of our house-painter. But as the *Guardian* said, it had
reached 'an honoured resting place' and it is to be hoped that people
will visit Congress House to see it.

The fate of the banners Robert painted wasn't so fortunate. The only one surviving when I came on the scene depicted, inset in a shield, the writhing serpent Capitalism being strangled by a shirt-sleeved worker. It was decorated on each side with torches wreathed in scrolls, the whole a typical piece of the symbolism of the time. The design, says Poynton, was derived from Walter Crane, the well-known socialist artist.

Cruttenden had possession of this banner for years, and in 1929 when a new branch of the Independent Labour Party was formed in Hastings, it was handed over to that body by agreement with John Whitlock, one of the old-timers of the SDF, and was inscribed with the ILP heading.

In 1910 it had first been used at a beach meeting addressed by Tom Kennedy. In 1937 it was carried through the streets of London from Blackfriars to Hyde Park by the Hastings contingent in a huge May Day procession, which was four miles long, one of the largest ever seen.

And then for the second time in the history of the banner war intervened and once more it disappeared, again in the custody of the ILP. I am told that it was taken to someone in the Birmingham area at the height of the invasion scare in 1940, probably to save it falling into the hands of Hitler, for Hastings was in the line of invasion, and there it disappeared because the caretakers moved. The Secretary of the ILP was unable to locate it after the war and its whereabouts is still unknown. It may well be stored in someone's attic.

Hastings itself has a small memorial. On 2 June 1962, during the week of the TUC Annual Congress of Trades Councils in Hastings, a seat donated from subscriptions organized by the Hastings Trades Council and made by Hastings Corporation carpenters was set up as a memorial to Robert at Carlisle Parade on the promenade, and presented to the town by Sir Tom O'Brien, General Secretary of the National Association of Theatrical and Kine Employees, in the presence of the Mayor of Hastings, Councillor (later Alderman) D.W. Wilshin, MBE, Mr Victor Feather and other officials of the TUC, and many other distinguished guests, including Mr Len Green whose family had been Robert's friends.

Immediately following this ceremony was another on the steps at 115 Milward Road, when a marble tablet on the wall, placed by the Hastings Trades Council, was unveiled by Councillor F. Watts, Secretary of the Essex Federation of Trades Councils.

37

Still alive?

There had been another strange twist to the story nearly twenty years earlier when Unity Theatre first staged their dramatization.

On 3 August 1949, the secretary of the theatre wrote to say they had a postcard from a man in Ilkeston, Derbyshire, claiming that he was Robert Tressell and asking for royalties on the play. The letter continued:

> On formally requesting Mr xxxx to give further particulars of his claim, he writes back to say that the manuscript is in his handwriting, and strangely enough . . . there is some similarity between his writing and the manuscript you brought to London.

The secretary enclosed the postcard for me to make comparisons with Robert's handwriting and give any information I might have about the claimant. I hadn't any, but before I could reply to Unity's letter I received one myself. The italics and other special features are the sender's.

> Mr. Ball.
> Dear Sir,
>   Writing in a hurry on one of my deceased dad's bill-heads. Please excuse condition of notepaper. I am *the author* of *The Ragged Arsed Philanthropists*. I have all the notes of the book. I have photographs of my calling and self taken during the last fifty years, as an acrobat, gasworker, plus in civilian attire if I may coign an expression. I have the book that preceded Ragged Trousers, crammed with the word bloody. I was writing 10 to 12 years 'ere the ragged trousers was written. The Tories know I wrote it. They barged me into the Army, year 1906. I could do nothing right in the Army. I was a marked man. I did not know the book was published in 1914. 15 years elapsed 'ere I made the discovery. When I discovered the book was mine I instituted a system if agitation but I got the sack

from the gasworks and the Post Office. I had two half time jobs of work. So instead of getting royalties I got my arse well and truly kicked. Most of my enemies are now crossed the mythical river Jordan. (Of course there is a river Jordan but does it lead to heaven)'.

P.S. The notes of the book have been seen by Mr. Strong of the Author's Club, London. He was a Solicitor. He said they constituted ample proof. I visited the Club in London.

My life alone (in biography) would make a best seller.

Twice wounded in 1914.

What is it worth to you in hard cash?

A world traveller, U.S.A., Australia, Africa, Germany, France, Belgium, etc. I travelled to garner knowledge and worked at many different jobs, always however, having to come back to painting and paperhanging. Even now at 70 years of age I am doing gardening, a small window cleaning round, hanging paper and painting houses. In my spare time writing books. Just finished Black Jack, a tale of coal-mining industry full of swear words.'

This letter was followed by more in similar vein and it was four years before this sad correspondence came to an end:

'Dear Mr. Ball,

Political enemies are still pulling down my garden fence . . . I believe the dirty dogs are LABOUR IDIOTS.'

The hand-writing did indeed bear some resemblance to that of the Tressell manuscript and the photograph in a privately printed novel the writer had sent me had a definite superficial likeness to some photographs of Robert.

In the meantime in March 1953, Richards Press forwarded the letter from Mr R.A.H. Barltrop of Chingford, Essex, already quoted which caused me to think for a while. Mr Barltrop in the course of lectures to working men's organizations about books and *The Ragged Trousered Philanthropists* in particular had, he said, come across one or two people with some first hand knowledge of the author. Said Mr Barltrop:

During a conversation with a remarkable old man named McLoughlin, he gave me various reminiscences of Noonan, whom he used to meet at the Communist Club and the *Club Autonomie*, both of which were in the Tottenham Court Road area. I mentally dismissed as an elderly man's mistaken recollection his claim that Noonan was alive, well and active in 1913. Some of his information could be checked – for instance, he told me of Noonan's figuring in a strike demonstration, and this could probably be verified from newspaper or labour paper files. I could without difficulty arrange for you to meet McLoughlin.

I have no record of what I wrote in reply to Mr Barltrop but I didn't make any arrangement to see him. I decided that Mr McLoughlin was mistaken. Now I wish I had met him and that I had read Meek at that time because Meek himself mentions visits he paid to both the Communist Club and the *Club Autonomie* some years before his book was published in 1910 and he may have visited it after that – and Mr McLoughlin may well have been referring to George mistakenly for Tressell.

I have often wondered, too, what I missed on the winter's day in 1952 when a man who, said my wife, 'looked as if he was on the road' had called at the house when I was out at work and had told her he had information about Robert Tressell and when would I be home? I was home about 5.30 p.m. but the traveller didn't return and we never heard from him again.

38

1962: a return from the dead

On Monday, 29 May 1967, the *Radio Times* carried an announcement that the production that week on the television programme Theatre 625 on BBC2 would be a dramatization by Stuart Douglass of *The Ragged Trousered Philanthropists* by Robert Tressell, produced by Michael Bakewell.

There was a most extraordinary sequel to this historic event.

On Monday, 5 June my brother rang me from London asking whether I had seen a report in *The Times* that day of an interview with Kathleen Noonan which also carried a picture of her. Kathleen Noonan? I was incredulous. Kathleen had been dead nearly fifty years. Robert's friends had said so, had given me the story of the motor accident, and Kathleen's own cousin had told me about it. Newspapers had reported it. *The Times* would have checked, there could be no doubt about that, but I still couldn't believe it. Surely something would have been heard of her in all those years, something would have reached the ears of her father's friends and her relations, or even the publishers. Yet here she was living right here in England, in Gloucestershire, but I was sure I would know definitely when I saw the photograph and sure enough when I got a copy of the paper the portrait was unmistakably that of Kathleen. Now, of course, I could hardly wait to see her and ask the innumerable questions which would set everything right in her father's story, and after I had obtained her address I wrote saying who I was and asking if I might visit her.

The arranging of this took three weeks and in the meantime I sent her a copy of *Tressell of Mugsborough* that she might acquaint herself with her father's story as it was then known. At last on 29 June 1967, my wife and I travelled down from Hastings by train.

And there took place a meeting which I had never even contemplated as possible. For twenty-five years I had been in one way or another concerned with the life of this woman and her father and never once had I imagined the possibility of this meeting. But I would have recognized this vigorous and alert lady of seventy-five as Tressell's daughter, I'm sure, even in a crowd. I could no longer have had any doubts even if I'd not already been convinced by *The Times* picture. We were received very cordially and Kathleen introduced us to two other people in the room – her daughter Joan and Joan's husband Mr Reg Johnson.

So Tressell had a grand-daughter, the baby who had been reported killed with her mother in 1918.

How had *The Times* rediscovered Kathleen? *The Times* hadn't. Mr Johnson had written to the paper, upon seeing the announcement of the forthcoming television production, saying that the author's daughter was still alive, and *The Times* had sent down a reporter. His story told how Kathleen had been unable to watch the play because she was an old age pensioner and couldn't afford a television set.

She had, she said, only returned to England in September 1962.

What happened in the meantime?

Immediately after the publishing of her father's book she had begun making preparations for joining Paul in Canada. 'I think', she says, 'that Paul went to Canada because his family paid his fare and made him a small allowance – possibly they thought it would break up our "romance" but there was not much chance of that as we wrote weekly letters.'

The twenty-five pounds which she had received for the publication was sufficient for travelling expenses and gave her the opportunity.

She went back to Hastings to say good-bye to her aunt and cousins and gave a copy of the book to the Cruttendens.

'My aunt was all right about it. She knew I was going out to marry Paul and wasn't enthusiastic but hoped everything would be all right with us. She gave us a Queen Anne silver tea-service for a wedding present, which was to be sent on later.'

In June 1914 she sailed from Bristol on the *Royal George*. Mrs Mackinlay and the two daughters had seen her off in London. She says:

> All my luggage came with me on the 'George', I think I had three trunks and I had a marvellous trousseau. It still makes me laugh and here it is for your amusement.
>
> The whole tray of one trunk was filled with stockings rolled together in pairs; I had a dozen wincey nightdresses (I was still selling them when we were short years afterwards in Canada); six

pairs of long-sleeved and long-legged woollen combinations (I was going to a cold country you see); and several full-length knitted vests to wear under my night-dresses, besides dresses and costumes for summer and winter, and a fur-lined coat.

The ship docked at Quebec and then went on to Montreal and she finally arrived at Regina, Saskatchewan, where Paul met her, on Wednesday, 1 July 1914, and they were married on the following Sunday, 5 July at St Peter's Church by Special Licence, on which occasion she swore the affidavit mentioned earlier.

Paul was described on the marriage certificate as a 'Gasoline Engineer, Bachelor'. He was working for the firm Massey Harris. Kathleen gave her parents' names as Robert and Madeline Noonan.

On 4 August war was declared and Paul was thrown out of work. A few weeks later Paul, who had told his relations that he had been on stage in Canada before Kathleen's arrival, although he was servicing farming equipment as the 'Gasoline Engineer' when they married, saw an advertisement by a theatrical company casting for a transcontinental tour. Says Kathleen:

> Paul went to see them. They wanted a 'heavy' (that is one to play serious parts) and an 'ingenue' (a girl to play the innocent) and agreed to hear me read – after which we were both taken on.
>
> In England and when he first went to Canada, Paul had called himself 'Edward Cornwallis' but now he adopted the stage name of 'Edward Lynne' and I was known as 'Mrs Lynne' and on the stage as 'Gabrielle Devereaux' because they said 'I looked French.' Only when we were first married and Paul was working as a gasoline engineer were we known as Mr and Mrs Meiklejon.
>
> We studied and rehearsed in a small Ontario town. We couldn't have been out of work very long, as it was while we were studying one day in a cemetery (it was like a park) I lost my wedding-ring and we had only been married three months when that happened. I'm not sure when we started on the road but we did one-night stands through Saskatchewan and Alberta and three weeks' repertory at Brandon, Manitoba, where we gave two perfomances on Christmas Day 1914.
>
> Part of our proceeds were supposed to go to the Red Cross. At some towns we did very well and stayed longer and at others the halls were half-empty. It was a very interesting life for me – seeing

Canada on the way; dashing from one station to another to make connections; having to put up scenery when we arrived, for we carried, and had to use, our own in most places, as it was only an occasional town that had a real theatre.

Part of the time we stayed at hotels or boarding-houses; sometimes we took rooms and boarded ourselves, buying supplies at farmhouses or village shops.

I became pregnant and was gradually having to change the dresses I wore on the stage. I'm not sure when we closed down but we had come to Winnipeg for Joan's birth on 7 November 1915 and it was here we lost a trunk we had left at Winnipeg Station when we went on tour, because we couldn't afford the storage charges. It contained books, photographs, letters, manuscripts, etc. and also probably copies of the *Evening Ananias* [the 'paper' Robert edited on the ship from South Africa] and other material which would be of interest now.

Paul got an office job and we lived in rooms. Apart from the small flat we had when first married we never had a home – always furnished rooms. Paul wanted to go East but when I was offered a free fare to Toronto with Joan, through a railwayman friend of ours, I grabbed it and took Joan and stayed with Auntie Pat and Uncle Alfred (the managers of the show) who had moved there. Then we got a wire from Paul to say that he had sold up our few things and was joining me. Joan was between one and two years old. So we were in rooms again and Paul got another office job. Whether it was confinement to routine or whether his liver was affected then I don't know but I used to dread his return at night as I never knew what mood he would be in. It was just that we were mentally incompatible, he had been spoiled and I suppose I had too. The undermining had begun.

Paul became acquainted with a man who was getting together a vaudeville company. I don't remember what he wanted Paul to do but there was a part for me in it, only I would have to wear tights on the stage. Imagine Katie, who wouldn't shake a duster out of the window without first pulling down her sleeve, in tights with a frill round the middle. The pay was very good and Paul was furious because I wouldn't do it.

However, the chap taught us some secrets of a mind-reading act which was to be part of his show. For some reason or other he never went on the road but had no objection to us using the act so we were on the way again. Paul would go on ahead to make bookings and put up posters – 'Gabrielle Devereaux, the Girl Mystic'. We would generally put on our act at picture shows between films. By that time we were dividing our takings and expenses, where before we had them in common.

I nearly left him several times but couldn't do it when things were a bit difficult. Finally our show folded up when we were in a small country town and when our money was practically gone and Paul couldn't find a job there, I worked in the kitchen of the hotel to pay for our board and room, Paul still trying to find work. When at last he got a job in a shoe factory, and his wages were enough to keep him, I told him that I really was going. I had enough money, sixteen dollars, in the bank to take me to Toronto and I could stay with friends until I got a job. He didn't believe I really meant it and came down to the station to see us off. He said whatever should he tell the family and I said 'Oh, tell them I'm dead!' I went to Toronto and stayed with Auntie Pat and Uncle Alfred.

When I was quite young I had wanted to be an actress, but Robert would never have allowed that. In those days, I think, perhaps they were not considered respectable. My first ambition was to be a nun and that was taboo. I suppose I couldn't have chosen a greater contrast. Then I would be a teacher. So I became a teacher, I became an actress, but it does not seem that I shall ever be a nun!

I arrived in Toronto just before Armistice Day 1918. Excitement was wild, everyone waving flags, banging pots and shaking talcum powder over passers-by.

I got Joan a small flag and she waved it as I pushed her in her go-cart, saying 'Peace, Peace.' She thought the flag was 'peace'.

Paul came to the house in Toronto once to find us but was told it was no use and he went round to the back entrance and called out 'Baby Joan, Baby Joan.' I thought I saw him on one occasion. He said if I didn't go back he'd have Joan taken away from me and put into a home but I knew he'd never be successful in that and he finally realized I wouldn't go back. He wanted my theatrical trunk which had a lot of posters and things in it so I let him have that and the next thing he was advertising for a girl for a mind-reading act – must have long fair hair and be really pretty. My friends teased me about that. But he never bothered me again and I suppose that was when he invented the motor accident. It was unheard of to think I should leave him. He might have said we'd died from the influenza epidemic which was raging just then, but that would not have been so dramatic.

Kathleen reflected that they were probably both to blame for the breakdown – 'Our upbringing had been so diametrically opposite – he a "poor little boy with a bad leg" waited on hand and foot by family and maids, me convent-bred and when not sheltered behind walls, living in an atmosphere of service and compassion for the underdog.'

But in fact the marriage was doomed from the start, for her attitudes to men and marriage had been formed in the shadow of that extraordinarily intense relationship with her father – who, incidentally, 'started more than he knew' when he invited Paul to dinner on meeting him by chance in the street after many years.

'My husband was the first man in my life,' Kathleen told me, 'and the only man to kiss me until years later and that only in greeting . . .,

I had lived a very sequestered life with no male companions beyond the 'How do you do' state, never any conversations except with a few older men, for instance Robert's school-teacher friend. I rather think Robert would have objected to us marrying just as much as Mary Jane, and for the same reason, and my aunt never brought in my father's name. She missed a cue – it *might* have made a difference to me. If he had not died I doubt very much whether I'd have married anyone.

I had never thought of getting married but only of keeping house for Dad and when I told Mrs Beney that I was engaged she said, 'Oh your father would have been so happy as he used to think you were unnatural in never wanting to marry – he used to ask all those young men to the house and you would always go out. . . .

I remember one time when we were out together and it was after dark, I don't remember where it was but it was a woodland path or something and I grabbed his hand and I said, 'Oh Dad there's a man', and he said, 'Oh he won't hurt us' or something to that effect. But I don't know whether it was my aunt who had instilled the fear of men into me but I know when I left my other aunt's and went up to London Paul was supposed to meet me at Charing Cross and he wasn't there when my train got in. I don't know how long I waited but I saw a man looking at me so I got on the tube and went to my destination. . . . [Paul] was probably worried off his head wondering what had happened to me. I was probably worried about the white slavers and Jack the Ripper although he was a bit before my time.

If my aunt had had any sense (it's easy to be wise after the event) she would have arranged for me to meet some other young men for I suppose I was at the ripe time to fall in love with any nice young man. As it was I was grieving for Dad, and Paul was grieving over the loss of his current girl-friend.

39

Family secrets

Kathleen stayed on in Toronto for some years and continued to call herself 'Mrs Lynne', as, she says, 'Meiklejon was so uncommon it would be easier to trace if Paul were trying to find me.' To this day for passport, bank and other purposes she signs herself Kathleen Meiklejon Lynne, another example of the family trait of cloaking the identity.

Kathleen did not seek maintenance from Paul, telling friends who suggested it that she had no moral right to it. 'If he had left *me*,' she said, 'then I would have claimed it.'

For some time she maintained herself and Joan at a job where she could live in and have Joan with her, caring for an invalid, then she took a job at St John's Hospital, Toronto, run by Anglican Sisters, where she stayed for seven years.

'I never starved nor lacked a place to stay but I always had to watch my pennies. Once when I was making up a parcel "for the poor." Joan said, "We're poor aren't we mummy?"'

Paul of course reported home that Kathleen and Joan had been killed and this was accepted by all relations and friends alike, but it didn't reach the ears of Grant Richards.

On 24 November 1920, he wrote a letter:

Dear Mrs. Meiklejon,

I have for some time been trying to find your address. You will remember that you sold to this firm the copyright of *The Ragged Trousered Philanthropists*. The book, as you know, was originally published at 6/- and went out of print. We then reissued it in cheaper form, and it has sold, and is still selling well. When I am certain of your address I hope to be able to send you some additional payment. Please let me hear from you. I write in this way as there seems to be no certainty that this letter will reach you.

The letter did reach her because some while later Richards sent her another twenty-five pounds and this was the last time they were in communication.

In 1923 Joan was taken seriously ill with rheumatic fever and was confined to her bed for over a year, making her mother's problems of caring for her and earning a living at the same time still more acute. She supported herself by private nursing until she joined the staff of the Victorian Order of Nurses, Public Health Department, where she remained for another fifteen years.

And here Kathleen was to follow in her father's footsteps as a social reformer in an entirely different context, one he perhaps would hardly have foreseen. Both she and Joan became members of the Social Service Study Group of St John's, and of the Social Services Committee of the Diocesan Synod of Montreal, and here under the auspices of the Anglican Fellowship for Social Action, Kathleen, with the help of a member of the staff of the *Montreal Daily Star*, produced a pamphlet and helped the Fellowship campaigns on slums and social conditions with something of her father's outspokenness, for her title *Dirty Old Montreal* was changed to *Hovels For God's Children* on the advice of the newspaperman who thought it might bring a libel action. But even so there are echoes of her father:

> Your brother and sisters – sons of God as you and I – live rotting in infested hovels fit for . . . but rats and lice. Don't stand there – do something . . . go see for yourself. . . . Find out who owns them, who operates them, who derives revenue from them.
>
> Find out if, directly or indirectly, you derive income from such places, if your parish does – or your diocese. Demand action of your Congregation . . . your diocesan representatives, your Alderman, your M.P., of Government and private enterprise. The time has come that judgement must begin in the House of God.

In 1945 they were advised to leave Canada for the sake of Joan's health, and finally went down to Tampa, Florida, to take ship for Kingston, Jamaica – a journey, says Kathleen, that took five and a half days. In Tampa, in the consul's office, there was another curious coincidence. When Kathleen applied for a passport in her name Mrs Meiklejon-Lynne (she had added the Lynne from her stage-name) the consul apparently was actually working on a passport for a Mrs Lynne-Meiklejon – Paul's second wife, who was going to England to settle her husband's estate. Kathleen had heard of Paul and his new wife once, back in 1922, and now learned that he had died in 1942. The consul showed her a photograph of Paul and his wife but he asked no questions and Kathleen kept silent.

They had sold all their belongings, says Kathleen, but once landed in Jamaica she soon got work at the Nuttall Hospital and Joan worked in various hotel offices. But both of them developed very bad throats (from dust, says Kathleen), and were advised by their doctor to leave the island and in 1947 they returned to Canada. Kathleen applied for the post of Assistant Matron at Trinity College, Toronto, was accepted and stayed there seven years.

Joan had always wanted to become a missionary (the missionary spirit seems to have been strong in the Tressell family) and she was finally offered training in England in 1956. There Joan made inquiries about possible surviving relations, none of whom she had ever seen and who, of course, did not even know she was alive. 'And so,' Kathleen says, 'we came to the motor accident, and until Joan came to England in 1956 I didn't realize I had been buried.' It was Robert's niece Alice who told Joan the story of the report of Kathleen's death.

In 1958 Joan received part of a legacy from her father's estate and was able to bring her mother over for a holiday, and Kathleen saw England for the first time since 1914.

At this time she was working at the Women's College Hospital, Toronto, and Joan, too, returned to Canada. But in 1962 Alice died, and Joan received the balance of her legacy from her father's share of the family estate, and she and Kathleen decided to return and live in England.

No one but Alice surviving from Robert's circle of friends and acquaintances knew or had even heard of this strange return from the dead, and she, one of my original informants, neither told me of this extraordinary development, nor Joan about my biography of her grandfather. So of course the Tressells remained 'dead' for another ten years.

It wasn't until this reappearance that we knew anything about the stay in Cape Town.

And in 1969 I was able to tell Kathleen that the name of the mother she had never known and whom she had called 'Madeline' on her marriage certificate was in fact 'Elizabeth'.

'Strangely enough,' she said, 'I had never missed her until after Joan was born and then I often wished that she was with me.'

And in another of those twists, strange in view of her father's opinions, in this story that never turns out as expected, she had achieved happiness and peace through religion.

Robert couldn't have invented a stranger story than his own, and the marvellous reappearance of his daughter.

But what of the other child who used to love him and who became a model for Frankie in the book?

'I had not seen Arthur for some years,' says Kathleen, 'when I left England. He was only seventeen, if that, when I sailed, and was only nine or ten the last time I remember seeing him.'

Fate had a different destiny for Arthur. In the First World War he joined the Royal Flying Corps and became an Aircraftsman. Among the long list of names on the War Memorial in Alexandra Park, Hastings, is that of First Air Mechanic A.G. Rolleston.

Kathleen made another discovery in England – the reputation of her father's book. 'It was a shattering revelation to discover what had been happening to it over the years,' she said. She and Joan discussed it but decided that as Kathleen had sold it outright, nothing could be done about it. She heard a few references to it abroad – that it was being used as a textbook in the London School of Economics, and that Penguin Books had published it.

Lawrence and Wishart sent her a copy of the full edition and she says of the Grant Richards version: 'I think when I saw the 1914 book my first disappointment was that Barrington was out, for he and Owen were a composite picture of Robert – possibly the reason for removing him, if Robert was supposed to be a house-painter, but I had no idea until reading the Lawrence and Wishart edition how badly the book had been mutilated.'

Lawrence and Wishart also sent her a cheque and I believe the BBC did likewise. Kathleen herself had never blamed Richards or anyone else for the fact that she had no rights in the book. In any case the copyright had run out in 1964.

She had told the *Times* reporter:

I sold the book for a mess of pottage, £25 to be exact. It was a lot of money to me and the publishers were taking a chance. Nobody knew whether it would be a success so I suppose it was a very fair price. I keep kicking myself for my own stupidity, but I don't think there is anything I can do about the book now. I don't want to be rich but I would like to be able to buy some new curtains. And I would like to have seen the play on television. I wonder if they got the casting right? After all, I knew the people my father put into the book.

The remark about the curtains was typical of the sardonic touch of humour Kathleen had inherited from her father.

To Joan, Robert's grand-daughter, who herself had known hard times, the television production was the last straw, she told me, and this led her husband to write and let the world know that the daughter of the man who had written the book and was buried in a pauper's grave, was still alive. Yet Kathleen herself was philosophical: 'If I had had a TV set,' she said, 'I would probably still be "dead" and we would never have met.'

In August 1968 Kathleen, with her daughter, was able to visit Hastings, the first time she had returned since June 1914, an interval of fifty-four years. While she was here Mr David Haines, a local writer, took some historic film shots of her revisiting places associated with her father and their life in Hastings.

There had been much discussion among leading trade unionists and Tressell fans in Hastings, sparked off by the idea that his own daughter couldn't afford a television set when the book had made a lot of money for other people. There seemed something a little immoral about it.

So the Hastings and District Trades Council had decided to address an appeal to Sussex trade unions and others to raise a fund for the presentation of a television set to her, and at last on 13 December 1968, Mr Les Harman, Chairman of the Trades Council, presented her with the set, a licence, an aerial and a cheque in the presence of a large company at the Railway Staff Association Club, St Leonards.

And she had another surprise at the presentation. Rose Cruttenden had been brought down from Tonbridge to meet her again after fifty-four years.

It was only with difficulty that Kathleen had finally been persuaded to accept this gift, and at last on 19 June 1969 she was able to watch the television film of the book when it was reshown on BBC1.

And now I was able to ask Kathleen the questions I had spent years trying to answer. What was her father's real name and what was the truth about his family? But Kathleen had no positive evidence. She could only tell me, she said, what her father had told *her*. Robert wrote in Kathleen's birthday-book, 'Born April 17th 1870, Dublin, Ireland', and *told* her that the address was Merrion Square West, and that his father was Sir Samuel Croker, an officer in the army. She never knew his mother's name or family origins. Kathleen enlarged on this with a few stories told her of Samuel and his wife. Samuel was injured in 'the Phoenix Park Riots' and had a silver plate in his skull. Robert often spoke of his father's courage for on another occasion he went alone to arrest a 'rebel' known to be hiding in a remote cabin, knocked on the door and called out that the place was surrounded. The 'rebel' came out and Samuel rode back with the man mounted in front of him on the same horse.

Kathleen remarked to me that this arrest seemed more in line with the duties of the Royal Irish Constabulary, but that she always understood Samuel was a soldier.

Samuel, perhaps as a result of his head injury, had died raving, and on the same day a large picture of him on horseback, which hung on the staircase landing, fell down.

Robert's mother was frivolous, vain and proud of her tiny feet; she had married off her eldest daughter 'at a very early age because a girl of that age dated the mother'.

Kathleen did not know where her father went to school, but all the girls went to convent schools and were well educated. I wrote to all the convents in Dublin and to Roman Catholic and Protestant schools but no records of the children either as Croker or Noonan could be found. Robert spent some of his childhood in London and on one occasion, as a small child dressed in a Jack-Tar suit, ran away from home and was found by a London policeman sleeping under a tree with a loaf of bread and a carving knife.

Kathleen believes the family also had estates in Ireland 'for the father left the collecting of rents to agents and lived in comfort himself without bothering about the conditions of his tenants and Robert who was, or was about to become, a student at Trinity College, left home when he decided he could not live on an income from absentee rentals'.

She had never heard talk of a stepfather, or of Alice's story about Samuel's death when Robert was a child and the mother's remarriage. On Mary Jane's, his eldest sister's, marriage certificate of 1875, her father's name is given as 'Samuel Noonan, deceased', yet Kathleen never heard of any talk of half-brothers and half-sisters. There were three boys and three girls in the family and the three in Hastings certainly took the name Noonan, although Kathleen says they all thought of themselves as Croker.

There is no record of Robert at Trinity College.

Robert said he had an uncle Charles who wrote fairy-stories and I found a Dr Charles Philip Croker at 7 Merrion Square West, but no records of any writings, and further inquiries in Dublin failed to disclose any connection with a Samuel Croker. And a Lady Croker, wife of Edward Croker, lived in Merrion Square but I have not been able to link her with Robert. Reference may be made here to John Wilson Croker, MP, Secretary of the Admiralty, also a writer who died in 1857, and to Thomas Croften Croker, collector of Irish legendry, who died in 1854, but apparently not related, both of whose physical descriptions, and certain personality traits, strongly resemble Robert's own. Dr Charles had a daughter Mary Croker, who died unmarried and whose will shows no connection with a Samuel Croker.

Thus from all my researches so far, there is nothing more positive to link Robert with any Crokers than the birth certificate of 18 April 1870 linking a Robert Croker with a Samuel Croker and a Mary Noonan. So we still don't know. But Kathleen mentions one telling little anecdote. When thinking of a pen-name as author of his book, Robert didn't want to use 'Noonan', and said, 'I can't use "Croker" or they'll say "Croker" by name and croaker by nature.'

40

The painter

On 19 August 1970, David Haines and his two teenage sons were walking past St Andrew's Church in Queen's Road and noticed a gang of workmen busy on the building. Some of the windows of the church were knocked out and in the churchyard a notice written in chalk on a piece of slate carried the information 'Pews for sale.' In answer to David's inquiry the men said that the church was being demolished. David knew the story of Robert's decoration of the chancel back in 1905 and also knew that these murals had been over-painted in 1966.*

David was curious and asked if he might have a look in the chancel and there he scratched off some of the white overpaint with a penny-piece and came upon gold-leaf and colour. He was almost certain that he had uncovered some of Robert's original. He immediately notified the Curator of the Hastings Museum, Mr Mainwaring Baines, the *Hastings and St Leonards Observer* and myself. The next morning I took my wife and my daughter Clare, aged ten, and together with the Haines' we began scraping various parts of the lower walls. The original decoration had covered the whole chancel, an area of about forty by twenty feet.

I had with me a photograph given to me by Kathleen of the original and we soon recognized what we had uncovered. But now we had to

*The vicar, the Reverend T.H.Walters, later told us that it had been done after vandals had dabbed the walls in 'bright, orange paint with French slogans and obscenities. I came in early on Sunday morning and could hardly hold the service with this filth in the background. . . .

'Some parishioners hastily set about scrubbing the walls and as they did this inevitably a great deal of damage was done to the painting. . . . It had been a drab dark area, the prevailing colour being a gloomy green. The church council decided that it should be repainted in a mid-white emulsion. This transformed it into an attractive, light and airy sanctuary.'

He said that he had had no idea of the significance of the mural, and knew little of Tressell. Some of the gloom mentioned by the vicar was due to the accretion of dust over the years. When we cleaned off parts we found the colours vivid and bright as they must have looked when the work was first painted.

make a quick decision. The demolition men were about to pull the roof down and were already removing slates and with the huge beams and stonework, the church floor would soon be several feet deep under the remains of the roof. Would we have time to try and save something of the mural and if so what could we do and how.

We were told, quite rightly, that the demolition could not be held up for us, delay was a costly business, and there was a contract date, but the workmen told us we had about two days before the roof came in.

We rapidly began cleaning off to try and find a definite part of the design and came upon the outline of one of the fourteen panels which formed the lower half of the mural. Working over the week-end with such doubtful aids as paint removers and detergents we uncovered part of the panel and David took colour transparencies of this fragment.

After the week-end we could only get to work when the demolishers weren't actually taking the roof off and even then we managed sometimes to be tucked away in the chancel while parts of the main roof were coming down and the whole place was filled with clouds of dust and falling slates and rubble.

In the meantime the *Hastings and St Leonards Observer* published an account of the find and people began to arrive on the site, some to offer help, some as interested spectators and some to complain about us.

One gentleman on the second day had walked in and offered us ten pounds towards expenses, but we decided not to accept at that stage. Various journalists and photographers came and took statements and pictures.

On Wednesday, 26 August, we and the church were still there, although now a large part of the roof was on the church floor, when accounts and pictures appeared in that day's *Guardian* and *Morning Star*. The *Morning Star* featured an appeal for help, not, incidentally, from us, but which showed that Tressell still had many devoted fans.

The *Guardian* headed its article, by Martin Woolacott, 'Hastings Still Fails Robert Tressell'.

It went on to say:

Hastings ... has received the news with total indifference. The Hastings *Observer*, which figures in Tressell's book as the 'Obscurer', gave the story six inches on the inside page.* The Council – which

*As the story developed the *Hastings and St Leonards Observer* in fact gave full coverage.

Tressell called 'The Forty Thieves' or 'The Brigands' – has evinced no interest in the affair. Everybody on the church side connected with the demolition ... seems either to be on holiday or unaware of what is happening. Hastings has never been proud of Tressell. Nothing is made of him in the schools and the Education Committee even turned down a recent offer by a London school to put on a dramatized version of *Philanthropists* for Hastings children.

Tressell's centenary... has been marked in Hastings by a minuscule display in the central library ... the fate of his fresco is perhaps evidence that Hastings is as unwilling to be reminded of his ideas in 1970 as it was in 1914.

With this article it might be said that the balloon went up and if someone had blown up the church and us with it or had knocked David's engine-driver-type cap off his head I wouldn't have been overcome with astonishment. Various strong-silent-type men began to look in the door or walk over the rubble to inspect the chancel and stand in small groups in conference in the churchyard. Most of them never said a word to us and I began to wonder whether they were detectives or MI5 or irate churchwardens, but I think many of them were councillors and Borough Council officials having a quiet look and wondering whether they could or ought to throw us out or whether the mural could be saved and was worth saving.

As the *Hastings and St Leonards Observer* said under the heading 'Storm Over Painting':

The goings on in St. Andrew's and in particular certain Press reports have aroused a great deal of controversy both locally and nationally. Local residents seem bent on proving that Hastings is interested in Tressell. Both Mr Ball and the *Observer* have received countless phone calls offering assistance. The report angered officials in the Church Commission, who claimed that all this had been going on behind their back.

The views of the objectors were perhaps best summed up by a letter signed 'Old Hastonian' which said:

What's all this nonsense about Robert Tressell? Why should the town recognize him or try to save some of his worthless art? What good did he ever do Hastings? He slandered the town and its residents. To me it seems sacrilege that one of his paintings should adorn a house of God. It seems foolish that your paper should consider him so important.

Others spoke of our 'desecration'.

But one Tressell fan had already, unknown to us, set about relentlessly importuning the Mayor himself to do something and in fact the Mayor came to have a look and wished us success.

Mr Mainwaring Baines, Curator of the Hastings Museum, himself busy on the old wreck of the Dutch ship, *Amsterdam*, lying off St Leonards, gave what advice he could and promised to make available money from a private fund at the museum, not under the control of the local authority, and to house in the museum anything we might save, if only a pictorial record of the painting and this event. In retrospect, I have to admit that it had never occurred to either David or myself to seek financial help from the town authorities. The real problem was time. We were assured daily that tomorrow or the next day the chancel roof would be pulled down and that is why we didn't attempt to organize a fund. That would take time and it would need a lot of money to pay the contractors to stop work, even if that could be done. Mr Mainwaring Baines called in the Superintendent of Building Works Department, Mr Sands, who examined the walls and told us that short of time and scientific method there was no prospect, in his opinion, of our saving anything intact, but offered us the loan of any available equipment we might need. To leave nothing untried I telephoned the British and the Victoria and Albert Museums who told me just what would be involved in the latest methods of taking the painting itself off the plaster. There were neither time, money nor experts to do this. David, however, who had been put in charge of the job by Mr Mainwaring Baines, had already decided to concentrate principally on one panel and not to clean it off completely for a photographic record but to first cut behind the cavity wall and attempt to take out the entire course of bricks on which the panel was painted or, failing that, to take off the plaster from the wall in pieces for reassembly.

In the meantime, offers of help in the form of labour, money, and technical advice continued, from friends, from strangers in various parts of the country, from workmen, artists, professional men, students. Another report in the *Guardian* said that the Labour Party was considering intervening to save the painting and that it was suggested that the fresco, rescued and restored, could be put up in the Clarion Youth Hostel, a Labour Party establishment some thirty miles from Hastings, but no one came to see us and that was all we knew of this project. Another report stated that an official of the TUC Education Department visited the site and asked for all the murals when uncovered to be photographed in colour so that a record might be kept at the Labour Party Memorial Museum.

The Hastings Trades Council rang us and offered help but again time and money to halt the demolition were the factors. It would take more money than could be raised locally and we were still daily being told that tomorrow or the next day would be our last.

The roof and half of the walls were now already down and the church was a great mass of timbers, stone, slates and rubble over which we had to climb, and the chancel walls were themselves damaged with parts of the roof overhanging which made the operation somewhat dangerous. The Bank Holiday was approaching, which we were told was our last chance in any case, because we had been visited by three representatives of the Church Commission, and I will not describe their attitude as cordial.

But we were trespassers, the Commissioners had a demolition contract, and that had a deadline. The demolition had been advertised months before. Why hadn't we come forward then?

After assuring us that we were wasting their and our time in our attempts to salvage something of the mural, they gave us permission to work over the Bank Holiday week-end, provided that we took out insurance against personal accident for all those working on the mural, permitted no uninsured volunteers, and excluded from the church all sightseers and others. We made no promise on the last point which we thought preposterous as we couldn't enforce it.

During the week a BBC Television unit arrived to take pictures and while they were there the contractors decided to pull down the remaining part of the roof, that over the chancel, which seemed to us at that stage of the demolition to be arbitrary and David swore that it was a final attempt – inspired elsewhere – to keep us out. He had, with the forty pounds we had from Mr Mainwaring Baines, come to terms, we thought, with the workmen and with the boss himself, who visited the site in a huge American car and had, to give him credit, allowed us to stay on.

David commented that the *men* would pull down Canterbury Cathedral itself for the right money.

He had already covered our panel with strips of paper and glue to hold the plaster together, and covered that with hardboard and a wooden frame to protect it from falling; luckily, it held as we stood outside watching men climb up on to the beams of the roof and fix winching cable and after a long struggle, so strong was the timbering, pull it in, while the BBC cameramen, at some considerable risk, filmed it crashing towards the camera.

Now of course the chancel floor was itself several feet high with the remains of the roof and the walls damaged and jagged with over-hanging chunks of brickwork and we realized the significance of the Commissioners' demands concerning insurance.

On Thursday, 28 August, David and I insured ourselves at fifty shillings a head for which we received cover of two thousand pounds for death or ten pounds per week for 'Temporary Total Disablement'.

On the Friday, we collected iron clamps and braces kindly loaned by the Building Works Depot. It was our intention, which David had already arranged with the workmen, to get them to start at the top of the now roofless chancel wall and cut away the inner course of bricks from the cavity wall, down to our panel, which we would then clamp and brace, aiming to take out the section of brickwork entire which even we doubted could be done and so did the workmen.

So on the Saturday morning we watched a workman walk up a plank sloping from the floor to the top of the twenty foot wall and hack away with a pickaxe a few feet of the inner course so that he could get a foothold and stand on it, leaning against the back courses while he hacked the inner away. It gave me a touch of vertigo but I had watched these men climbing about the roof and up the steeple. They certainly earned their money whatever it was! How can men do it? I asked.

'We all know we'll get ours some day,' he replied, 'but its part of the job, id'nit?'

We waited expectantly as he gradually came down the wall and on the way 'putting his pickaxe through the Prince of Peace' to quote David – until suddenly he stopped:

'Solid,' he said, 'you've had it!' And true enough the cavity ended almost at the top of our panel and this put an end to our plan of cutting behind it.

The workman retired to London and his week-end, and David now put into operation his alternative plan. We collected some unofficial (and uninsured) volunteers, staff from the Borough Library, already on standby, and an assortment of hammers, knives and hack-saw blades – anything with a flat surface which we could get behind the plaster, for the plan was to remove the plaster in sections. Before we could get to the panel we had to move a load of brick, timber and rubble round it – in fact the only way through the church and chancel was by walking across the beams fallen from the roof. David marked off the panel in sections and numbers with coloured chalk, cut away the plaster round it and the task began.

The adhesive and paper held well and prevented the plaster from crumbling as the work proceeded but it was a ticklish job as it varied in thickness from about three-quarters to one-quarter of an inch and was much perished in places. Boxes were put below the panel to catch even the smallest piece and once the workers got the hang of the thing and the right tool, which turned out to be Mr Powys's table knife, the operation got under way. There was room for only two men, one using hammer and knife and the other holding the plaster to the wall as it was loosened. Of course, as anticipated, it came away in pieces of several sizes ranging from an occasional chunk down to tiny chips, but it all went carefully into the boxes, which were also numbered to correspond with the section of the panel.

By late afternoon on Sunday we began transferring the boxes to a room at the library annexe kindly lent by the Borough Librarian, Mrs O'Nions. They were to be in charge of the Head of the Reference Library, Mrs Pam Haines, wife of David.

There had been many sightseers and souvenir-hunters this afternoon and an extraordinary gesture. One youngish man and his wife – skilled workers from London – had come down to see the paintings and the man quietly took me aside and offered me six hundred pounds, which I thought might be their life's savings, if we could still halt the contractors. It was, of course, impossible to accept this generous offer.

By eight o'clock on Sunday evening the entire panel was off the wall and stored and we went back to the church to collect our tools.

We had finally got our painting, even if only in fragments. David had paid forty pounds to the men, which amounted to a payment of forty pounds for the two hours or so that one man spent fruitlessly knocking down the chancel wall for us, although we believe that the prospect of this money had perhaps contributed to our being allowed to remain on the site. The pieces we finally managed to save still lie in their boxes awaiting the complicated process of reassembly and cleaning off, after which what is restored will be put into the Hastings Museum, as the last known physical reminder of Tressell's work. For this reason above all, and irrespective of any intrinsic merit the murals may have possessed, was the salvage operation undertaken. The rest (and a large part of the murals had survived because we cleaned off various small areas on different parts of the wall to find out) is now rubble.

In another of the strange twists in Tressell's story it was discovered that only just prior to the demolition the original templates from which he had worked on the murals were found in the stores of his old employers and destroyed because it wasn't realized that they were of any particular significance.

Robert may have been against 'institutional religion' but he put all his loving craftsmanship and a lot of his own time and thought into this work, and his detractors understand nothing of the quality of his spirit. This chapter may fittingly close with the words of someone who does. Of the many offers of help we received only one was accepted at the time because the sender, who, I imagine, was a lady, didn't give a name and address.

Headed merely 'St Albans, Herts', this letter, obviously inspired by the stories of young helpers and the picture of my young daughter working on the wall, enclosed thirty shillings and said:

> Dear Young Philanthropists,
>
> Thank you for trying to preserve something of Tressell's. The quality of his work as an *artist* is not important – the quality of his mind and values is what matters.
>
> He may have died in 1911 in a Pauper's grave in Liverpool, but there will always be those who will love and respect this darling Iconoclast.
>
> So Mr. Ball is going to buy you something with the enclosed to ease those dry and dusty throats as you work on his murals – and together we will remember and salute Robert Tressell – he would have liked it this way – because what you are doing now makes *all* that he did even more worth while.
>
> Yours sincerely,   D.M.H.

41

A grass plot, a jam jar, and *The Ragged Trousered Philanthropists*

In 1943 when I obtained Robert's death certificate from the Royal Liverpool United Hospital (now the United Liverpool Hospitals) I also made inquiries about his burial-place but was told there was no record of this. I tried again in 1948 with the hospital and with the municipal authority with the same result.

This added much to the mystery of his final resting-place. There was no record of him in the Hastings Registers. For this book I tried yet again in August 1968 and a full search was made of all Corporation cemeteries and the crematorium in Liverpool, yet again without success. He had given only the name Robert Noonan when admitted to hospital and the death certificate gave this name. He apparently didn't use the 'Phillipe'.

The municipal authority, however, after the search, passed on my letter to the City Librarian to whom I had also written, as I was told that some records were kept there, but the reply stated that for 1911 only those for St James's were available and there was no trace of Robert Noonan.

I had been told by a native of Liverpool that the burial of a pauper would most probably be at Walton Park or Smithdown Road, and the City Librarian advised me to write to the individual cemeteries and gave me a list of the six still in use which were there in 1911. Accordingly I wrote to all six. The Roman Catholic authorities replied that there was no record of the burial in their cemeteries; one didn't reply, and three, apparently without making an individual search, sent on my letters to the municipal authority – who had already said they had no record and who wrote again to tell me so.

I had nearly resigned myself to failure, but there was still one cemetery I hadn't cleared and I didn't know which that was as the municipal authority hadn't listed those to whom I had sent letters.

And then on 13 September a letter came from Walton Park:

> Dear Sir,
> I have traced the burial of Robert Noonan in this Cemetery.

The entry had been found by Mr William Marsden, the Superintendent. Evidently it had not been recorded in the Registers of the Municipal Authority. I sent for a copy of the Register entry and this showed that Robert had been buried under a Relieving Officer's Order, that is, as a pauper, from the Royal Liverpool Infirmary, under the name Robert Noonan, in Plot T.11 on 10 February 1911, aged forty, the burial service being conducted by the Reverend A.V. Atkinson, Curate.

I also asked Mr Marsden for any information he might be able to give me about the cemetery and circumstances of burial, and he very kindly sent me the following which he has permitted me to quote.

> The deceased was buried in a pauper's grave (T.11.) and I should imagine the ritual would be the same then as now, i.e. full service attended by Clergyman, Cemetery Superintendent and undertaker's assistants. The fees would be paid out of the rates. This cemetery is a private one belonging to Liverpool Parish Church, but was formerly the burial ground of the Overseers of the Poor for Liverpool. The Cemetery is adjacent to Walton Hospital which in 1911 was Walton Workhouse.

No one in the family including Kathleen knew where he had been buried.

One of the first things which struck me was that the burial didn't take place until seven days after death. Paupers of course were buried one on top of another and perhaps a number were buried together. And there he had lain in his anonymous grave, unmarked by any stone for nearly fifty-eight years.

And then towards the end of 1970, when BBC Television made a short film about Robert and his work in Hastings during which Kathleen was taken to the Mayor's Parlour, was received by the Mayor, Councillor E.P. Nye, and signed the Distinguished Visitors' Book – the first sign of any kind of official recognition of the existence of Robert Tressell and his work in this borough – the BBC team also went to Liverpool and sought out the grave in Plot T.11. A lady attendant looked up a plan of the cemetery and told them 'It's over here,' and walked across to a large grassy patch, like an overgrown field, to Plot 'T.' and paced out eleven paces. 'He's down there,' she said. There was nothing to mark the grave in this paupers' section, nothing to photograph but the long grasses and wild plants which would flower in the summer, and the cameraman stuck an empty jam-jar he found into the ground to focus on.

The plot was only a few yards from the walls of Walton Gaol where many a murderer had been hanged. And as if to point the irony of the scene and of the extraordinary coincidences of Tressell's life, his grave is within a few yards of a family tombstone inscribed to members of a family named – Owen.

Owen, who had turned, startled, and seen the apparition standing at the door, an apparition of man's own creating, a monstrous blood-sucking grotesque like Blake's ghost of a flea, a gaoler of Hell to haunt him through life. And all his kind. Or was it an apparition of man, haunting himself, a child playing at ghosts? But children must grow into men and the apparitions were, of course, mere grotesques and properly belonged to man's infancy and the terrors of the childish night and cries in the dark, and would fade with the morning. Or children quarrelling over the sharing of toffee? But children would grow into men.

Owen, who could shed other people's tears, laugh with the innocent, and scorn grown-up children squabbling over toffee and the size of their hats and calling it a social 'system'.

Owen, 'one of the damned', whose story of 'twelve months in Hell' was written down in *The Ragged Trousered Philanthropists* by Robert Tressell, who had been there with him.

List of authors quoted

Louis Creswicke, *South Africa and the Transvaal War*, T.C. and E.C. Jack, Edinburgh, 1901.

Michael Davitt, *The Boer Fight For Freedom*, Funk and Wagnalls Co., London and New York, 1902.

P.S.O'Hegarty, *History of Ireland under the Union*, Methuen and Co., London, 1952.

C. Desmond Greaves, *Life and Times of James Connelly*, Lawrence and Wishart, London, 1961.

R.W. Postgate, *The Builders' History*, National Federation of Building Trade Operatives, London, 1923.

G.D.H. Cole and Raymond Postgate, *The Common People*, University Paperbacks, Methuen and Co., London, 1966.

E.J. Hobsbawm and George Rude, *Captain Swing*, Lawrence and Wishart, London, 1969.

Sidney Webb, *English Poor Law History*, Vol. 2. Longman and Co., 8 Vols. London, 1906–29.

Frank Swinnerton, *The Adventures of a Manuscript*, The Richards Press, London, 1956.

Marjorie Plant, *The English Book Trade*, Allen and Unwin, second edition, London, 1965.

Grant Richards, *Author Hunting*, Hamish Hamilton, London, 1934.

George Meek, *George Meek, Bath Chairman*, Constable, London, 1910.

Samson Low, *Times History of the War in South Africa*, 7 Vols., London, 1900–1909.

W.T. Rodgers and Bernard Donoughue, *The People Into Parliament*, Thames and Hudson, London, 1966.

R.H. Hilton and H. Fagan, *The English Rising of 1381*, Lawrence and Wishart, London, 1950.

Appendix

For the convenience of the reader here is a concise bibliography of all editions to date as comprehensive as the publishers' and my own research can supply and which I believe to be complete up to and including 1973.

Grant Richards Home Editions

First editions				*Abridged editions*	
First published	April	1914		May	1918
Reprinted	May	1914		October	1918
	October	1935		February	1921
	February	1938		February	1925
	August	1943		October	1926
	April	1944		June	1927
	July	1944		October	1927
	December	1944		August	1932
	March	1945			
	April	1946			
	March	1947			
	October	1948			
	November	1949			
	November	1951			
	February	1954			

Grant Richards Foreign Editions or pirated

1914	American
1914	Canadian (English copies)
Early 1920s	Russian (? Pirated translation)
1925	German translation

Penguin Books

April	1940
May	1940
January	1941
May	1942

Australian Edition October 1942

One of the Damned

Lawrence and Wishart full text

Home	Foreign and Translation
1955	1957 Russian (English)
1956	1958 German (GDR) translation
1959	1961 Czech translation
1962	1962 American
1966	1964 Bulgarian translation
1968	1971 Japanese translation
1971	In preparation Swahili translation

Panther Classics series

Reprints by Lawrence and Wishart of the full text: 1965, 1967, 1969, 1971, 1976, 1978

Index

Index